A GUIDE TO
SOVIET RUSSIAN
TRANSLATIONS
OF AMERICAN
LITERATURE

BY GLENORA W. BROWN
AND DEMING B. BROWN

COLUMBIA SLAVIC STUDIES

A SERIES OF THE
DEPARTMENT OF SLAVIC LANGUAGES, COLUMBIA UNIVERSITY
ERNEST J. SIMMONS, GENERAL EDITOR

A GUIDE TO
SOVIET RUSSIAN TRANSLATIONS OF AMERICAN LITERATURE

BY GLENORA W. BROWN
AND DEMING B. BROWN

KING'S CROWN PRESS
COLUMBIA UNIVERSITY, NEW YORK, 1954

King's Crown Press is an imprint established by Columbia
University Press for the purpose of making certain scholarly
material available at minimum cost. Toward that end, the
publishers have used standardized formats incorporating
every reasonable economy that does not interfere with legibil-
ity. The author has assumed responsibility for editorial
style and for proofreading.

Library of Congress Catalog Card Number: 54-8836

Published in Great Britain, Canada, India and Pakistan
by Geoffrey Cumberlege, Oxford University Press,
London, Toronto, Bombay and Karachi

Manufactured in the United States of America

ACKNOWLEDGMENT

THE preparation and publication of the several series of works under SLAVIC STUDIES have been made possible by a grant from the Rockefeller Foundation to the Department of Slavic Languages of Columbia University.

Ernest J. Simmons
Executive Officer

PREFACE

THE research for this book was begun in 1948. Interrupted
by the birth of our second child, two serious illnesses, and
innumerable lesser events, it has remained as prominent an
element in our lives as the kitchen stove.

We have collaborated closely at every stage in its preparation. In general, however, the Checklist itself is the work
of Mrs. Brown, and the essay, the introduction to the Checklist and the tables are mine.

We have tried to organize the Checklist so as to ensure
the utmost clarity and convenience for its potential users.
Only after extensive consultation with librarians, editors
and other interested specialists did we decide upon its final
arrangement. The organization of the Checklist is described
in the Introductory.

A number of persons have assisted us at various times
in the preparation of the book. We are grateful to the writers Langston Hughes, Albert Maltz, Upton Sinclair and
Elmer Rice for help in identifying certain translations of
their works. The staff of the Slavonic Division of the New
York Public Library has given us liberal assistance. Joseph
Komidar, Head of the Reference Department of the Northwestern University Library, has provided much valuable
technical advice, and M. Helen Perkins, Reference Assistant,
has been helpful to us in many ways. Josephine Hayford,
Mary F. Miller and Gloria Sosin have each made important
contributions. To Jenta Winternitz, who typed a particularly
difficult manuscript, we offer special thanks.

Finally, we are particularly grateful to Professor Ernest
J. Simmons, whose initial encouragement and continued un-
flagging support have been indispensable.

D.B.

Northwestern University
January, 1954

TABLE OF CONTENTS

Part I

Soviet Russian Translations of American Literature, 1917-1947

Part II

Checklist

Tables

Indexes

PART I

SOVIET RUSSIAN TRANSLATIONS

OF AMERICAN LITERATURE

1917-1947

SOVIET TASTE IN AMERICAN LITERATURE

AT the time of the October Revolution, the Russians based their conception of American culture on a combination of impressions derived from books of fact and fiction, travelers' tales, reports in a generally attentive press, and a vast amount of theoretical speculation from thinkers as widely divergent as Dostoevsky and Lenin. There was no dearth of facts about the United States, but there were huge quantities of misinformation and myth.

American literature in tsarist times had done little to regularize this haphazard conception, for the pre-revolutionary reading public had known relatively few American writers. Only eight of them—James Fenimore Cooper, Bret Harte, Jack London, Henry Wadsworth Longfellow, Edgar Allan Poe, Harriet Beecher Stowe and Mark Twain—had achieved a durable popularity among significant numbers of Russians. A few additional authors—Edward Bellamy, Ralph Waldo Emerson, Benjamin Franklin, Nathaniel Hawthorne, O. Henry, Washington Irving, Upton Sinclair and Henry David Thoreau among them—had appeared in book form at one time or another, and others had appeared in random periodical pieces. But all of these had failed to make a deep or lasting impression. The list of American writers who had appeared in translation before 1917 does bespeak a lively and catholic interest on the part of many Russians. Many of America's most prominent literary figures had been represented. Nevertheless, the literature thus circulated was relatively small in volume. Further, the pattern of preferences which had developed by the time of the Revolution indicates a heavy reliance on writings of the early and middle years of the nineteenth century. With few exceptions, the American writers available to the Russian readers in the decades immediately preceding the Revolution presented a picture of our country that was far outdated.

The appearance of American authors on the Russian scene had been largely accidental, governed by such factors as their popularity in Western Europe, the whims of publishers, the suspicions of the Tsar's censors, and the un-coordi-

nated decisions of Russian men of letters in selecting works
to translate and promote.

This absence of a coordinating principle indicates a fundamental difference between the pre-revolutionary and post-
revolutionary approaches to American culture. Before the
Revolution, American literature was presented to the Russians in terms of isolated fragments. In the years following
the upheaval, the Russians examined American political,
social, economic and cultural phenomena with heightened interest and in much greater detail. Their intellectual leaders
mulled over the contradictions and paradoxes existing in the
American past and present and, in the light of a steady influx of new information, marshaled them into a doctrinal
view of American development. (This process of discovery
and analysis was governed chiefly by the gradual formation
of Soviet Marxism as a national intellectual and ideological
discipline.) In the course of consolidating and reinforcing
this fuller, if more doctrinaire, interpretation of American
culture, the Soviet regime made available to the public a
quantity and variety of American literature vastly exceeding
that which had been available before the Revolution.

As a consequence, American literature for the first
time was allowed to provide a relatively comprehensive ac-
count of our culture to the Russian people. In comparison
with the body of ideas about the United States that existed before the Revolution, the Soviet conception has arrived at a
large degree of homogeneity. And it is obvious that this
homogeneity has been attained, in many respects, at the ex-
pense of objective truth. Nevertheless, despite a censorship
which has excluded many works which militate against the official Soviet interpretation, America has, to some extent,
been permitted to speak for herself through her literature.
The present survey attempts to determine the patterns of
that literary expression, in terms of specific periods within
the Soviet epoch.

The Period of War Communism, 1918-1921:
While the change in publishing practices after the Revolution was relatively sudden, it did not happen all at once. In
the chaotic years immediately following the Soviet seizure of
power, Russians were more enthusiastic then effective in
their approach to the problem of overcoming their cultural
lag. Book publication in general was at a very low ebb. Even
had the paper and presses been available, it is doubtful

whether the country, which was preoccupied with the civil
war, the intervention, and the first efforts of reconstruction,
could have sustained a program involving the translation of
hundreds of new American books. In the years of War Communism the works of only eight American authors were published in book form, and these in small quantities. Six of
these eight authors—Longfellow, Twain, Whitman, Harte,
London and Sinclair—had been well known in tsarist Russia,
and it is probable that one of the remaining two—Lafcadio
Hearn—was not unknown. Only Albert Edwards (Arthur Bullard), whose novel, Comrade Yetta, was translated in 1919,
can have been new to the Russians.

In these lean years Soviet publishing houses relied for
their American quota on literature whose attractiveness for
the Russian reader had already been proved. Consequently,
the public was merely encouraged to confirm its traditionally
fragmentary impression of America. Soviet intellectuals,
however, recognized the need for a program of translating
foreign literature as early as 1919. In that year a group of
professors, academicians, literary scholars and writers
banded together to form an organization called Vsemirnaya
Literatura [World Literature], whose intention was "to pub-
lish for the new Soviet intelligentsia all the best books,
wherever they existed on earth ... in the very best Russian
translations," and whose larger purpose was to "serve the
ideal of the brotherhood, comradeship and mutual understanding of people."[1] After a year's deliberation this group drew
up a plan of publication which, according to its leading spirit,
Maxim Gorky, would set before the Russian people "a vast
historical-literary chrestomathy, which will give the reader
an opportunity to acquaint himself in detail with the rise,
triumph and fall of literary schools, with the development of
poetic and prose techniques, with the mutual influences of
the literatures of various nations and in general with the
whole course of literary evolution in its historical se-
quence."[2]

The World Literature publishing house existed from
1919 to 1927 and, according to contemporary testimony, did
much to familiarize the new Soviet generation with foreign
writers.[3] The 120 freshly translated and edited volumes
which it produced were widely representative of world literature. But the organization fell far short of its original goal,
which had been to place 4,000 foreign titles in the hands of

Soviet readers.[4] Further, its selection from American literature was conservative. The five Americans whom it sponsored—London, Poe, Sinclair, Twain and Whitman—were already well known in Russia. Nevertheless, the very existence of such an organization as early as 1919 indicates the
spirit in which the Soviet intelligentsia, at the very outset,
faced the problem of establishing cultural ties with the outside world.

Other characteristics of book production in the period of
War Communism also affected the publication of American
literature. In this era of crisis, the Soviet leaders knew that
the fate of their Revolution hung in the balance. The publishing industry, no less than other sectors of the economy, was
enlisted in the service of the Revolution. Both the foreign
and the domestic literature which it issued tended to stress
revolutionary themes. Books were selected not so much for
their literary worth as for their utilitarian importance in
terms of the historical moment. Many of the works of Whitman, London, Sinclair and Longfellow which were chosen
for publication at this time expressed sentiments of social
protest or revolt. The selection of Edwards' Comrade Yetta
also indicates an inclination toward revolutionary subject
matter. Of the thirty-one American titles listed for the period from 1918 through 1921, ten are clearly hortatory in
nature.

Another characteristic of this period was the publication of animal, nature and adventure stories, chiefly those
of London. Russians had developed a taste for this kind of
literature long before the Revolution, and London had already
become a favorite in this respect. The trend toward such
reading continued, for fourteen of the thirty-one titles from
1918 through 1921 fall into this category. The prominence of
this type of writing in the period of War Communism indicates three trends which were to continue strong to the
present day. First, while many such works were issued for
adult consumption, the publishers, even at this early date,
also had in mind the youth of Russia. Young people's literature developed tremendous importance as the Soviet period
progressed, and the American contribution to that literature
was large. Second, the Russian love of animal stories and
tales of primitive adventure, so prominently indicated even
in the first years of the Revolution, continued to obtain in
later years, and increasing numbers of American works

were published to satisfy this appetite. Third, the printing
of such books in these years of extreme social, political and
economic crisis shows that the controllers of Soviet publishing recognized the reader's need for relaxation and escape
from the omnipresent tensions of the Revolution. This trend,
too, has continued to the present. Much of the American literature which has been translated during the Soviet era has
provided Russian readers with sheer entertainment, divorced
from political and ideological didacticism.

One more practice, adopted under War Communism,
continued to characterize Soviet publishing in later years.
One Soviet spokesman has described this as the process of
"simplification, popularization, of drawing near to the mass
reader in the production of translated literature."[5] Foreign
books were frequently shortened and abridged, and some-
times even re-written for the purpose of making them accessible to large numbers of unsophisticated readers. The
practice was not infrequent in pre-revolutionary Russia,
but it was given new impetus by publishing policies immediately after the Revolution, and has continued, with varying
frequency, to the present.[6] Its aim was at least partly educa-
tional—to familiarize large numbers of Soviet readers with
the literature of foreign countries as economically as possible.

However strong the artistic objections to this practice
might have been (and several critics did object), something
of the sort needed to be done. The "liquidation of illiteracy"
was one of the initial tasks of the Soviet regime, and the
accomplishment in this field was enormous. Nevertheless,
no newly literate population can be made to enjoy and appreciate good literature overnight. The method of simplifying
imported works was probably, in large measures, designed
to make the transition from illiteracy to enlightenment as
painless as possible. The popularization of world literature
among the masses was only one of the devices for accom-
plishing this, but it was an important one.

The practice of editing foreign works also provided an
opportunity for political and ideological censorship, and
there were numerous incentives for this throughout the entire Soviet period. The present study makes no attempt to
determine the degree of fidelity with which individual American works were reproduced. Nevertheless, it is certain that
editing with an ideological purpose did take place.

The Period of the New Economic Policy, 1922-1928:

Book production in pre-revolutionary Russia had reach-
ed its peak in 1912-13. The output had declined fairly steadily
until 1921, when it was less than half that of 1913.[7] Consequently, as War Communism gave way to the New Economic
Policy (NEP), the Russians were in the midst of a literary
famine. Those who had already developed a taste for reading
before the Revolution were now joined by millions of new
literates in demanding books of all kinds. In response, the
rehabilitated and expanding publishing industry of the NEP
brought forth a flood of books, both native and translated.
Russia developed into a nation of insatiable readers, and
foreign books in translation became standard fare.

American literature played an important role in this development. During the five years from 1923 through 1927, for
example, 24 percent of the foreign titles published in the
Soviet Union were American, and only French literature,
which represented 30 percent of the total, exceeded ours in
popularity. In 1924 and 1925, our literature led the field, and
in the former year over one-third of the foreign titles published in Russia were American.[8]

The most significant fact, however, is that during the
seven years of the NEP at least 80 American authors entirely
new to the Russian people were published in book form. In
addition, four writers who had been known before the Revolution, but whose works had not been published during War
Communism, now reappeared in Russian print. Also, seven
of the eight Americans whose books had been issued under
War Communism continued to be published under the NEP.
This means that the works of at least 91 different American
authors appeared in book form in Russia from 1922 through
1928, representing more than a tenfold increase over the
period of War Communism and a fivefold increase over the
entire pre-revolutionary period.

The achievement of the NEP becomes even more im-
pressive when one considers that there were at least 900
printings[9] of American books during this period, as compared
to a total of 38 under War Communism.[10]

What was the nature of this tide of American literature?
What aspects of our writing did it represent, and how ac-
curately did it reflect American life and thought? Within the
NEP period there were several independent and contradic-
tory trends in publication of American literature, so that it

is difficult to generalize about the period as a whole. Never-theless, it is possible to discern four fairly distinct categor-ies among the hundreds of American works translated.

The chief representatives of the first three of these categories were Jack London, O. Henry and Upton Sinclair, respectively. From 1922 through 1926, these three writers together accounted for over 70 percent of the printings of American works in Russia. Their relative popularity declined in the following two years, but even in 1927 and 1928 their combined works accounted for over 40 percent of the total.[11] The early preference for these writers is symptomatic of three trends which have continued to the present.

The fondness for London, which originated before the Revolution, remained alive during the austerity of War Com-munism, and blossomed during the NEP into a phenomenon of fundamental literary importance, indicates a major trait in the Soviet appetite for American literature. During the NEP and, to a lesser extent, later periods, Soviet publishers looked to America for romantic narratives of adventure in exotic settings, animal stories and nature tales. London was by far the most popular author of such stories, but others soon come to share his vogue. In 1922, Edgar Rice Bur-roughs' Tarzan of the Apes was translated, and achieved six printings in the following two years. Tarzan and its numer-ous sequels, along with Burroughs' Martian stories, came out in twenty-one printings altogether from 1922 through 1924. The publication of a volume of poems by the Canadian, Robert W. Service, was inspired, no doubt, by the success of London's Klondike stories.[12] Another writer in the London tradition, James Oliver Curwood, attained great popularity from 1925 through 1928, when forty-three volumes of his stories appeared. Rex Beach, also in this tradition, had novels published in Russia in 1926 and 1928. Even Zane Grey made his way into Russian print, when three of his novels came out in 1927, 1928 and 1929. Two other Americans who held a similar appeal for the Russian reader in the late twenties were James Stevens and Stewart Edward White. By the end of the NEP, the vogue for Burroughs, Curwood, Grey and Beach was over, but the taste for American stories of the great outdoors continued, and Jack London remained the favorite American author in Russia.

Also, toward the end of the NEP, Soviet publishers fostered a revival of the long-standing Russian interest in

stories of American Indians and frontiersmen by increased
publication of the works of James Fenimore Cooper, who had
been a pre-revolutionary favorite. Cooper continued to be
popular in the thirties, and his tradition is also responsible
for the interest in James Willard Schultz and Mayne Reid,
whom many Russians persisted in considering an American.
The American Indian's grip on the Russian imagination is
at least partly responsible for the continuing success of
The Song of Hiawatha, upon which its author's Russian reputation is almost solely based. This poem, also a pre-revolutionary favorite, was re-published in 1928 after a hiatus of
ten years, and continued to reappear until 1941. Finally, the
Soviet affection for Bret Harte, which also had its roots in
the Russian past, sprang from this fascination with the American wilderness and the frontier as a narrative setting.

The above grouping of writers, which includes such
widely diverse authors as Zane Grey and Longfellow, is of
course rather loose. The purpose of such a grouping, however, is not so much to show similarities between the authors
themselves as to indicate the Russian cultural impulse which
led to their publication. From this standpoint, it is evident
that the surge of publishing activity which began in 1922 included a large number of American writers whose main
appeal is to the reader's love of primitive nature, raw adventure and stories of action in remote settings. This aspect
of Russian interest in America, particularly in the first decade after the Revolution, was largely the product of curios-
ity about life in the Wild West, the Far North and the primitive forests of our continent. Many Russians may also have
felt a sense of identification with these stories, for frontier
life was very much a part of the Soviet scene too. And while
this interest was also in large measure simply a product of
the universal love for the exotic, it was undoubtedly based on
romantic misconceptions about American civilization, in
which large numbers of Russians assumed that the frontier
atmosphere of the nineteenth century in the United States
still obtained in large sections of our country.

One of the main tendencies of Soviet publication in the
NEP period, then, was to draw from that section of American literature which depicted life of the periphery of civilization, or which showed our culture in its frontier, formative
period. To the extent that this treatment was romantic and
anachronistic, Soviet publication tended to create for the

reader an inaccurate picture of contemporary America. As
the years passed, however, other strains of our literature
became dominant in Russia, so that the reader could more
easily distinguish between fact and romantic fiction about
the United States. Nevertheless, this latter kind of literature
has continued to be popular in the Soviet Union, for the Russian love of nature and adventure has not ceased.[13]

O. Henry illustrates the second category of American
literature to become prominent during the NEP. Beginning
in 1923, his books appeared in Russia by the hundreds of
thousands, and, within a short time, brought with them the
works of many other Americans who were diverting because
of their humor, their ability to capture American local color,
or their sheer narative charm. This group is equally as
heterogeneous as the one associated with London, but its
members do have decided characteristics in common. First,
most of them worked closely within the framework of American society, and were interested in the atmosphere at the
center of our civilization rather than its outskirts. Consequently, they tended to write about twentieth-century America, and to reflect her standards more fully than others.
Second, their chief function was to amuse rather than to edify,
and thus they represented, if not a lesser, then certainly a
less profound aspect of contemporary American writing. On
the whole, they brought to the Russian reader of the twenties
the kind of literature that his American counterpart was
reading at the same time.

Before discussing further this group associated with O.
Henry, I must mention one other author, not of the twenties,
whom it is extremely difficult to classify. This is Mark
Twain, whose Russian reputation has been larger than that
of any other American, excepting Jack London. He was well
known before the Revolution, and new editions of his works
have appeared steadily throughout the entire Soviet period.
His popularity has not been as spectacular as London's, but
its persistence indicates that he may continue to be a classic in Russia long after London has been forgotten. From
this, it would obviously be inaccurate to associate Twain
solely with the wave of diverting, "civilized" Americans,
headed by O. Henry, who appeared in Russia during the NEP.
For one thing, Twain, like Bret Harte, devoted some of his
writing to the American frontier. Another and perhaps even
more important reason is that as a humorist, satirist and

realist, Twain stands head and shoulders above the rest of these writers. For the present purpose, however, Twain must be associated with this group, for he, like the others, was concerned with the life of organized American society and the amusement that can be derived from its mores and foibles.

Twain and O. Henry alone represented this literature of manners and local color in America for the Russians in 1922 and 1923. In 1924 and 1925, they were joined by Irvin S. Cobb, Konrad Bercovici, David Freedman, Joseph Hergesheimer, Fannie Hurst, T. S. Stribling and Jean Webster. In 1926, the humorists Ellis Parker Butler, Octavus Roy Cohen and Twain's contemporary, Artemus Ward, appeared in Russian, along with the novelists Edna Ferber and Martha Ostenso. By 1927, the stream of such literature had swelled to include Jack Bethea, Jack Black, Maxwell Bodenheim, Frank Elser, Ellen Glasgow, Montague Glass, Ben Hecht, Paul Kimball, Anita Loos, M. Sublette and Tristram Tupper. More Americans of this type were printed in 1928, the final year of NEP publishing, than ever before or since. In addition to many of those already named, the following authors came out in Russia in that year: Gertrude Atherton, Louis Bromfield, Robert Carse, George Randolph Chester, Zona Gale, Susan Glaspell, Harry Clay Hervey, Kathleen Norris, Bertha Pearl and Donald Ogden Stewart.[14]

This stream of popular American fiction ceased flowing to Russia during the early years of the First Five-Year Plan, and it never resumed. In 1929, books by Donn Byrne, Edwin C. Hill and Booth Tarkington came out, and in 1930 Thomas Bailey Aldrich's The Story of a Bad Boy, together with works by Jack Bethea, Fannie Hurst, Sophie Kerr and Jean Webster were published. But these were the very last driblets. The writings of Twain and O. Henry continued to be issued in large numbers, it is true, but, with rare exceptions, Russian publishers ceased employing the criterion of success in the American popular market in selecting books for translation.

The significance of this decision is great, for the seven years of the NEP had been the only period in all of Russian history when the average reader could come in contact with the books which the masses of middle-class Americans were currently reading. It is a moot question whether, had the Russian reader been given the opportunity to continue his

acquaintance with current American popular fiction, his
opinion of our literature, and therefore of our culture, would
have been higher or lower than it became in succeeding
years. But it is certain that, by knowing what Americans
were reading, he would have understood better the cultural
forces which shape our country. Short-lived as it was, this
experience with the more popular segments of current American literature must have given the Russians an entirely new
understanding of the ways of contemporary America. To a
great extent, the literature which accomplished this was
superficial, romantic, sentimental and generally mediocre.
But the very presence on Soviet bookshelves of works which
exemplified the current mass American taste in literature
was a phenomenon entirely new to Russian culture.

The works of Upton Sinclair exemplify the third category of American literature to become prominent in Russia during the NEP. The group of writers representing this
trend is large and varied, but its members have in common
an orientation toward art that is basically sociological
and political, and most of them display a left-wing (though
not necessarily Marxist) bias toward the problems of American life. Publication of this kind of writing began in the period of War Communism, and it gathered impetus as the Russian output of books increased.

At first, NEP publishers confined their efforts in this
category (as in the other two categories mentioned above)
largely to authors who had already proved themselves in
Russia. In 1922 and 1923, books by London (who, because of
the socialist content of his books and his interest in the
class struggle, must be considered in this category also),
Albert Edwards, Sinclair and Whitman were published, and
the only new authors were Leroy Scott and John Reed. Ernest
Poole's The Harbor and a book of Albert Rhys Williams'
reportage on the Russian Revolution came out in 1924. Most
of these same authors continued to be published in 1925 and,
in addition, Claude McKay, William E. Dubois, Michael Gold
and Walter White first appeared in Russian print in that
year. From 1926 through 1928, the volume increased steadily. By the end of the NEP, the following additional authors
had been published: Samuel Hopkins Adams, Lester Cohen,
E. Haldeman-Julius, Robert Herrick, Harry Kemp, Charles
Norris, David Graham Phillips, Dan Poling, Carl Van Vechten and W. E. Woodward.

The above classification includes muckrakers, novelists and poets of protest, political and social satirists, and writers whose chief distinction is a preoccupation with some minority group. Many of them have little in common, but all them are either specifically or implicitly critical of life in capitalist America, and this trait draws them together. Several of them exhibited qualities or wrote about topics which would have interested Russians, even had they not been criticial of America. But the Soviet regime created an increasingly favorable atmosphere for the dissemination of literature exposing the negative side of capitalist civilization. Publishing houses under the NEP (and even more so under the Five-Year Plans) tended to stress the anti-capitalist criterion above all else in selecting American works.

Sinclair was the most prominent of these novelists in Russia. Also, his depiction of America's troubles was the most comprehensive. But there were others of similar scope, such as Adams, Herrick, Norris and Phillips. Still others were more specialized in their interests, and the most numerous were those who concentrated on the American proletariat. The works of authors of this type published under the NEP emphasized mainly the class struggle and the revolutionary opposition between workers and capitalists. But there was another kind of American proletarian literature which appealed to the Soviet public at this time—the literature of tramps, vagabonds and the American "hobo." This liking for hobo literature embraced not only the more picaresque works of such men as Twain, London, Harte and O. Henry, but also the contemporary writings, usually autobiographical, of Harry Kemp, Jim Tully, Glen Mullin and others. These books appealed more to the Soviet reader's taste for romantic adventure than to his class consciousness. Nevertheless, Soviet publishers cannot have overlooked their proletarian relevance.

A more important trend that began in the NEP was the choice of large quantities of literature written by American Negroes, or about them. The situation of colored people in America had long been a subject of concern to educated Russians. Uncle Tom's Cabin had been a favorite for decades. In 1925 appeared books by Dubois, McKay and Walter White, in which the American Negro spoke for himself to the Russian people. (White's novels continued to come out until 1927, and McKay's writings continued to appear until 1930.)

A book by Jessie Fauset was published in 1927, and in 1928
Carl Van Vechten's novel of Harlem, Nigger Heaven, was
translated, together with a collection of Negro humor by
William Pickens. The stream of such literature swelled in
the thirties, when many of the works of Roark Bradford, Du
Bose Heyward, Joel Chandler Harris, Langston Hughes,
Angelo Herndon and Richard Wright were published. Soviet
publishers in the thirties were alert for the appearance of
new works by and about Negroes, and particularly those with
a strong ingredient of social protest. The translation of all
of these writings is an expression of the same impulse that
led to the publication of Upton Sinclair. The appearance of
such works in Russia as late as 1951 can be traced back to
the wave of American literature that began in 1922.

No single writer symbolizes the fourth category of
American literature that became prominent under the NEP.
This was the school of critical realism, which began to
appear in Russian translation in 1924, when novels by Sherwood Anderson, John Dos Passos and Sinclair Lewis were
published. The translation of their works gave Russia its
first opportunity to know the best of current American writing, and established a trend of deep respect for contemporary
American literature. The writers in this group did much to
dispel the anachronistic, hazy, romantic and generally erron-
eous impression of America that obtained in the early and
middle years of the NEP. In contrast to the popular and
largely ephemeral fiction of such writers as Edna Ferber and
Ben Hecht, the works of these authors made a lasting impression on the Soviet reader. Also, they received much more
attention and a much higher evaluation from Soviet critics,
who soon recognized their superiority and promoted their
cause. Finally, this group, together with the more politically
tendentious authors of the next two decades, dominated
Soviet publication of American literature in the thirties and
forties.

These writers appeared simultaneously with many of the
socially conscious writers whom I have associated with Sinclair, and in a topical and thematic sense the two groups are
not mutually exclusive. (For example, Stribling and Herrick
might well be associated with the critical realists.) The chief
characteristic of this fourth group, however, was that its
members continued prominent in the Russia of the thirties
and, to some extent, in the forties, and were considered by

the critics to be on a higher esthetic level. The preference
for these writers indicates a Soviet tendency to appreciate
the best of American literature in an era when many other
avenues to cultural understanding were closed.

In 1925, works of Theodore Dreiser and Eugene O'Neil
joined those of Anderson, Dos Passos and Lewis in Russia.
The new Soviet awareness of American critical realism
also became evident in the publication of turn-of-the-cen-
tury works by Frank Norris and Ambrose Bierce in 1925
and 1926, respectively, and in 1926 a book of Waldo Frank
came out. By 1928, most of these writers were represented
in Russia by several books each, and in the decade which
followed, these writers, plus several who appeared in the
thirties, signified for Soviet Russians the highest attainment
of American literature in the twentieth century.

All of this indicates that during the seven years in which
the New Economic Policy governed Soviet publishing, there
were tremendous changes in the amount and variety of American literature available to the Russian public. This virtual
flood of books disclosed whole new areas of American
thought, new regional and cultural landscapes, heretofore
undiscovered facets of the American character, and many
new points of view regarding the American scene. The farm,
the factory and the office; the small town and the big city;
the North and South and Middle West; the soldier, the flapper,
the capitalist and the union organizer—seen from the American perspective of the twenties—came before the Russian
reader for the first time. Dozens of unfamiliar writers, past
and contemporary—realists, humorists, satirists, decadents,
sentimentalists, romancers, provincials, Bohemians,
Freudians and Marxists—became accessible.

The selection of American books for translation from
1922 to 1928 was eclectic as it had never been before in
Russia, and much more so than it was to be in the next two
decades. Several aspects of this era in Soviet development
help to explain this. First, the Soviet government made
strong efforts to foster the production of books, in line with
the revolutionary aim of raising the mass cultural level.
The increase in output of books made possible a greater
variety. Second, the production of native Soviet Russian literature, especially fiction, grew relatively slowly in the
twenties in comparison with the rapidly increasing number
of readers. Third, Soviet cultural authorities consciously

fostered the circulation of new foreign literature, in an
effort to make Russians world-conscious. Fourth, America,
as the technologically most progressive country in the
world, became a subject of intense practical and even romantic interest to all Russians. (Henry Ford's autobiography
ran to four printings in 1924.) There was a tendency to print
anything American, solely because of its glamorous origin.

But the Russian people, starved for knowledge of the outside world, would undoubtedly have welcomed, in their ig-
norance, any selection of American literature, regardless of
its bias. The relatively catholic choice of American works
in this period was encouraged by two additional factors
peculiar to the NEP. The first of these was the atmosphere
of amnesty toward non-proletarian literature which was
established by the 1925 Party resolution favoring collabora-
tion with fellow-traveling and petty-bourgeois writers. This
resolution was aimed toward smoothing relations between
warring factions in the Soviet literary world, and toward
making it possible for writers who were as yet incapable of
adopting a wholly orthodox point of view to continue as cre-
ative artists. While the Party decision mainly concerned Soviet writers, it probably had ramifications in the publishing
world. Editors could feel relatively free to select foreign
works whose political or ideological content did not harmo-
nize with the current outlook of the Party and the government.

The second factor was the existence of private publishers during the NEP, firms which competed against each
other and against various state publishing houses in a relatively free literary market. Under such conditions, publishers were bound, above all, to seek works that would sell.
The wide variety of American literature published in this
period was probably, in part, the result of experimentation
in search of authors who would develop a lucrative Russian
following. Publishers from both the socialized and private
sectors of the NEP economy engaged in such experimentation. One might have expected that the state publishing
houses, which received government subsidies and were not
as subject to the vicissitudes of the market as were private
entrepreneurs, would restrict themselves to books directly
useful to the Revolution, politically and ideologically. The
fact is that state firms and private publishers alike intro-
duced such writers as Ben Hecht, Edgar Rice Burroughs,

Zane Grey and many others. Credit for the genuinely representative character of American literature in Russia in the
twenties belongs equally to state and private enterprises.
Ultimate responsibility for this, of course, belongs to the
Soviet government, which, through the Commissariat of Ed-
ucation and its censorship organ, Glavlit, examined and
sanctioned each of these books. The influx of American literature during the NEP could never have been accomplished
without the sufferance and active aid of the Soviet government.

The Period of the First Three Five-Year Plans, 1929-1941:
    With the inauguration of the First Five-Year Plan the
circulation of American books in the Soviet Union began to
drop. In 1929 the number of American authors in new Russian printings was only half that of 1928. The number continued to dwindle steadily, until in 1932 the works of only 9
Americans were published in book form, as compared to 52
in 1927. Even more striking is the contrast in number of
printings: in 1927 there were 177; in 1932 there were 14.
    The situation improved somewhat during the middle
thirties. The decline continued in 1933 and 1934, but in 1935
the number of printings rose to 25, in 1936 to 39, and in 1937
to 40. After that, the number again fell, so that in 1941 there
were only 9 new printings. In terms of the number of copies
of American books produced, however, the contrast between
the twenties and thirties is not as great. The average size of
printings increased considerably, so that in 1936, for example, 39 printings totaled 1,277,430 copies, whereas in
1927, 177 printings had totaled 1,788,550 copies. Nevertheless, the twenties produced nearly twice as many copies as
the thirties.
    A great many American writers disappeared from the
Russian scene as a result of the new publication policies.
Well over half of those who had been known in the twenties
were no longer printed in the thirties. A good share of these
writers would undoubtedly have been forgotten in any case,
just as they lost prominence in America. Others, however,
would probably have held their readers, had their books been
available. The most prominent of those who ceased to appear
were Konrad Bercovici, Rex Beach, Maxwell Bodenheim,
Irvin S. Cobb, James Oliver Curwood, Edna Ferber, Zona
Gale, Zane Grey, Ben Hecht, Joseph Hergesheimer, Fannie
Hurst and Charles Norris. Soviet publishing continued to fol-

low its searching, experimental pattern, but its choice of
fiction ceased having any correlation with American best-
seller lists. The period of relative catholicity in publication
of American books had come to an end.

Under the First Five-Year Plan, Soviet literature itself
underwent a vast transformation. Toward the end of 1928
writers were instructed to create, and publishers were or-
dered to print, works in direct support of the drastically
accelerated program of industrialization and collectivization.
Literary effort was evaluated in terms of its immediate and
practical application to the economic, political and social
tasks at hand. Further, the proportion of non-literary works
published—technical books on agriculture, industry and science, and books of political, economic and social indoctrina-
tion—increased rapidly. With the entire publishing apparatus
mobilized in the service of the Plan, translation of foreign
works not likely to contribute politically, psychologically
or ideologically to its fulfillment was discouraged.

Another element which may have affected the selection
of American works for publication was the closing down of
private publishing houses at the end of the NEP. These
firms, judging from their output in the twenties, had enjoyed
relative freedom in choosing foreign works, and had exer-
cised it widely. When they ceased to exist a certain specula-
tive, exploratory drive in Russian publishing undoubtedly
died with them.

The final, and probably the most substantial, cause for
the change in Soviet publication is political and ideological.
As the NEP gave way to the Five-Year Plans, the Party
assumed increasingly active control over all publishing.
Marxism as a critical tool became more widely used and
highly developed, and as its principles became clearly de-
fined along the lines which the Party wished to establish,
Soviet critics grew more exacting in their demands on
Western literature. Fewer and fewer current American
works of the type that had been acceptable, or at least toler-
ated, in the twenties, were now looked upon with favor by
the Party.

While Soviet literary doctrine was sharpening, the
character of American literature was changing. The Depression and the rise of international fascism brought about a
marked increase in the American literature of political,
economic and social discontent. Some of this writing was

clearly Marxist in orientation, some was partly derived
from Marxist theory, and much of it was merely protest literature of no particular ideological parentage. All of it had
in common a strong inclination to indict contemporary in-
stitutions and to plead the necessity for radical alterations
in the existing order if further economic and social suffering,
and war, were to be prevented. All of it painted contemporary
America in dismal colors, and suggested that the capitalist
world was in distress.

This type of literature displaced the popular bourgeois
writers who had been so prominent in Russia in the twenties. By 1931, the relatively small amount of American literature issued in Russia was clearly weighted in favor of left-
wing writing. Of the eleven authors published in book form
in that year, seven—John Dos Passos, Michael Gold, Charles
Harrison, Robert Herrick, David Gordon, Upton Sinclair and
Jim Tully—can be considered writers of social protest. In
1932, all but two of the nine authors—O. Henry and Walt
Whitman—were in this category, and in the case of Whitman
the distinction is doubtful. In 1933 and 1934, books by the
following fourteen authors were published: Thomas Bailey
Aldrich, Sherwood Anderson, Pearl Buck, Dos Passos,
Dreiser, Ernest Hemingway, Langston Hughes, London,
Longfellow, Sinclair, Agnes Smedley, John Spivak, Sophie
Treadwell and Twain. Not all of these can be associated
with left-wing writing, but the pattern is clear. By 1941,
books of social protest by the following additional writers
had been translated: Erskine Caldwell, Jack Conroy, Albert
Halper, Josephine Herbst, Josephine Johnson, Sidney Kingsley, Grace Lumpkin, Albert Maltz, Edward Newhouse, Clifford Odets, Elmer Rice, John Steinbeck and Mary Heaton
Vorse. These were only the most prominent, for many others
in this category were published in these years.

But publishers by no means confined themselves to contemporary literature of social protest. In the first place,
the well-established liking for Twain, London and O. Henry
was perpetuated by frequent new printings. Other favorites
of long standing, such as Cooper, Harte, Mrs. Stowe, Whitman
and Longfellow continued to be published in numerous editions. Several other excellent American writers became
available for the first time. Stephen Crane was translated,
Pearl Buck's novels became very popular, a volume of Ring
Lardner came out, and several anthologies, representing the
best American prose and poetry, were issued.

Among twentieth-century writers, the school of critical realism became equally as prominent as the school of immediate social protest. In number of books circulated and frequency of new printings, such authors as Caldwell, Dreiser, Mrs. Buck, Dos Passos, Steinbeck and Hemingway far exceeded such writers as Conroy and Gold. Most of the protest writers, with the notable exception of Sinclair, were represented by only one or two works, and few of these achieved more than a single printing. The only reason for considering them prominent is the size of their group, which indicated that publishers were searching among the new American left-wing writers of the thirties for proletarian literature which would be both ideologically acceptable and appealing to Soviet readers.

Thus, the group of Americans who became genuinely popular as individual writers in Russia in the thirties cannot, for the most part, be identified as proletarian. Most of these critical realists displayed some measure of left-wing bias, it is true. But their chief traits were psychological profoundity, faithfulness in observation of human relationships, breadth of social understanding and, above all, the ability to write well. These qualities, rather than exact conformity to Soviet ideological demands, perpetuated the Russian interest in such men as Anderson, Frank and Lewis, and established the fondness for Hemingway, Steinbeck, Caldwell and Wright. On the whole, the Soviet public was given an opportunity to read, and showed a preference for, much of the best contemporary American literature.

Periodicals played an important role in the thirties. Over a hundred American authors appeared in Russia in at least 23 magazines from 1930 to 1941.[15] Stories and excerpts from the novels of Ernest Hemingway appeared at least 25 times in Soviet periodicals from 1934 to 1939; Dos Passos was represented 21 times from 1930 to 1934; Caldwell 26 times from 1934 to 1944. Langston Hughes' poems were printed at least 22 times from 1932 to 1940. Five or more works of each of the following writers were published in magazines: Sherwood Anderson, Gold, Lewis, Agnes Smedley, Dreiser, Pearl Buck, Lardner, Maltz, Bierce, Twain, Whitman and O. Henry. Whole novels, or large sections of them, were published serially, representing such writers as Mrs. Buck, Steinbeck, Halper, Hemingway and Lewis.

A series of periodicals devoted to foreign literature had

existed since 1922. In the twenties, however, their contribution was insignificant.[16] Further, these magazines tended increasingly to favor American literature of the extreme left. In 1932, however, the magazine Internatsionalnaya Literatura [International Literature] was founded. The establishment of this periodical reflected an important change in official Soviet literary policy. The Party, dissatisfied with the results of its increasingly rigid and intolerant insistence on narrowly utilitarian literature, redefined its attitude and declared an amnesty toward Soviet writers who were generally sympathetic toward the regime but who had been unable completely to embrace official ideology. This by no means signified a relaxation of Party controls over Soviet writers. But it did result in greater tolerance toward deviations, and a greater willingness to accept foreign writers on their own terms. Also, within the next few years, the Soviet Union developed its United Front foreign policy. The number of foreign writers whom the Soviet literary world could treat as allies increased.

Internatsionalnaya Literatura was a salutary product of this change. Its literary standards were high. While there was no mistaking its left-wing orientation and its hostility to "bourgeois culture," it succeeded in the next decade in presenting an excellent cross section of the best of American literature, past and contemporary. A whole issue in 1933 was devoted to American writing. In the following years, dozens of representative Americans who had not heretofore been published in Russia came to the Soviet reader through its pages. Among them were Willa Cather, Carl Sandburg, William Faulkner, William Saroyan, Robert Frost, Sidney Howard, Edwin Arlington Robinson, Archibald MacLeish, Vachel Lindsay, Frank Stockton, Manuel Komroff and Irwin Shaw. The magazine also published much literary criticism, and regularly reviewed current American books. Further, it served as a testing ground, and the appearance of several of our writers in book form in Russia was undoubtedly a consequence of enthusiastic response to their original publication in Internatsionalnaya Literatura. This was by no means the only Soviet magazine in the thirties which performed a similar function, but it was the most effective. Its planned and systematic presentation of American works undoubtedly did much to stimulate Soviet interest in our culture.

Periodicals, however, gave only an ephemeral sampling of American works. Book production provided a truer indication of literary policy, and in this field Soviet publishers were much less liberal in their choice of American works than they had been in the twenties. It will be recalled that during the seven years of the NEP, 91 American authors had been published in book form, and that 80 of these were new to Russian readers. In contrast, during the thirteen years from 1929 through 1941, the books of 84 American authors were published, of whom 53 were new. Further, of these 53 new authors, at least 35 can be considered writers of social protest. The Soviet publishing industry, which had been directed to eschew American "bourgeois" popular fiction, now concentrated on the left-wing writing born of the Depression.

Simultaneously, however, this highly centralized and ideologically directed publishing apparatus continued to print, in hundreds of thousands of copies, the works of traditional favorites such as London, Twain and O. Henry. And it continued to issue the works of many of America's best contemporary critical realists.

The Period from 1942 through 1947:

During the Second World War and the initial period of reconstruction, Soviet publishing developed a pattern quite similar to that of War Communism. Printing of American belles-lettres was sharply curtailed, and the selection of titles became conservative. Of the fifteen writers whose books were published at this time, nine—Twain, Sinclair, O. Henry, Poe, London, Whitman, Harte, Cooper and Dreiser—were favorites of long standing. Three others—Caldwell, Steinbeck and Maltz—had established their Russian reputations in the thirties. Only three—Stuart Engstrand, Edgcum Pinchon and Lillian Hellman—were new. Periodicals also followed this pattern, and confined their new translations, for the most part, to the political and military reportage of such persons as Martha Dodd, Florence Borden Harriman, Quentin Reynolds, Ralph Ingersoll and Elliott Roosevelt.

This retrenchment in publication of American literature merely paralleled a general curtailment of "non-essential" activity in the Soviet Union. The publishing industry, like everything else, was mobilized for war service. It is interesting, moreover, that the American authors who did continue to be printed were in many cases the same ones who had been singled out in previous times of crisis. Writers such as Twain, Sinclair, London, Whitman, Harte and Cooper had come to be regarded as sources of cultural stability. Russians could rely on them during a period of grave national danger.

A Note on Publication since 1947:
Statistics for the present study end with 1947. This year also marks the disappearance of practically the last vestiges of liberalism in Soviet choice of fresh American works for translation. A new anti-Western cultural policy, unprecedented in its rigidity, has excluded all contemporary works which do not directly support the official Soviet thesis of American decadence. The author who enjoys the greatest official favor today is Howard Fast, and the only other prominent twentieth-century writers who have been published since 1947 are London, O. Henry, Dreiser, Lincoln Steffens, Maltz and Sinclair Lewis. (Lewis' Kingsblood Royal was translated because of its exposure of American race prejudice.) Many writers who enjoyed great popularity in the thirties and forties—such as Sinclair, Hemingway, Caldwell, and Steinbeck—have either been officially denounced or quietly discarded. A few standard nineteenth-century authors, such as Whitman, Twain, Mrs. Stowe and Harte have come out in recent editions, but only because their remoteness from the present renders them ideologically "harmless."

The Soviet reader of today probably thinks of American literature in terms of the works of Jack London and O. Henry, a small number of nineteenth-century classics, and a handful of officially approved left-wing contemporaries. If he is fortunate, he may occasionally be able to find an old and worn copy of A Farewell to Arms or Elmer Gantry. But if his memory goes back three decades, he probably recalls wistfully the wealth of American literature that was once available to him.

NOTES

1. K. Chukovski, "Kak ya polyubil anglo-amerikanskuyu literaturu," Internatsionalnaya literatura, No. 9-10 (1941), p. 236.

2. N. Ashukin, "'Vsemirnaya literatura,'" in Literaturnaya entsiklopediya (Moscow, 1929), II, 325.

3. R. Culle, "American Writers and Literature in Soviet Russia," Russki golos, Nov. 6, 1927, p. 4.

4. Ashukin, op. cit., p. 326.

5. Lev Vaisenberg, "Perevodnaya literatura v Sovetskoi Rossii za desyat let," Zvezda, No. 6 (1928), p. 115.

6. In the absence of the large number of Russian texts which would be required for measuring and analyzing the results of this practice, it is nevertheless evident that it was most common in the early years of the New Economic Policy. The entries in Knizhnaya Letopis frequently specified that this had been done, and rough comparisons of the number of pages indicated for a Russian title with the number of pages in its American counterpart show that this was done more frequently than the entries in Knizhnaya Letopis specify. Also, a critic in 1928 mentioned "the custom of our publishing houses of ordering the translator to shorten the translation, without mentioning this in the title." (Book review by E. Lann, "Lester Kouen [Lester Cohen], Musor," Pechat i revolyutsiya, No. 4 [1928], p. 214.)

7. Helen Lambert Shadick (trans.), Book Publishing in Soviet Russia: An Official Survey Based upon the Data of the All-Union Book Department, Washington, D.C., (Public Affairs Press, 1948), p. 2.

8. The figures in this paragraph are from Vaisenberg, op. cit., p. 116.

9. The entries in Knizhnaya Letopis frequently make it impossible to distinguish between an "edition" and a "printing." Henceforth, the term "printing" will be used to denote both categories.

10. The total number of copies of American books pub-

lished under the NEP was 10,479,980; under War Communism the total was 351,450. The annual average number of
copies under the NEP was 1,497,140; under War Communism
it was 87,863.

11. London alone continued to dominate the field, however. In 1929, his books accounted for 65 percent of the total
copies of American works published.

12. Another Canadian writer of the out-of-doors,
Ernest Thompson Seton, achieved a major success with Soviet readers. Over 1,500,000 copies of his works are listed
in Knizhnaya Letopis.

  13. Here it is appropriate to mention the stream of
American children's literature which began in 1922 and
which, with qualitative changes, has continued to flow to
Russia during the entire Soviet period. Several of the American authors who had been published in pre-revolutionary
Russia had appealed to youth as well as to adults. Irving,
Cooper, Twain, Mrs. Stowe and London must have had many
young readers before the Revolution, and they continued to
attract the youth of the Soviet period. (Many Soviet editions
of their works are designed specifically for children.) But
the influx of our literature under the NEP also brought many
contemporary children's writers, including such current
American favorites as Mary Mapes Dodge, Lucy Fitch Perkins and Lucy Sprague Mitchell. Likewise, such writers as
Burroughs, Curwood, Grey, Schultz and O. Henry must have
had many youthful readers. The importation of contemporary
juvenile favorites from America ceased, for the most part,
in 1929, with the publication of Booth Tarkington's Penrod
and Dorothy Canfield Fisher's Understood Betsy. During the
thirties and forties, the publication of young people's books
was largely confined to two categories: (1) outdoor stories
of adventure and animals and (2) favorites of long standing
in Russia, such as Twain, Mrs. Stowe, O. Henry and Irving.
Soviet publishers ceased to import contemporary American
youth literature for two probable reasons: first, a large body
of indigenous Russian literature for youth was accumulating,
inspired by the official emphasis on the cultural development
of the new Soviet generation, and this made it unnecessary
to import foreign works. Second, the political and ideological
strictness which accompanied the inauguration of the Five-
Year Plans undoubtedly discouraged editors from selecting

works which showed American life and culture in a favorable light, and children's books were more likely than others to affirm American standards.

14. Slightly outside this category are the popular romances of Richard Connell, Reginald Kauffman and Johnston McCulley, which also appeared in Russia in this period. Their presence indicates that Soviet publishers scarcely overlooked a single aspect of American popular fiction during the NEP.

15. Sixty-four of these authors appeared only in periodicals, and were never published in book form.

16. The first of these, Sovremenny Zapad [Contemporary West], was sponsored by the World Literature organization, came out in six issues, and ceased publication in 1924. The second was Vestnik Inostrannoi Literatury, which began in 1928, and was the organ of the International Union of Revolutionary Writers. This was superseded by Literatura Mirovoi Revolyutsii [Literature of the World Revolution], also an organ of the IURW, in 1931.

PART II

CHECKLIST

INTRODUCTORY

THIS Checklist includes Russian translations of American works published in book and periodical form in the Soviet Union during the years 1917-1947. The material consists chiefly of novels, short stories, poems, plays, sketches, autobiographical and biographical writings, memoirs and essays. Movie scenarios have also been included, together with certain historical and journalistic writings which it seemed feasible to classify as "literature."

While a comprehensive picture of American literature in the Soviet Union is presented, there are a number of omissions. We have excluded translations in the non-Russian languages of the USSR. This means that editions representing millions of copies of American works published within Soviet borders are not mentioned in the present context. (The works of Jack London alone have been translated into 29 Soviet languages.) Likewise, we have omitted books published in English in Soviet editions. Canadian writers are not included. We have also excluded works written solely for juvenile readers.

Other omissions were not of our own choosing, but rather the result of inadequate source materials. Very few Soviet Russian translations of American literature have found their way to the United States. Consequently, we have had to rely heavily on Soviet bibliographical sources. The most important of these is Knizhnaya Letopis, a periodical publication which is roughly equivalent to the American Cumulative Book Index. Knizhnaya Letopis, which has provided the foundation for the present study, does not include complete listings of all books issued by Soviet publishers, although it is impossible to measure the degree of its incompleteness. Also, there are large gaps in the files of this publication in American libraries for the years after 1941. Our next most important source is Zhurnalnaya Letopis, a periodical publication roughly corresponding to the American Readers' Guide to Periodical Literature. While it has been extremely valuable, it is probably even less comprehensive in its coverage than Knizhnaya Letopis. The number of magazines whose contents it listed fluctuated widely and frequently. In contrast to <u>Knizhnaya Letopis</u>, which was published over the entire period, <u>Zhurnalnaya Letopis</u> was founded only in 1926. Also, the available files of this publication end with 1940.

We have endeavored to supplement these two main sources, wherever possible, by noting titles mentioned in Soviet book reviews, literary articles and encyclopedias. Our chief effort in this respect, however, has been to examine the files of Soviet literary periodicals available in this country. All magazine printings listed here for the years 1917-1925 and 1941-1947, and a considerable number of those listed for the intervening period, have been found in this manner.

The makeup of both <u>Knizhnaya Letopis</u> and <u>Zhurnalnaya Letopis</u> changed frequently, both in respect to the organization of their material and the form of the entries. During most of the period under study, each issue of these publications was divided into sections representing separate topical fields, such as history, economics, geography and belles-lettres (<u>khudozhestvennaya literatura</u>). For the years in which this system of organization obtained, we have confined our research in these publications to the <u>khudozhestvennaya literatura</u> sections. In doing so, we have accepted the Soviet editors' interpretation of the boundaries of "belles-lettres." Since their interpretation is relatively broad, however, it is probable that most works of an even remotely "literary" nature that were listed in <u>Knizhnaya Letopis</u> and <u>Zhurnalnaya Letopis</u> have been included here. Nevertheless, it is possible that certain American literary works of particularly pronounced political, economic, historical or sociological content have been omitted because they happened to be listed in other sections of these publications.

Soviet publishers have re-titled translated works with great frequency. With few exceptions, both <u>Knizhnaya Letopis</u> and <u>Zhurnalnaya Letopis</u> provide only the Russian titles of translated works, and list the authors' names only in their transliterated Russian form. Neither discriminates between works of English and American origin. Fully half of the time we have spent in compiling this list has been devoted to identifying authors from their bizarre transliterated names; determining whether or not they are American; and, most difficult of all, identifying a large number of works whose

Russian titles bear only slight resemblance, if any, to their
American titles. While we have succeeded in tracking down
a great many of these titles and identifying them by a variety of means, there remain numerous titles which have
proved impossible to identify. We have included such works,
and have provided English translations of their Russian
titles in the hope that future investigators may have better
success than we.

We have organized the materials in this book in the
following fashion. The entries in the main body of the
Checklist are arranged alphabetically by author, except for
the anthology section, which is arranged alphabetically by
Russian title. Under each author heading, collected works are
listed first, in chronological order of their appearance in
the Soviet Union. These are followed by separately published
works, listed alphabetically by Russian title. Where there
was more than one edition of a single Russian title, these are
listed chronologically. All printings within a single edition,
however, are listed together, so that the chronological order,
in some cases, is not absolute.

The individual entries are presented in the following
manner: Russian title; American title (if identified—other-
wise the Russian title is translated in brackets); translator;
editor and author of introduction (if any); publisher of book
or name of periodical; place of publication; date of publication; pagination; number of copies (if the entry refers to a
book for which this information was available); Russian
source; classification symbol.

Russian title. All Russian titles have been rendered as
they appeared in the sources. Single American works may
appear under several different Russian titles. For example,
Upton Sinclair's The Jungle will be found listed under four
separate Russian titles: Chashcha, Dzhungli, Debri and Okovy
Sbrosheny. For this reason, it is particularly important for
users of this book to consult the Index, which lists together
under the American title all printings of a single work.

American title. The American title is provided where-
ever it has been possible to identify a work with certainty.
For unidentified items, and for excerpts for which the publishers have invented titles, a translation of the Russian
title is provided in brackets. There are a few instances in
which the Russian title is not translatable.

Translator. If there is no translator listed in an entry,

the name of the translator was omitted from the Russian
source.

   Publisher of book or name of periodical. The more
frequently mentioned publishers and periodicals are given
in abbreviated form. See the Table of Abbreviations.

   Place of publication. The following abbreviations are
used: M.—Moscow; P.—Petrograd; L.—Leningrad; N.N.—
Nizhni Novgorod. All other place names are given in full.

   Russian sources. For every item which was found in
either Knizhnaya Letopis or Zhurnalnaya Letopis, a number
is provided, referring to the issue in which the item is
located. (KL 17948.27, for example, refers to Knizhnaya
Letopis, item No. 17948 for the year 1927; ZL 23647.39
refers to Zhurnalnaya Letopis, item No. 23647 for the year
1939.) These numbers are provided for users who wish to
refer to the original sources for further bibliographical
information. We have also supplied references for items
derived from other sources. For items which we have taken
directly from the periodicals in which they appeared, and for
available translations in book form, no source references
have been supplied.

   Classification symbols. These symbols have a twofold
function: to assist the user in identifying translations by
indication of their literary form, and to indicate the nature
of the Russian editions in which these translations were published. A list of classification symbols is included in the
Table of Abbreviations.

   References to American sources. These references are
provided to aid the user in locating English versions of
translated works. They do not purport to indicate first editions. For well-known works which are readily available in
American libraries, we have not provided such references.
Also, there are a few items whose American sources we
have been unable to establish.

TABLE OF ABBREVIATIONS

Book Publishers and Periodicals

Dalgiz. — Dalne-vostochnoye Gosudarstvennoye Izdatelstvo
Detizdat. — Izdatelstvo Detskoi Literatury
Gosizdat. —Gosudarstvennoye Izdatelstvo
Gosizdat R.S.F.S.R. — Gosudarstvennoye Izdatelstvo Rossi-
    skoi Sovetskoi Federativnoi Sotsialisticheskoi Respub-
    liki
Goslitizdat. — Gosudarstvennoye Izdatelstvo Khudozhestven-
    noi Literatury
In. Rab. — Izdatelstvo Inostrannykh Rabochikh v S.S.S.R.
Int. Lit. — Internatsionalnaya Literatura
Inter. Mayak — Internatsionalny Mayak
Inter. Molodyozhi — Internatsional Molodyozhi
Kniga i Rev. — Kniga i Revolyutsiya
Knizh. Nov. — Knizhniye Novinki
Kras. Gaz. — Krasnaya Gazeta
Kras. Nov — Krasnaya Nov
Kras. Prolet. — Krasny Proletari
Len. GIKHL — Leningradskoye Gosudarstvennoye Izdatelstvo
    Khudozhestvennoi Literatury
Lenizdat. — Leningradskoye Gosudarstvennoye Izdatelstvo
Lit. Mir. Rev. — Literatura Mirovoi Revolyutsii
Lit. Sov. — Literaturny Sovremennik
M.O.D.P. i K. — Moskovskoye Obshchestvo Dramaticheskikh
    Pisatelei i Kompositorov
Mezhrabpom. — Mezhdunarodnaya Rabochaya Pomoshch
Mol. Gvard. — Molodaya Gvardiya (publishing house)
Mol. Gvard. — Molodaya Gvardiya (periodical)
Nizh. Kom. — Nizhegorodskaya Kommuna
Nov. Vsemir. Lit. — Novinki Vsemirnoi Literatury
Pechat i Rev. — Pechat i Revolyutsiya
Sov. Prob. — Sovremennyie Problemy
Teatr i Dram. — Teatr i Dramaturgiya
Ts. K. Mopr. — Tsentralny Komitet Mezhdunarodnoi Organ-
    izatsii Pomoshchi Bortsam Revolyutsii

Ts.K.R.K.S.M. — Tsentralny Komitet Rossiskovo Kommun-
  isticheskovo Soyuza Molodyozhi
Ts.K.S.T. — Tsentralny Komitet Soyuza Tekstilshchikov
Tsedram. — Tsentralnoye Upravleniye Po Rasprostraneniyu
  Dramaturgicheskikh Produktsi
Uchpedgiz. — Gosudarstvennoye Uchebno-pedagogicheskoye
  Izdatelstvo
Univ. Bib. — Universalnaya Biblioteka
V.Ts.I.K. — Vserossiski Tsentralny Ispolnitelny Komitet
  (RSFSR)
V.Ts.S.P.S. — Vsesoyuzny Tsentralny Sovet Professionalnykh
  Soyuzov
Vkhutein. — Vysshi Khudozhestvenno-tekhnicheski Institut
Voyenizdat. — Voyennoye Izdatelstvo
Voyenmorizdat. — Voyenno-morskoye Izdatelstvo
Vsemir. Lit. — Vsemirnaya Literatura
Zhurn. Gaz. Obyed. — Zhurnalno-gazetnoye Obyedineniye
ZIF — Zemlya i Fabrika

Classification Symbols,
Place Names and Bibliographical Terms

Amer. — American
(autobiog.) — autobiography
(biog.) — biography
c. — copies
(coll.) — collection; (coll. s.) — collection of short stories;
  (coll. p.) —collection of poems; etc.
ed. — edition
introd. — introduction
KL 17948.27 — Knizhnaya Letopis, item No. 17948 for the
  year 1927
L. — Leningrad
M. — Moscow
MLRA — Library of Congress, Monthly List of Russian Ac-
  cessions
(n.) — novel
N.N. — Nizhni Novgorod
no. — number
P. — Petrograd
(p.) — poem
p., pp. — pages

(pl.) — play
Pol. sob. romanov — Polnoye sobraniye romanov (complete
    collected novels)
Pol. sob. soch. — Polnoye sobraniye sochineni (complete
    collected works)
pub. — publisher
(rep.) — reportage
(s.) — short story
(sk.) — sketch
Sob. soch. — Sobraniye sochineni (collected works)
trans—translated
ZL 23647.39 — Zhurnalnaya Letopis, item No. 23647 for the
    year 1939

ANTHOLOGIES

1. Amerika: izbrannyie proizvedeniya Teodora Draizera,
   Eptona Sinklera i). O. Genri [America: selections from the
   works of Theodore Dreiser, Upton Sinclair and O. Henry].
   Nizhegorodskaya Kommuna, N.N., 1928. 48 p., 4100 c.
   KL 15106.28
   Contents: Theodore Dreiser, Do groba (The lost Phoebe).
   Upton Sinclair, Dvoye: iz romana "Okovy sbrosheny"
   [two: an excerpt from The jungle]. O. Henry, Spustya
   dvadtsat let (After twenty years).
   "The Lost Phoebe" is from Free and other stories;
   "After twenty years" is from The four million.

2. Amerika: sbornik novykh proizvedeni [America: a collec-
   tion of new works]. Edited by R. A. Rozental. Izvestiya,
   M., 1924. 100 p., 12,000 c. KL 6060.24 (coll. s.)
   Contains works by Jack London, O. Henry, Upton Sinclair,
   W. [William] Morrow, L. [Lawrence] Mott, Sherwood An-
   derson, Claude McKay. Titles not listed in KL.

3. Amerikanskaya novella [the American short story].
   Trans. by V. A. Azov, L. Gausman, O. Przhetslavskaya.
   Atenei, P., 1923. 156 p., [no. of copies omitted]. KL
   11.23
   Contains stories by Ambrose Bierce, Joseph Conrad,
   William Morrow, Lawrence Mott. Titles not listed in KL.
   The error of including Conrad was subsequently noted by
   Soviet critics.

4. Amerikanskaya novella XIX veka [the American short
   story of the 19th century]. Edited and with an introd. by
   A. Startsev. Goslitizdat., M., 1946. 478 p., 25,000 c.
   Contents: Washington Irving, Rip Van Vinkle (Rip van
   Winkle). Edgar Allan Poe, Zolotoi zhuk (The gold bug),
   Bochonok Amontilyado (The cask of Amontillado). Nathan-
   iel Hawthorne, Sedoi zastupnik (The gray champion), Opyt
   doktora Kheideggera (Dr. Heidegger's experiment),
   Molodoi Braun (Young Goodman Brown), Gibel mistera
   Khigginbotoma (Mr. Higginbothom's catastrophe). T. B.
   Thorpe, Bolshoi medved iz Arkanzasa (The big bear of
   Arkansaw from The hive of the bee-hunter). Edward E.

[Everett] Hale, Chelovek bez rodiny (The man without a country). Bret Harte, Kompanyon Tenessi (Tennessee's partner), Kak Santa Klaus prishol v Simpson-Bar (How Santa Claus came to Simpson's Bar). Mark Twain, Znamenitaya skachushchaya lyagushka (The celebrated jumping frog of Calaveras county), Zhurnalistika v Tenessi (Journalism in Tennessee), Bankovy bilet v 1000000 funtov sterlingov (The £1,000,000 banknote). Thomas Bailey Aldrich, Mardzhori Dou (Marjorie Daw from Marjorie Daw and other stories). George Cable, Posson Dzhon (Posson Jone' from Old Creole days), Zhan-akh! Poklen (Jean-ah-Poquelin from Old Creole days). Joel Chandler Harris, Skazki dyadyushki Rimusa [tales of Uncle Remus]. Henry James, Dezi Miller (Daisy Miller). Hamlin Garland, Vozvrashcheniye soldata (The return of a private from Main-travelled roads), Pod lapoi lva (Under the lion's paw from Main-travelled roads). Frank Norris, Sdelka s pshenitsei (A deal in wheat). Ambrose Bierce, Zapolnenny probel (A resumed identity from Can such things be?), Kuvshin siropa (A jug of sirup from Can such things be?), Diagnoz smerti (A diagnosis of death from Can such things be?). Stephen Crane, Na temu o nishchete (An experiment in misery from Men, women and boats), Voyenny epizod (An episode of war from Men, women and boats), Tyomnoryzhaya sobaka (A dark-brown dog from Men, women and boats).

5. Amerikanskaya novella XX veka [the American short story of the 20th century]. Selected and edited by A. Gavrilov, I. Kashkin, N. Eishiskina, A. Yelistratova. Goslitizdat., M., 1934. 371 p., 5000 c. KL 939.35 Contents: Stephen Crane, Taina geroizma [the secret of heroism; not identified], Shlyupka (The open boat from Men, women and boats). Henry James, Biografiya pisatelya [biography of a writer; not identified]. Ambrose Bierce, Pokhorony Dzhona Mortonsona (John Mortonson's funeral from Can such things be?), Sluchai na mostu cherez Soviny ruchei (An occurrence at Owl Creek bridge from In the midst of life). Jack London, Lyubov k zhizni (Love of life from Love of life, and other stories). O. Henry, Gorod bez proisshestvi [city without incident; not identified]. Ring Lardner, Chempion (Champion from the collected short stories of Ring Lardner). John Reed, Noch na Brodveye (Night on Broadway from Daughter of the

revolution). Sherwood Anderson, Pogibshi roman (The
lost novel from Death in the woods and other stories),
Chto zastavlyayet malchika boyatsya [what compels the
boy to be afraid; not identified, but possibly The man who
became a woman from Horses and men]. Ernest Hemingway, Alpiskaya idilliya (An Alpine idyll from The fifth
column and the first forty-nine stories). William Faulkner,
Kogda nastupayet noch [when night falls; not identified,
but possibly That evening sun from Collected stories of
William Faulkner]. Erskine Caldwell, Pustaya komnata
(The empty room from We are the living), V subbotu
dnyom (Saturday afternoon from Jackpot), Polnym polno
shvedov (Country full of Swedes from We are the living).
George Milburn, Kabluk, nosok i raz-dva-tri (Heel, toe
and a 1, 2, 3, 4 from O'Brien, The best short stories of
1932). Agnes Smedley, Vdova muchenika (The martyr's
widow from Chinese destinies), Synovni bunt (A Chinese
son rebels from Chinese destinies). Langston Hughes,
Smirennaya Kora (Cora unashamed from The ways of
white folks). Jack Conroy, Bezdomnyie [homeless ones;
not identified, but possibly They won't let us birds roost
nowheres from New Masses, June, 1933, p. 18], Artel
mostovshchikov (Paving gang — on a job in Missouri from
New Masses, Feb., 1932, p. 20). Whittaker Chambers,
Slyshite li vy ikh golosa (Can you hear their voices? from
New Masses, March, 1931, p. 7). Michael Gold, Malchik,
kotory umer za Tammani (The boy who died for Tammany
from New Masses, Jan., 1932, p. 18), Svobodny! [free; not
identified].

6. Amerikanski yumor [American humor]. Trans. by P.
   Okhrimenko. Biblioteka Zhurnala "Ogonyok," M., 1927.
   48 p., 15,000 c. KL 5244.27
   Contains works by Rube Goldberg, Ellis Parker Butler,
   Stephen Leacock, Henry Hanemann, Oliver Herford,
   Christopher Ward, Josh Billings. Titles not listed in KL.

7. Amerikanskiye komedii [American comedies]. Trans. by
   L. Shiffers. Iskusstvo, M., 1940. 170 p., 1075 c. KL
   14407.40
   A collection of one-act plays. Contents not listed in KL.

8. Amerikanskiye rasskazy [American short stories]. Trans.
   by Yuri Smirnov. Zhurn. Gaz. Obyed., M., 1937. 39 p.,
   50,000 c. KL 11081.37

Contents: John Wexley, Shosse No. 51 (Southern Highway
51). Dzhei Dzherlando [this writer not identified],
Oshibka [The mistake; not identified]. Albert Maltz,
Chelovek na doroge (Man on a road). Len Zinberg, Bolshiye ruki (Big hands). Marcelo Salinas, Zashchitnik
(The protector). Jack Conroy, On — tysyachi (He is
thousands).
"Southern Highway 51" is from O. Henry memorial award,
1934; "Man on a road" is from The way things are; "Big
hands" is from New Masses, July 2, 1935, p. 22; "The
protector" is from New Masses, Feb. 25, 1936, p. 19;
"He is thousands" is from New Masses, May, 1932, p. 18.

9. Angliskiye i amerikanskiye pyesy v odnoi deistvi [English
and American one-act plays]. Trans. by L. Shiffers.
Iskusstvo, M. & L., 1946. 135 p., 5000 c. KL 11682.46
Contents: Florence Ryerson and Colin Clements, Takov
Gollivud (That's Hollywood). Josephine Niggli, Byka
otravali (This bull ate nutmeg). The volume also contains
plays by Allan Monkhouse, Ronald Mitchell, Herbert Farjeon,
Bernard Cronin, and Stanley Houghton, all British dramatists.
"That's Hollywood" is from Mayorga, The best one-act
plays of 1939; "This bull ate nutmeg" is from Kozlenko,
Contemporary one-act plays.

10. Antologiya negrityanskoi poezii [an anthology of Negro
poetry]. Selected and trans. by R. Magidov. Zhurn. Gaz.
Obyed., M., 1936. 46 p., 50,000 c. KL 8615.36
Contents not listed in KL.

11. Antologiya revolyutsionnoi poezii [anthology of revolutionary poetry]. Edited by Vasili Kazin and Sergei
Obradovich. Izvestiya, M., 1924. 108 p., 13,000 c.
Contains selections from three American poets: Walt
Whitman, Bei! bei baraban! (Beat! beat! drums!), Gody
sovremennyie (Years of the modern). Henry Wadsworth
Longfellow, Nevolnik v proklyatom bolote (The slave in
the dismal swamp). Claude McKay, Proklyatiye porabashchennovo [curses of the enslaved; not identified], V plenu
[in captivity; not identified].

12. Deti Ameriki [children of America]. Detizdat., M., 1943.
[no. of pages and no. of copies omitted]. Znamya (M.),
1944, No. 3, p. 161 (coll. s.)
Contents: John Steinbeck, Ryzhi poni (The red pony).
Irwin Shaw, Zemlyanichnoye morozhenoye (Strawberry

ice cream soda). Ernest Hemingway, Na Big-River (Big two-hearted river). Erskine Caldwell, Moi starik (My old man). James Stevens, Amerikanski Gerkules [American Hercules; not identified, but probably a selection from Paul Bunyan or The Saginaw Paul Bunyan].
"The red pony" is from The long valley; "Strawberry ice cream soda" is from Sailor off the Bremen; "Big two-hearted river" is from In our time; "My old man" is from Jackpot.

13. Mekhanika vyborov v stranakh kapitalizma: v izobra-zhenii khudozhestvennoi literatury [the mechanics of elections in capitalist countries as described in belles lettres]. Kommunist (Kuibyshev), 1937, No. 17-18, pp. 36-39. ZL 45526.37
Contents: Mark Twain, Kak menya vybirali v guberna-tory (Running for governor). T. S. Stribling, Vyborny vagon (The sound wagon).
"Running for governor" is from Sketches new and old; "The sound wagon" is an excerpt from the novel The sound wagon.

14. Na podyome: almanakh proletarskoi i revolyutsionnoi literatury zapadnoi Yevropy i Ameriki [on the ascent: an almanac of proletarian and revolutionary literature of Western Europe and America]. Selected by M. S. Zhivov; edited by A. Gorlin. Goslitizdat., M. & L., 1932. 416 p., 200 c.
Contains selections from the following American writ-ers: Mary Heaton Vorse, Zabastovka (Strike!). Michael Gold, Pogonya za kuskom khleba [pursuit of a piece of bread; not identified], Dopros s pristrastiyem [a biased interrogation; not identified]. Joseph Kalar, Syn shakh-tera [miner's son; not identified]. Hyug Kein [this writer not identified], Predannost [devotion; not identi-fied]. Norman MacLeod, Ovechye stado [a flock of sheep; not identified]. John Dos Passos, Ueslei Everest (Paul Bunyan). A. B. Magil, Tak on umer [thus he died not identified]. Joseph Freeman, Dzhentlmen iz Arkanzasa [gentleman from Arkansas; not identified].
"Strike" is an excerpt from the novel Strike!; "Paul Bunyan" is an excerpt from the novel 1919.

15. Negrityanskaya narodnaya poeziya [Negro folk poetry].

Trans. by Yu. Anisimov. Int. Lit. (M.), 1934, No. 5,
pp. 86-88.
Contents: Pesni kandalnykh artelei [songs of the shack-
led trade unions; not identified]. Vorovskaya pesn
[theives' song; not identified, but possibly Death of Do
Dirty from Fine clothes to the Jew by Langston Hughes].
Toska [yearning; not identified].

16. Negrityanskaya poeziya [Negro poetry]. Trans. by Yu.
Anisimov. Int. Lit. (M.), 1935, No. 11, pp. 63-65.
Contents: Iz negrityanskikh pesen protesta [from Negro
songs of protest; not identified]. Sterling Brown, Deti
Missisipi (Children of the Mississippi). Langston
Hughes, Dom v mire (House in the world). Everett
Hawkins, Prometei [Prometheus; not identified].
"Children of the Mississippi" is from Southern road.
Unable to locate source for "House in the world."

17. Pesni i ballady amerikanskikh poetov XX veka [songs
and ballads of American poets of the 20th century]. Int.
Lit. (M.), 1937, No. 4, pp. 125-134. ZL 26824.37
Contents: Ben Lucien Burman, Kak Mak Farlandy s
Kobbami bilis (Oh, the Cobbs an' McFarlands are fight-
in'). Vachel Lindsay, Kongo (The Congo), Dzhon Braun
(John Brown). Edward O'Connor, Nikto ne proidyot (No-
body knows). Aunt Molly Jackson, Golodnyie pesni
(The hungry blues).
"Oh, the Cobbs an' McFarlands are fightin'" is from
Century Magazine, Jan., 1925, p. 384; "The Congo" and
"John Brown" are from Vachel Lindsay, Collected
poems; "The hungry blues" is from New Masses, Dec.,
1931, p. 4. Unable to locate source for "Nobody knows."

18. Poeti Ameriki XX veka [American poets of the 20th
century]. Selected and trans. by Ivan Kashkin and M.
Zenkevich; introd. by Ivan Kashkin. Goslitizdat., M.,
1939. 287 p., 10,000 c.
Contains selections from the poetry of Edwin Arlington
Robinson, Carl Sandburg, Vachel Lindsay, Robert Frost,
Edgar Lee Masters, John Gould Fletcher, Hilda Doo-
little, Edna St. Vincent Millay, Elinor Wylie, William
Carlos Williams, Ernest Walsh, Alfred Kreymborg,
Louis Untermeyer, Robinson Jeffers, Archibald Mac-
Leish, Ernest Hemingway, Arturo Giovannitti, Michael
Gold, Joseph Kalar, A. B. Magil, Joe Hill, Edward

O'Connor, Aunt Molly Jackson, Ben Lucien Burman,
Lawrence Gellert, Countee Cullen, Sterling Brown and
Langston Hughes.

19. Rasskazy molodykh amerikanskikh pisatelei [stories
    of young American writers]. Trans. by Yu. Smirnov.
    Zhurn. Gas. Obyed., M., 1938. 48 p., 50,000 c. KL
    3270.38
    Stories by Len Zinberg, Richard Bransten, Dee Brown,
    Albert Maltz, Irene Merrill, Joseph Starobin, Peter
    Quince. Contents not listed in KL.

20. Sem amerikanskikh yumoristov [seven American humor-
    ists]. Trans. by Ye. Tolkachev. Proletari, Kharkov,
    1928. 178 p., [no. of copies omitted]. KL 597.28
    Contents not listed in KL.

21. Skazki severo-amerikanskikh indeitsev: O tom, otkuda
    poyavilsya mokh; O tom kak vykhukhol i bobyor pomen-
    yalis khvostami; O tom, kak possorilis krolik s rysyu
    [tales of the North American Indians: Where moss
    came from; How the muskrat and the beaver exchanged
    tails; How the rabbit quarreled with the lynx; not iden-
    tified]. Trans. and adapted by V. Isakov. Leningrad
    (L.), 1940, No. 3, p. 17. ZL 23052.40

22. Stikhi imazhistov [poetry of the Imagists]. Trans. by
    Ivan Kashkin. Int. Lit. (M.), 1937, No. 2, pp. 128-131.
    Contents: John Gould Fletcher, Iz knigi "Izlucheniya"
    [from the book Irradiations]. Hilda Doolittle, Znoi
    (Heat), Ostrova (The islands), Kormchi (The helmsman).
    William Carlos Williams, Metricheskaya figura (Metric
    figure), Rassvet (Dawn). Elinor Wylie, Pesenka
    bezumnovo (Madman's song). Ernest Walsh, Lyubovnaya
    pesn (A love song).
    "Heat" and "The helmsman" are from Sea Garden;
    "The islands" is from Hymen; "Metric figure" and
    "Dawn" are from The collected earlier poems of William
    Carlos Williams; "Madman's song" is from Elinor
    Wylie, Collected poems; "A love song" is from Ernest
    Walsh, Poems and Sonnets.

INDIVIDUAL AUTHORS

ADAMS, Samuel Hopkins

23. Razgul (Revelry). Trans. from the 9th Amer. ed. by S.
Zaimovski; foreword by V. G. Boss. Gosizdat., M. & L.,
1928. 312 p., 7000 c. KL 3462.28 (n.)

24. Tyoploye mestechko [warm little town]. Lit. Sov. (L.),
1937, No. 12, pp. 219-24. ZL 4781.38
An excerpt from Revelry.

ALDRICH, Thomas Bailey

Mardzhouri Dou (Marjorie Daw). See 4.

25. Vospominaniya amerikanskoyo shkolnika (The story of
a bad boy). Trans. and adapted by T. Gabbe and Z.
Zadunaiskaya. Gosizdat., M. & L., 1930. 174 p., 10,000
c. KL 27284.30 (n.)
A juvenile publication.

26. Same. 1934. 208 p., 25,325 c. KL 16346.34

ANDERSON, Sherwood

Collected works

27. Sobraniye sochineni [collected works]. With critical
material edited by Yev. Lann. ZIF, M. & L., 1925. KL
15306.25
KL lists only one volume in this edition. See 40.

Separate publications

Chto zastavlyayet malchika boyatsya. See 5.

28. Dver lovushki (The door of the trap). Trans. by P.
Okhrimenko, with an introd. by the translator.
Sovremenny Zapad (L.), 1923, No. 3, pp. 96-105. (s.)
From The triumph of the egg.

29. Istoriya rasskazchika (A story teller's story). Trans.
by Ye. Romanova. Int. Lit. (M.), 1935, No. 10, pp. 107-
118; No. 11, pp. 98-114. (autobiog.)
Excerpts.

ANDERSON, Sherwood (Continued)

30. Same. Trans. by Ye. Romanova; introd. by S. Dinamov; annotated by R. Z. Magidov. Goslitizdat., M., 1936. 318 p., 10,000 c. KL 8571.36

31. Koni i lyudi (Horses and men). Trans. by M. Volosov. Petrograd, L. & M., 1926. 249 p., 4000 c. KL 20250.25 (coll. s.)

32. Loshadi i lyudi (Horses and men). Trans. by M. Kovalenskaya. Gosizdat., M. & L., 1927. 250 p., 15,000 c. KL 16767.27

33. Po tu storonu zhelaniya (Beyond desire). Trans. by P. Okhrimenko; introd. by S. S. Dinamov. Goslitizdat., M. & L., 1933. 320 p., 5000 c. KL 24887.33 (n.)

34. Pogibshi roman (The lost novel). Trans. by A. V. Krivtsova. Lit. Mir. Rev. (M), 1932, No. 9-10, pp. 72-74. (s). From Death in the woods and other stories.

    Same. See 5.

35. Smert v lesu (Death in the woods). Trans. by Yel. Romanova. Int. Lit. (M.), 1934, No. 3-4, pp. 180-185. (s.) From Death in the woods and other stories.

36. Same. Trans. by Val. Stenich. Lit. Sov. (L.), 1934, No. 10, pp. 67-75. ZL 7602.35

37. Sudebny sluchai [a legal occurrence; not identified]. Trans. by I. S. Makarov. 30 Dnei (L.), 1934, No. 12, pp. 41-44. ZL 12286.35 (s.)

38. Torzhestvo yaitsa (The triumph of the egg). Trans. by P. Okhrimenko. Sov. Prob., M., 1925. 257 p., 5000 c. KL 1070.25 (coll. s.)

39. Uainsburg, Ogaio (Winesburg, Ohio). Trans. by P. Okhrimenko; foreword by M. Levidov. L. D. Frenkel, M. & L., 1924, 248 p., 3000 c. KL 5202.24 (n.)

40. Same. Trans. by P. Okhrimenko. ZIF, M. & L., 1925. 360 p., 5000 c. Sob. soch., Vol. II. See 27. KL 15306.25

41. Uinsberg Okhaio (Winesburg, Ohio). Trans. by S. D. Matveyev. Gosizdat., M., 1924. 224 p., 3000 c. KL 12178.24

42. V nogu! (Marching men). Trans. by Mark Volosov;
    foreword by V. Lavretski. Mysl, L., 1927. 232 p.,
    5000 c. KL 7457.27 (n.)

43. Yaitso (The egg). Trans. by P. Okhrimenko. Biblioteka
    Zhurnala "Ogonyok," M., 1926. 63 p., 14,000 c. KL
    22270.26 (coll. s.)
    From The triumph of the egg. Other titles not listed in
    KL.

ARKWRIGHT, James

44. Stikhi [poetry; not identified]. Trans. by G. Fish.
    Zvezda (L.), 1931, No. 4, pp. 138-142.

ASCH, Nathan

45. Doroga (The road: in search of America). Trans. by
    O. Romm. Goslitizdat., M., 1938. 200 p., 20,000 c.
    KL 19894.38 (coll. sk.)

46. Kontora (The office), with an introd. by Joseph Free-
    man. Trans. by I. Streshnev; foreword by I. Kashkin.
    Krug, M., 1927. 248 p., 5000 c. KL 13334.27 (n.)

47. Povest o devushke Mertl [the story of a girl named
    Myrtle]. Trans. by A. Romm. Inter. Molodyozhi (M.),
    1938, No. 1, pp. 34-35. ZL 7424.38 (sk.)
    An excerpt from The road.

48. Zateryannaya preriya [remote prairie]. Trans. by N.
    Kamionskaya. Int. Lit. (M.), 1936, No. 11, pp. 185-188.
    (sk.)
    An excerpt from The road.

ATHERTON, Gertrude

49. Ubistvo Mistera Bolfema (Mrs. Balfame). Trans. by
    N. A. Sakharova. Mysl, L., 1928. 312 p., 5200 c. KL
    21203.28 (n.)

AUSTIN, Mary

50. Gost iz stolitsy [guest from the capital; not identified].
    Trans. from the manuscript by M. Gorkina. Oktyabr
    (M.), 1934, No. 4, pp. 91-116. ZL 30705.34 (s.)

BEACH, Rex

51. Khishchniki Alyaski (The spoilers). Trans. by N. M.

BEACH, Rex (Continued)

Tsymovich. Mysl, L., 1926. 279 p., 4000 c. KL 4442.26 (n.)

52. Zapozdavshi vzryv (Cool waters). Trans. and adapted by S. Lyalitskaya. G. F. Mirimanov, M., 1928. 18 p., 10,000 c. KL 4875.28 (s.)
A juvenile publication. From The goose woman and other stories.

BELLAH, James Warner*

53. Lyotchiki [aviators; not identified]. Trans. by P. Okhrimenko. Goslitizdat., Sverdlovsk, 1942. 39 p., 50,000 c. KL 14324.44 (s.)

54. Obyknovenny Anglichanin (Jonathan Brasenose). Trans. by T. Ozerskaya. Int. Lit. (M.), 1941, No. 11-12, pp. 140-148. (s.)
From Saturday Evening Post, Aug. 23, 1941, pp. 16-17.

BENGAL, Ben

55. Pervyie pobegi (Plant in the sun). Trans. by Ye. Kalashnikova. Int. Lit. (M.), 1940, No. 2, pp. 136-150. (pl.)
From Kozlenko, The best short plays of the social theater.

BERCOVICI, Konrad

Collected Works

56. Sobraniye sochineni [collected works]. Sov. Prob., M., 1927. KL 6089.27
KL lists only one volume in this edition. See 67.

Separate Publications

57. Doch ukrotitelya (The bear tamer's daughter). Trans. by P. Okhrimenko. 2nd ed. Sov. Prob., M., 1925. 206 p., 5000 c. KL 18232.25 (coll. s.)
From Ghitza and other romances of gypsy blood. Other titles not listed in KL.

---

*Mr. Bellah has asked the compilers to state that his works were translated into Russian "without the permission or knowledge of the author."

59. Same. 1927. 206 p., 3000 c. KL 19295.27

60. Fanutsa (Fanutza). Trans. by P. Okhrimenko. Biblio-
    teka Zhurnala "Ogonyok," M., 1927. 64 p., 16,000 c.
    KL 929.27 (coll. s.)
    From Ghitza and other romances of gypsy blood. Other
    titles not listed in KL.

61. Same. 1927. 64 p., 16,000 c. KL 13339.27

62. Kino-akter (The troubles of a perfect type). Trans. by
    P. Okhrimenko. Gosizdat., M. & L., 1926. 64 p.,
    15,000 c. KL 11208.26 (coll. s.)
    From Dust of New York. Other titles not listed in KL.

63. Lena [Lena; not identified, but possibly Iliana from
    Iliana: stories of a wandering race, or Ileana from Love
    and the gypsy]. Trans. by Mark Volosov. Mysl, L.,
    1927. 89 p., 5200 c. KL 20351.27 (coll. s.)

64. Poyushchi veter (Singing winds). Trans. by A. V.
    Krivtsova. Krug, M., 1927. 239 p., 4000 c. KL
    13940.27 (coll. s.)

65. Schastye (Happiness). Trans. by P. Okhrimenko. Sov.
    Prob., M., 1926. 247 p., 5000 c. KL 19189.25 (coll. s.)
    From Iliana: stories of a wandering race. Other titles
    not listed in KL.

66. Semya (Seed). Trans. by P. Okhrimenko. Biblioteka
    Zhurnala "Ogonyok," M., 1927. 52 p., 30,000 c. KL
    2505.27 (s.)
    From Iliana: stories of a wandering race.

67. Svadebny gost (The marriage guest). Trans. by T.
    Shchepkina-Kupernik. Sov. Prob., M., 1927. 235 p.,
    4000 c. Sob. soch., Vol. IV. See 56. KL 6089.27 (n.)

68. Tsyganskaya krov [gypsy blood]. Trans. by L. S.
    Sovelev. Seyatel, L., 1926. 78 p., 15,250 c. KL
    9550.26 (coll. s.)
    Contents not listed in KL.

69. Tsyganskiye rasskazy [gypsy stories]. Trans. by P.
    Okhrimenko. Biblioteka Zhurnala "Ogonyok," M.,
    1926. 64 p., 12,500 c. KL 11683.26 (coll. s.)
    Contents not listed in KL.

70. Vetry poyushchiye (Singing winds). Trans. by Mark Volo-
    sov. Priboi, L., 1927. 199 p., 5000 c. KL 14491.27 (coll. s.)

BERCOVICI, Konrad (Continued)

71. Zhenskoye serdtse [woman's heart; not identified].
Trans. by P. Okhrimenko. Gosizdat., M. & L., 1926.
61 p., 15,000 c. KL 18997.26 (coll. s.)

BETHEA, Jack

72. Gluboki shram (The deep seam). Trans. by A. A.
Gavrilova. Gosizdat., M. & L., 1927. 260 p., 5000 c.
KL 16769.27 (n.)

73. Same. 1930. 252 p., 5000 c. KL 27240.30

BIERCE, Ambrose

Diagnoz smerti (A diagnosis of death). See 4.

74. Drozd (The mocking-bird). Trans. by G. Yarros. 30
Dnei (L.), 1937, No. 1, pp. 58-67. ZL 15339.37 (s.)
From In the midst of life.

75. Kapitan Rensom (One kind of officer). Trans. by G.
Yarros. 30 Dnei (L.), 1936, No. 7, pp. 51-59. ZL
47236.36 (s.)
From In the midst of life.

Kuvshin siropa (A jug of sirup). See 4.

76. Lyubimitsa moyei tyotushki (Curried cow). Trans. by
M. Kessel. Int. Lit. (M.), 1935, No. 2, pp. 111-114.
(s.)
From Negligible tales.

77. Nastoyashcheye chudovishche (In the midst of life).
Trans. and with an introd. by V. A. Azov. Vremya,
L., 1926. 163 p., 4150 c. KL 4441.26 (coll. s.)

78. Podvig (A son of the gods). Trans. by P. Okhrimenko.
30 Dnei (L.), 1938, No. 10, pp. 83-87. ZL 58227.38
(s.)
From In the midst of life.

Pokhorony Dzhona Martonsona (John Mortonson's funeral). See 5.

79. Rasskazy [short stories]. I. A. Kashkin, editor of translation; introd. by Ye. Yelistratova. Goslitizdat., M.,
1938. 152 p., 10,000 c. KL 28223.38 (coll. s.)
Contents not listed in KL.

80. Salto mistera Sviddlera (Mr. Swiddler's flip-flap).
Trans. by N. Daruzes. 30 Dnei (L.), 1937, No. 9, pp.
72-75. ZL 38934.37 (s.)
From Negligible tales.

Sluchai na mostu cherez Soviny ruchei (An occurrence
at Owl Creek bridge). See 5.

81. Vsadnik v nebe (A horseman in the sky). Trans. by P.
Okhrimenko. 30 Dnei (L.), 1936, No. 5, pp. 48-52.
ZL 32376.36 (s.)
From In the midst of life.

Zapolnenny probel (A resumed identity). See 4.

BISHOP, Ellen

82. Na peschanoi doroge (Along a sandy road). Trans. by
P. Okhrimenko. 30 Dnei (L.), 1936, No. 1, pp. 53-55.
ZL 16023.36 (s.)
From O'Brien, The best short stories of 1930.

BLACK, Jack

83. Zakon vsesilen (You can't win). Trans. by Mark Volosov.
Vremya, L., 1927. 287 p., 4150 c. KL 9821.27 (autobiog.)

BODENHEIM, Maxwell

84. Devyatoye avenyu (Ninth avenue). Trans. by M. Kuznets.
Puchina, M., 1927. 274 p., 5150 c. KL 13943.27 (n.)

BOIE, Mildred

85. Vesna v Karoline [spring in Carolina; not identified].
Trans. by Yu. Anisimov. Int. Lit. (M.), 1940, No. 7-8,
p. 65. (μ.)

BOOTHE, Clare (Mrs. Clare Boothe Luce)

86. Trizhdy ubity (Margin for error). Trans. and adapted
by Leonid Lench; edited by T. Rokotov. Int. Lit. (M.),
1942, No. 3-4-5, pp. 134-156. (pl.)

BOYD, Thomas Alexander

87. V mirnoye vremya (In time of peace). Trans. by K.

BOYD, Thomas Alexander (Continued)

Ksanina; foreword by T. Khmelnitskaya. Goslitizdat., L., 1940. 336 p., 10,000 c. KL 2352.41 (n.)

BRADFORD, Roark

88. Starik Adam i yevo deti (Ol' man Adam an' his chillun). Trans. by D. L. Maizels and I. I. Solovyova. Goslitizdat., L. & M., 1931. 168 p., 5140 c. KL 29971.31 (coll. s.)

BRADY, Robert

89. Stikhi ob interventsii [poetry about intervention; not identified]. Trans. and with an introd. by A. Birs. Zvezda Severa (Arkhangelsk), 1935, No. 7, pp. 3-5. ZL 55479.35

BROMFIELD, Louis

90. Khoroshaya zhenshchina (A good woman). Trans. by L. L. Domger. Vremya, L., 1928. 280 p., 4000 c. KL 13257.28 (n.)

91. Spravedlivost (Justice). Trans. by P. Okhrimenko. 30 Dnei (L.), 1939, No. 7, pp. 56-64. ZL 46502.39 (s.) From Awake and rehearse.

BROWN, Lee

92. Pered sobraniyem [before the meeting; not identified]. Trans. by Yu. Smirnov. Mol. Gvard. (M.), 1937, No. 10-11, pp. 23-54. ZL 45523.37

BROWN, Sterling

Deti Missisipi (Children of the Mississippi). See 16.

93. Na rassvete (Break of day). Trans. by M. Zenkevich. Int. Lit. (M.), 1940, No. 1, p. 87. (p.) From New Republic, May 11, 1938, p. 10.

94. Yuzhnaya doroga (Southern road). Trans. by Yu. Anisimov. Int. Lit. (M.), 1940, No. 7-8, p. 65. (p.) From Southern road.

BRYANT, William Cullen

95. Svoboda [freedom; not identified]. Trans. by T.

Shchepkina-Kupernik. <u>Zvezda</u> (M. & L.), 1924, No. 6, p. 112. (p.)

BUCK, Pearl

96. Mat (The mother). Trans. by N. Daruzes. <u>Int. Lit.</u> (M.), 1935, No. 11, pp. 3-34. (n.)
An excerpt

97. Same. Trans. by N. L. Daruzes. Golitizdat., M., 1936. 215 p., 10,000 c. KL 23275.36

98. Mesto v zhizni (Virgin birth). Trans. by T. and V. Ravinski. <u>Lit. Sov</u>. (L.), 1937, No. 5, pp. 117-136. ZL 26860.37 (s.)
From <u>Far and near</u>.

99. Pervaya zhena Yuana (The first wife). Trans. by B. Gendlyar. <u>Mol. Gvard</u>. (M.), 1937, No. 8, pp. 81-106. ZL 35001.37 (s.)
From <u>The first wife, and other stories</u>.

100. Synovya (Sons). Trans. by N. L. Daruzes. Goslitizdat., M., 1935. 396 p., 15,000 c. KL 22795.35 (n.)

101. Same. Trans. by N. Daruzes. <u>Kras. Nov</u>. (M.), 1935, No. 1, pp. 32-69; No. 2, pp. 108-143; No. 3, pp. 62-120. ZL 17202.35

102. Same. <u>Int. Lit</u>. (M.), 1935, No. 5, pp. 9-52.
An excerpt.

103. Yuan (A house divided). Trans. by L. Brodski. <u>Znamya</u> (M.), 1935, No. 12, pp. 102-158. ZL 2059.36 (n.)
An excerpt.

104. Zemlya (The good earth). Trans. by N. L. Daruzes; introd. by S. Tretyakov. Goslitizdat., M. & L., 1934. 267 p., 5000 c. KL 9522.34 (n.)

105. Same. Goslitizdat., M., 1935. 317 p., 50,000 c. KL 18548.35

106. Same. 1936. 285 p., 50,000 c. KL 536.37

107. Same. Trans. by N. Daruzes. <u>Int. Lit</u>. (M.), 1934, No. 2, pp. 34-57.
An excerpt.

108. Same. Trans. by A. D. Gurevich; foreword by Karl

BUCK, Pearl (Continued)

> Radek. Zhurn. Gaz. Obyed., M., 1935. 48 p., 40,000 c.
> KL 12815.35
> An excerpt.

BUCKNER, Robert L.

109. Chelovek, kotory vyigral voinu (Man who won the war).
Trans. by G. Yarros. Znamya (M.), 1937, No. 12,
pp. 164-174. ZL 47878.37 (s.)
From Atlantic Monthly, Feb., 1936, pp. 208-16.

BURMAN, Ben Lucien

> Kak Mak Farlendy s Kobbami bilis (Oh, the Cobbs an'
> McFarlands are fightin'). See 17.

BURNSHAW, Stanley

110. Ya—Dzhim Rodzhers (I, Jim Rogers). Trans. by Ye.
Polonskaya. Int. Lit. (M.), 1936, No. 10, pp. 57-58. (p.)
From Proletarian literature in the United States (New
York, International Publishers, 1935).

BURROUGHS, Edgar Rice

111. Bogi Marsa (The gods of Mars). A. M. Dmitriev, editor of translation. Novella, P., 1923. 282 p., 5000 c.
KL 12114.23 (n.)

112. Bogi na Marse (The gods of Mars). Trans. by E. K.
Brodersen. A. F. Marks, P., 1923. 189 p., 7000 c.
KL 12131.23 (n.)

113. Boksyor Billi [boxer Billy; not identified]. Trans. by
E. K. Brodersen. A. F. Marks, P., 1924. 163 p.,
5000 c. KL 721.24 (n.)

114. Doch tysyachi dzheddakov [not identified]. Trans. by
E. K. Brodersen. A. F. Marks, P., 1923. 141 p.,
7000 c. KL 11065.23

115. Priklyuchiniya Tarzana v dzhunglyakh (Jungle tales of
Tarzan). Trans. by B. Markovich. A. F. Marks, P.,
1923. 173 p., 3000 c. KL 8984.23 (coll. s.)

116. Same. 1923. 173 p., 3000 c. KL 18.24

117. Printsessa Marsa (A princess of Mars). A. M.
Dmitriev, editor of translation. Novella, P., 1923.
236 p., 5000 c. KL 11539.23 (n.)

118. Syn Tarzana (The son of Tarzan). Trans. by L. and N. Chukovski. A. F. Marks, P., 1923. 137 p., 8000 c. KL 9699.23 (n.)

119. Same. 1924. 189 p., 5000 c. KL 261.24

120. Tarzan (Tarzan of the apes). Trans. by N. Kamenshchikov. Moskovski Rabochi, M., 1922. 272 p., 10,000 c. KL 8529.22 (n.)

121. Same. 2nd revised ed. Edited by S. G. Zaimovski. Novaya Moskva, M., 1923. Part I, 276 p., 10,000 c. KL 7410.23

122. Tarzan i sokrovishcha Opara (Tarzan and the jewels of Opar). Trans. by F. Markushevich. A. F. Marks, P., 1924. 154 p., 7000 c. KL 261.24 (n.)

123. Tarzan i yevo zveri (The beasts of Tarzan). Trans. by E. K. Brodersen. A. F. Marks, P., 1923. 189 p., 8000 c. KL 9700.23 (n.)

124. Same. 1924. 137 p., 5000 c. KL 1252.24

125. Tarzan: priklyuchiniya v dzhunglyakh (Jungle tales of Tarzan). Trans. by A. O. Martyanova. Atenei, P., 1923. 176 p., 5000 c. KL 8381.23 (coll. s.)

126. Tarzan—priyomysh obezyany (Tarzan of the apes). Trans. by M. V. Vatson, A. F. Marks, P., 1923. 222 p., 7000 c. KL 11066.23 (n.)

127. Tarzan: vozvrashcheniye v dzhungli (The return of Tarzan). Trans. by M. K. Mysl, P., 1923. 240 p., 6000 c. KL 5830.23 (n.)

128. Vladyka Marsa (The warlord of Mars). Trans. by E. K. Brodersen. A. F. Marks, P., 1923. 128 p., 7000 c. KL 12783.23 (n.)

129. Vozvrashcheniye Tarzana (The return of Tarzan). V. A. Azov, editor of translation. Gosizdat., M. & P., 1923. 243 p., 7000 c. KL 8944.23 (n.)

130. Vozvrashcheniye Tarzana v dzhungli (The return of Tarzan). Trans. by S. Emden. A. F. Marks, P., 1923. 188 p., 5000 c. KL 7422.23

131. Same. 1923. 189 p., 5000 c.

132. Zakorenely prestupnik [a hardened criminal; not identified]. Trans. by E. K. Brodersen. A. F. Marks, L., 1924. 176 p., 5000 c. KL 11076.24

56

BUTLER, Ellis Parker

133. Blokhi vse zhe blokhi (Fleas will be fleas). Trans. by
Ye. Tolkachev; edited by M. Zenkevich. ZIF, M. & L.,
1928. 151 p., 5000 c. KL 7149.28 (coll. s.)
From American Mercury, Dec., 1907, pp. 152-160.
Other titles not listed in KL.

134. Krasny shnurok [the red cord; not identified]. Trans.
by P. Okhrimenko. ZIF, M. & L., 1926. 32 p., 15,000
c. KL 12707.26 (coll. s.)
Also contains stories by Eugene Field, Stephen Leacock and Josh Billings. Titles not listed in KL.

135. Modny mekh [modish fur; not identified]. Trans. by
Ye. Tolkachev. ZIF, M. & L., 1928. 32 p., 10,000 c.
KL 10865.28 (coll. s.)

136. Svini—vsegda svini (Pigs is pigs). Trans. by Ye.
Tolkachev. ZIF, M. & L., 1926. 39 p., 12,000 c.
KL 22274.26 (s.)

BYRNE, Donn

137. Dom palacha (Hangman's house). Trans. by Mark
Volosov; introd. by I. Zvavich. ZIF, M. & L., 1929.
325 p., 5000 c. KL 1566.29 (n.)

CABLE, George

Posson Dzhon (Posson Jone'). See 4.

Zhan—akh! Poklen (Jean — ah — Poquelin). See 4.

CAHAN, Abraham

138. Karyera Levinskovo (The rise of David Levinsky).
Trans. by S. I. Tsederbaum. Kniga, L. & M., 1927.
403 p., 4200 c. KL 16383.27 (n.)

CALDWELL, Erskine

139. Amerikanskiye rasskazy [American stories]. Selected
and trans. by I. A. Kashkin, with an introd. by the
translator. Goslitizdat., M., 1936. 281 p., 10,000 c.
KL 34510.36 (coll. s.)
Contents not listed in KL.

140. Same. 1937. 238 p., 3500 c. KL 5348.38

141. Babye leto (Indian summer). Trans. by I. Romanovich. Int. Lit. (M.), 1935, No. 11, pp. 48-53. (s.) From We are the living.

142. Balagan (Carnival) and Mukha v grobu (The fly in the coffin). Trans. by L. Nikitina and I. Volevich. 30 Dnei (L.), 1939, No. 5-6, pp. 97-101. ZL 36051.39 (coll. s.) From Southways.

143. Beglyanka (Runaway). Trans. by M. Volosov. Pravda, M., 1939. 48 p., 50,000 c. KL 10020.39 (coll. s.) From Southways. Other titles not listed in KL.

144. Bely medved (Hamrick's polar bear). Trans by L. Nikitina and I. Volevich. Rezets (L.), 1939, No. 6, pp. 10-12. ZL 22671.39 (s.) From Southways.

Bolshoi Bek (Big Buck). See 164.

Chto bylo, kogda mama uyekhala pogostit k tyote Bessi (The time ma spent the day at aunt Bessie's). See 151.

Chyornyie almazy (Black diamonds). See 147.

145. Desyat tysyach reshet pod cherniku (Ten thousand blueberry crates). Trans. by V. Toper. 30 Dnei (L.), 1936, No. 3, pp. 53-59. ZL 20433.36 (s.) From Jackpot

146. Dvoye (Man and woman). Trans. by L. Nikitina and I. Volevich. 30 Dnei (L.), 1939, No. 1, pp. 79-85. ZL 8368.39 (s.) From Southways.

147. Dzho Dzhendro (Joe Jendro), Chyorniye almazy (Black diamonds), and Eloiz (Where America died). Trans. by P. Vladimirov. Industriya sotsializma. (M.), 1939, No. 5, pp. 50-53. ZL 38333.39 (coll. sk.) Chapters from Some American people.

Eloiz (Where America died). See 147.

148. Indeyets Dzhon i Dzhordzh Khopkins (John the Indian and George Hopkins). Trans by L. D. Kislova. Int. Lit. (M.), 1935, No. 5, pp. 116-119. (s.) From Jackpot.

149. Izbrannyie rasskazy [selected stories]. Pravda, M.,

CALDWELL, Erskine (Continued)
> 1947. 63 p., 100,000 c. KL 7094.47 (coll. s.)
> Contents not listed in KL.
>
> Kak moi starik obzavyolsya upakovochnym pressom (My old man's baling machine). See 151.
>
> Kak propovednik Hausho uprosil nas pozvonit v kolokol (The day we rang the bell for preacher Hawshaw). See 151.

150.   Kendi Bichem (Candy-man Beechum). Trans by O. Kholmskaya. Na koleni pered voskhodyashchim solntsem (Kneel to the rising sun). Trans. by L. Kislova. Int. Lit. (M.), 1936, No. 4, pp. 48-61. (coll. s.)
From Kneel to the rising sun.

Khensom Braun i dlinnokhvostyie dyatly (Handsome Brown and the shirt-tail woodpeckers). See 151.

151.   Malchik iz Dzhordzhii (Georgia boy). Trans. by N. Volzhina. Novy mir. (M.), 1944, No. 8-9, pp. 95-122. (coll. s.)
Contents: Kak moi starik obzavyolsya upakovochnym pressom (My old man's baling machine). Kak propovednik Hausho uprosil nas pozvonit v kolokol (The day we rang the bell for preacher Hawshaw). Moi starik i solomennaya vdovushka (My old man and the grass widow). Chto bylo, kogda mama uyekhala pogostit k tyote Bessi (The time ma spent the day at aunt Bessie's). Khensom Braun i dlinnokhvostyie dyatly (Handsome Brown and the shirt-tail woodpeckers). Moi starik i melochka (My old man and the gypsy queen). Svobodny den Khensoma Brauna (Handsome Brown's day off). Moi starik na politicheskom postu (My old man's political appointment). Vizit dyadi Neda (Uncle Ned's short stay).

152.   Same. Trans. by N. Volzhina and I. Kashkin. Goslitizdat., M., 1945. 127 p., 10,000 c. KL 3598.46 (coll. s.)
Contents not listed in KL

153.   Medlennaya smert (Slow death). Trans. by N. Daruzes. 30 Dnei (L.), 1936, No. 6, pp. 52-57. ZL 44802.36 (s.)
From Kneel to the rising sun.

Moi starik (My old man). See 164.

Same. See 12.

Moi starik i melochka (My old man and the gypsy queen). See 151.

Moi starik i solomennaya vdovushka (My old man and the grass widow). See 151.

Moi starik na politicheskom postu (My old man's political appointment). See 151.

154. Moskovskiye vpechatleniya [Moscow impressions; not identified]. Trans. by P. Okhrimenko. Int. Lit. (M.), 1941, No. 11-12, pp. 228-231. (sk.)

Mukha v grobu (The fly in the coffin). See 142.

Na koleni pered voskhodyashchim solntsem (Kneel to the rising sun). See 150.

155. Narodny izbrannik (The people's choice). Trans. by N. Daruzes. Int. Lit. (M.), 1934, No. 3-4, pp. 186-190. (s.)
From We are the living.

156. Negr v kolodtse (The Negro in the well). Trans. by M. Umanskaya. 30 Dnei (L.), 1937, No. 1, pp. 38-43. ZL 15341.37 (s.)
From Southways.

Same. See 166.

157. Neskolko Amerikantsev (Some American people). Trans. by G. Prokulina. Int. Lit. (M.), 1936, No. 7, pp. 139-146; No. 8, pp. 92-95; No. 9, pp. 105-109. (coll. sk.)
Excerpts.

158. Nozh, chtoby rezat kukuruzny khleb (A knife to cut the corn bread with). Trans. by L. Nikitina and I. Volevich. 30 Dnei (L.), 1938, No. 11, pp. 91-96. ZL 3920.39 (s.)
From Southways.

159. Para prazdnichnykh bryuk (The corduroy pants). Trans. by L. Kislova. Int. Lit. (M.), 1935, No. 1, pp. 78-80. (s.)
From Jackpot.

160. Polevyie tsvety (Wild flowers). Trans. by L. Nikitina and I. Volovich. 30 Dnei (L.), 1939, No. 2, pp. 79-82. ZL 13085.39 (s.)
From Southways.

CALDWELL, Erskine (Continued)

161. Polnym-polno shvedov (Country full of Swedes). Trans. by I. Kashkin. V subbotu dnyom (Saturday afternoon). Trans. by N. Daruzes. Kras. Nov (M.), 1934, No. 10, pp. 86-98. ZL 54908.34 (coll. s.)
"Country full of Swedes" is from We are the living; "Saturday afternoon" is from Jackpot.

Polnym-polno shvedov (Country full of Swedes). See 5.

Pustaya komnata (The empty room). See 5.

162. Rechel (Rachel). Trans. by A. Yeleonskaya. Int. Lit. (M.), 1935, No. 11, pp. 43-47. (s.)
From We are the living.

163. Sluchai v Iyule (Trouble in July). Trans. by N. Daruzes. Int. Lit. (M.), 1940, No. 7-8, pp. 4-64. (n.)

164. Smert Kristi Tekera (The end of Christy Tucker). I. A. Kashkin, editor of translation. Pravda, M., 1941. 64. p., 50, 000 c. KL 14659.41 (coll. s.)
Contents: Smert Kristi Tekera. Bolshoi Bek (Big Buck). Moi starik (My old man).
From Jackpot.

Svobodny den Khensoma Brauna (Handsome Brown's day off). See 151.

165. Tabachnaya doroga (Tobacco road). Trans. by L. Slonimskaya; introd. by N. Rykov. Goslitizdat., L., 1938. 224 p., 10,300 c. KL 6758.38 (n.)

166. Tikhonya (Snacker) and Negr v kolodtse (The Negro in the well). Trans. by R. Rait. Lit. Sov. (L.), 1939, No. 7-8, pp. 111-123. ZL 48667.39 (coll. s.)
From Southways.

V subbotu dnyom (Saturday afternoon). See 161.

Same. See 5.

167. Vesenni pal (The grass fire). Trans. by N. Volzhina. 30 Dnei (L.), 1935, No. 12, pp. 60-64. ZL 2066.35 (s.)
From Jackpot.

Vizit dyadi Neda (Uncle Ned's short stay). See 151.

CALDWELL, Erskine, and Margaret Bourke-White

168. V tsarstve khlopka [in the kingdom of cotton]. Trans.

by N. Volzhina. Int. Lit. (M.), 1938, No. 4, pp. 131-142. (sk.)
An excerpt from You have seen their faces.

CARSE, Robert

169. Gorizont (Horizon). Trans. by A. G. Movshenson and
B. P. Spiro; edited by D. M. Gorfinkel. Vremya, L.,
1928. 232 p., 4150 c. KL 2538.28 (n.)

CATHER, Willa

170. Madam Gru (A chance meeting). Trans. by Ye.
Tselikov. 30 Dnei (L.), 1935, No. 6, pp. 52-58. (sk.)
From Literary encounters.

CHAMBERS, Whittaker

171. Slyshite li vy ikh golosa? (Can you hear their voices?).
Trans. by Ye. Kalashnikova. Lit. Mir. Rev. (M.),
1932, No. 2, pp. 38-50. (s.)
From New Masses, March, 1931, p. 7.

Same. See 5.

172. Smert kommunistov (Death of the Communists). Trans.
by Ye. Romanova. Lit Mir. Rev. (M.), 1932, No. 3,
pp. 54-57. (s.)
From New Masses, Dec., 1931, p. 10.

173. Tovarishch Menn (Our comrade Munn). Trans. by Ye.
Kalashnikova. Lit. Mir. Rev. (M.), 1932, No. 1, pp.
46-52. (s.)
From New Masses, Oct., 1931, p. 13.

CHESTER, George Randolph

174. Kak oni stanovyatsya millionerami (Get-rich-quick
Wallingford). Trans. by Teodor Levit. Puchina, M.,
1928. 336 p., 4150 c. KL 15137.28 (n.)

COBB, Humphrey

175. Puti slavy (Paths of glory). Trans. by N. Kotov.
Znamya (M.), 1936, No. 2, pp. 178-236. ZL 13504.36
(n.)

COBB, Irvin S.

176. Chetyre milliona i para naruchnikov [four million and

COBB, Irvin S. (Continued)

a pair of handcuffs; not identified]. Trans. by Mark Volosov. Seyatel, L., 1925. 48 p., 15,000 c. KL 13759.25 (s.)

177. Same. [no translator given]. Nizhegorodskaya kommuna, N. N., 1927. 53 p., 2500 c. KL 19313.27

178. Dulen — skandalist i kozlyonok [not identified]. Trans. by A. V. Krivtsova. Biblioteka Zhurnala "Ogonyok," M., 1926. 53 p., 15,000 c. KL 21750.26 (coll. s.)

COHEN, Lester

179. Musor (Sweepings). Trans. by Mark Volosov. Priboi, L., 1928. 278 p., 5000 c. KL 956.28 (n.)

COHEN, Octavus Roy

180. Oshibka [a mistake; not identified]. Trans. by Ye. Tolkachev. 30 Dnei (L.), 1927, No. 7, pp. 30-37.

181. Shokoladny nabor (Assorted chocolates). Trans. by P. Okhrimenko. Biblioteka Zhurnala "Ogonyok," M., 1926. 37 p., 12,500 c. KL 16793.26 (coll. s.)
Contents not listed in KL.

COLMAN, Louis

182. Dzhimmi Logan (Lumber). Trans. by Mark Volosov. Zhurn. Gaz. Obyed., M., 1937. 261 p., 25,000 c. KL 35629.37 (n.)

CONNEL, J. [sic.]

183. Krasny flag [red flag; not identified]. Trans. by A. Shmulyana. Leningrad (L.), 1940, No. 7-8, p. 3. ZL 34067.40 (p.)
This writer not identified.

CONNELL, Richard

184. Chelovek v kletke (The cage man). Trans. by Ye. Tolkachev; edited by M. Zenkevich. ZIF, M. & L., 1928. 210 p., 4000 c. KL 16647.28 (coll. s.)
From The sin of Monsieur Pettipon. Other titles not listed in KL.

185. Drug Napoleona (A friend of Napoleon). Trans. by Ye.

Tolkachev; edited by M. Zenkevich. ZIF, M. & L.,
1928. 32 p., 10,000 c. KL 6324.28 (s.)
From Apes and angels.

186. Same. Trans. by P. Okhrimenko. Biblioteka Zhurn-
ala "Ogonyok," M., 1929. 47 p., 20,000 c. KL 4458.29
187. Prints bolen svinkoi (The prince has the mumps).
Trans. by Ye. Tolkachev; edited by M. Zenkevich.
ZIF, M.& L., 1927. 32 p., 11,000 c. (s.)
From Apes and Angels.

CONROY, Jack

Artel mostovshchikov (Paving gang — on a job in
Missouri). See 5.

Bezdomnyie. Sec 5.

188. Detstvo v rudnichnom posyolke [childhood in a mining
village]. Trans. by O. P. Kholmskaya. Int. Lit. (M.),
1933, No. 5., pp. 26-34.
An excerpt from The disinherited.

189. Obezdolenny (The disinherited). Trans. by N.
Kamionskaya and M. Kovalenskaya; introd. by A.
Yelistratova. Goslitizdat., M., 1935. 300 p., 10,000 c.
KL 38278.35 (n.)

On — tysyachi (He is thousands). See 8.

COOPER, James Fenimore

Collected Works

190. Polnoye sobraniye romanov [complete collected novels].
Edited by N. Moguchi. ZIF, M. & L., 1927, 1928. 13
vols.

Separate Publications

191. Bluzhdayushchaya iskra (The wing-and-wing; or, Le
Feu-follet) and Priklyucheniya Milsa Vellingforda
(Afloat and ashore; or, The adventures of Miles
Wallingford). ZIF, M. & L., 1928. 272 p., 7000 c.
Pol. sob. romanov, Vol. XII. See 190.
KL 15495.28 (coll. n.)

Dva admirala (The two admirals). See 194 and 190.

Khizhina ná kholme (Wyandotte; or, The hutted knoll).
See 198 and 190.

COOPER, James Fenimore (Continued)

192. Koloniya na kratere (The crater; or, Vulcan's peak) and Morskiye lvy (The sea lions; or, The lost sealers). ZIF, M. & L., 1928. 228 p., 7000 c. Pol. sob. romanov, Vol. XIII. See 190. KL 21178.28 (coll. n.)

193. Kozhany chulok (Leather stocking tales). Gosizdat., R.S.F.S.R. and Dr. Selle and Co., Berlin, 1923. 316 p., [no. of copies omitted]. KL 11186.23
Contents not listed in KL.

Krasnokozhiye (The redskins; or, Indian and Injin). See 197 and 190.

194. Krasny Korsar (The red rover) and Dva admirala (The two admirals). ZIF, M. & L., 1928. 317 p., 7000 c. Pol. sob. romanov, Vol. VIII. See 190. KL 12497.28 (coll. n.)

195. Lev sv. Marka [lion of St. Mark; not identified]. Adapted by N. Moguchi. Mol. Gvard., M., 1930. 144 p., 10,100 c. KL 15191.30 (n.)
A juvenile publication.

196. Lotsman (The pilot) and Osada Bostona (Lionel Lincoln; or, The leaguer of Boston). ZIF, M. & L., 1928. 275 p., 7000 c. Pol. sob. romanov, Vol. IX. See 190. KL 8372.28 (coll. n.)

197. Mersedes iz Kastilii (Mercedes of Castile; or, The voyage to Cathay) and Krasnokozhiye (The redskins; or, Indian and Injin). ZIF, M. & L., 1928. 211 p., 7000 c. Pol. sob. romanov, Vol. XI. See 190. KL 7925.28 (coll. n.)

Morskiye lvy (The sea lions; or, The lost sealers). See 192 and 190.

Osada Bostona (Lionel Lincoln; or, The leaguer of Boston). See 196 and 190.

198. Penitel morya (The water-witch; or, The skimmer of the seas) and Khizhina na kholme (Wyandotte; or, The hutted knoll). ZIF, M. & L., 1927. 286 p., 10,000 c. Pol. sob. romanov, Vol. II, See 190. KL 15002.27 (coll. n.)

199. Same. 1930. 268 p., 5000 c. KL 16728.30

200. Posledni iz Mogikan (The last of the Mohicans).

Gosizdat. R.S.F.S.R. and Lutze & Vogt, Berlin, 1923. 360 p. [no. of copies omitted]. KL 11187.23 (n.)

201. Same. ZIF, M. & L., 1927. 260 p., 10,000 c. Pol. sob. romanov, Vol. V. See 190. KL 15575.27

202. Same. 1930. 260 p., 5000 c. KL 20007.30

203. Same. Trans. by Ye. M. Chistyakova-Ver and A. P. Repina. Detizdat., M. & L., 1936. 539 p., 25,000 c. KL 23423.36
A juvenile publication.

204. Same. 1938. 324 p., 61,000 c. KL 982.39

205. Preriya (The prairie). Introd. by V. Mlechin. Mol. Gvard., M., 1927. 299 p., 5000 c. KL 16385.27 (n.)

206. Same. Foreword by S. Dinamov. ZIF, M. & L., 1928. 268 p., 8000 c. Pol. sob. romanov, Vol. VII. See 190. KL 2964.28

Priklyucheniya Milsa Vellingforda (Afloat and ashore; or, The adventures of Miles Wallingford). See 191 and 190.

Satanstoe (Satanstoe; or, The Littlepage manuscripts). See 214 and 190.

207. Shpion (The spy: a tale of the neutral ground). Edited and with a foreword by N. Moguchi. ZIF, M. & L., 1927. 223 p., 10,000 c. Pol. sob. romanov, Vol. I. See 190. KL 5277.27 (n.)

208. Same. 1929. 223 p., 5000 c. KL 4459.29

209. Same. Trans. by Ye. Chistyakova-Ver. Detizdat., M. & L., 1946. 443 p., 50,000 c. KL 5063.47 (n.)
A juvenile publication.

210. Sledopyt (The pathfinder; or, The inland sea). ZIF, M. & L., 1927. 267 p., 10,000 c. Pol. sob. romanov, Vol. IV. See 190. KL 12811.27 (n.)

211. Same. 1929. 267 p., 5000 c. KL 10492.29

212. Same. M. Grits, editor of translation. Detizdat., M. & L., 1938. 488 p., 50,300 c. KL 3235.38
A juvenile publication.

213. U istokov Soskveganny (The pioneers; or, The sources of the Susquehanna). ZIF, M. & L., 1927. 235 p., 10,000 c. Pol. sob. romanov, Vol. VI. See 190. KL 20369.27 (n.)

COOPER, James Fenimore (Continued)

214. V Venetsii (The bravo: a Venetian story) and Satanstoe
      (Satanstoe; or, The Littlepage manuscripts). ZIF,
      M. & L., 1928. 272 p., 7000 c. Pol. sob. romanov,
      Vol. X. See 190. KL 9910.28 (coll. n.)

215. Zveroboi (The deeslayer; or, The first war-path).
      ZIF, M. & L., 1927. 232 p., 10,000 c. Pol. sob.
      romanov, Vol. III. See 190. KL 8450.27 (n.)

216. Same. 1929. 232 p., 5000 c. KL 4459.29

CRAM, Mildred

217. Billi (Billy). Trans. by P. Okhrimenko. 30 Dnei (L.),
      1937, No. 6, pp. 57-69. ZL 31163.37 (s.)
      From O'Brien, The best short stories of 1924.

CRANE, Stephen

218. Aly znak doblesti (The red badge of courage). With a
      foreword by Joseph Conrad. Trans. by A. V. Krivtsova
      and Yev. Lann; introd. by Yev. Lann. ZIF, M. & L.,
      1930. 230 p., 5000 c. KL 11172.30 (n.)

219. Same. Trans. by A. V. Krivtsova and Yev. Lann. Gos-
      litizdat., M., 1935. 261 p., 10,000 c. KL 42042.35

220. Beg yunosti (The pace of youth). Trans. by N. Kamion-
      skaya; foreword by R. Kennel. Biblioteka Zhurnala
      "Ogonyok," M., 1929. 40 p., 17,000 c. KL 10491.29
      (coll. s.)
      From Men, women and boats. Other titles not listed
      in KL.

      Na temu o nishchete (An experiment in misery). See
      4.

      Shlyupka (The open beat). See 5.

      Taina geroizma. See 5.

221. Tshcheslaviye (Showin' off). Trans. by A. Krivtsova.
      30 Dnei (L.), 1935, No. 1, pp. 49-59. ZL 17203.35 (s.)
      From Whilomville stories.

      Tyomnoryzhaya sobaka (A dark-brown dog). See 4.

      Voyenny epizod (An episode of war). See 4.

CROY, Homer
222. V chuzhom kupalnom kostyume [in another's bathing
suit; not identified]. Trans. by M. Urnov. Int. Lit.
(M.), 1935, No. 4, pp. 88-89.

CURWOOD, James Oliver
223. Brodyagi severa (Nomads of the North). Trans. by
M. P. Chekhov. Mysl, L., 1925. 192 p., 6000 c.
KL 19221.25 (n.)
224. Same. 1927. 192 p., 7000 c. KL 11460.27
225. Same. Trans. by O. Tselkhert. Kras. Gaz., L., 1928.
186 p., 40,000 c. KL 6327.28
226. Chyorny okhotnik (The black hunter). Trans. by M.
Volosov. Mysl, L., 1927. 236 p., 5000 c. KL 4150.27
(n.)
227. Same. 1927. 236 p., 10,200 c. KL 11729.27
228. Devushka na skale [the girl on the cliff; not identified].
Trans. by T. and V. Ravinski. Mysl, L., 1927. 264 p.,
5000 c. KL 270.27
229. Devushka severa [girl of the north; not identified].
Trans. by K. Ksanina. Kras Gaz., L., 1928. 232 p.,
50,000 c. KL 19014.28
230. Dolina bezmolviya (The valley of silent men). Trans.
by M. Irskaya. Kras. Gaz., L., 1928. 215 p., 50,000 c.
KL 16647.28 (n.)
231. Dolina molchalivykh prizrakov (The valley of silent
men). Trans. by M. P. Chekhov. Mysl, L., 1926.
200 p., 6000 c. KL 4963.26 (n.)
232. Same. 1927. 191 p., 5000 c. KL 11728.27
233. Grizzli (The grizzly king). Trans. by M. P. Chekhov.
Mysl, L., 1927. 168 p., 5000 c. KL 1732.27 (n.)
234. Same. 1927. 168 p., 10,000 c. KL 11727.27
235. Kazan (Kazan). Trans. by M. P. Chekhov. Mysl, L.,
1925. 280 p., 6000 c. KL 20276.25 (n.)
236. Same. 1927. 232 p., 5000 c. KL 4147.27
237. Les v ogne (The flaming forest). Trans. by L.
Vsevolodskaya. Mysl, L., 1927. 190 p., 5000 c.
KL 1306.27 (n.)

CURWOOD, James Oliver (Continued)

238. Same. 1927. 190 p., 10,000 c. KL 13970.27

239. Molniyenosny (Swift lightning). Trans. by V. I. Smetanich. Mysl, L., 1927. 231 p., 10,000 c. KL 9837.27 (n.)

240. Muzhestvo Kapitana Plyuma (The courage of Captain Plum). V. I. Smetanich, editor of translation. Mysl, L., 1927. 221 p., 5000 c. KL 13387.27 (n.)

241. Same. Trans. by V. Nikolai. Kras. Gaz., L., 1928. 160 p., 50,000 c. KL 12100.28 (n.)

242. Okhotniki na volkov (The wolf hunters). Trans. by A. N. Karasik. Mysl, L., 1925. 200 p., 5000 c. KL 15487.26 (n.)

243. Same. 1927. 200 p., 5000 c. KL 4148.27

244. Pogonya (The hunted woman). Trans. by M. P. Chekhov. Mysl, L., 1926. 291 p., 5000 c. KL 20743.26 (n.)

245. Pylayushchi les (The flaming forest). Kras. Gaz., L., 1928. 196 p., 50,000 c. KL 10371.28 (n.)

246. Severny tsvetok (Flower of the North). Trans. by Zin. Lvovski. Mysl, L., 1926. 263 p., 5000 c. KL 20994.26 (n.)

247. Same. 1927. 263 p., 6200 c. KL 13971.27

248. Skovannyie ldom serdtsa [hearts chained by ice; not identified]. Trans. by T. Bogdanovich. Mysl, L., 1926. 236 p., 5000 c. KL 16455.26 (n.)

249. Same. 1927. 230 p., 5000 c. KL 9393.27

250. Staraya doroga (The ancient highway). Trans. by A. M. Karnaukhova. Mysl, L., 1926. 224 p., 5000 c. KL 17945.26 (n.)

251. Same. Trans. by K. Ksanina. Kras. Gas., L., 1928. 252 p., 36,000 c. KL 2269.29

252. Syn Kazana (Baree, son of Kazan). Trans. by M. P. Chekhov. Mysl, L., 1926. 286 p., 5000 c. KL 15806.26 (n.)

253. Same. 1927. 247 p., 5000 c. KL 4149.27

254. Tam, gde nachinayetsya reka (The river's end). Trans. by Z. Lvovski. Mysl, L., 1926. 260 p., 5000 c. KL 20380.26 (n.)

255. Same. 1927. 260 p., 6200 c. KL 17913.27
256. U istokov reki (The river's end). Trans. by M.
Irskaya. Kras. Gaz., L., 1928. 170 p., 60,000 c.
KL 12101.28 (n.)
257. U polednei granitsy (The country beyond). Trans. by
T. and V. Ravinsky. Mysl, L., 1926. 278 p., 5000 c.
KL 17946.26 (n.)
258. Same. 1927. 278 p., 6000 c. KL 11461.27
259 V tyazhyolyie gody (The Plains of Abraham). Trans.
by Mark Volosov. Kras. Gaz., L., 1928. 216 p., 60,000
c. KL 19723.28 (n.)
260. Zolotaya petlya (The golden snare). Trans. by M. P.
Chekhov. Mysl, L., 1926. 209 p., 5000 c. KL 19008.26
(n.)
261. Same. 1927. 209 p., 6200 c. KL 18556.27
262. Same. Trans. by O. Bogdanova. Kras. Gaz., L., 1928.
156 p., 50,000 c. KL 2268.29
263. Zolotoiskateli (The gold hunters). Trans. by Zin.
Lvovski. Mysl, L., 1926. 239 p., 5000 c. KL 14858.26
(n.)
264. Same. 1927. 212 p., 5000 c. KL 8451.27

DAVIS, Elmer
265. Mister Priddl i potomstvo [Mr. Priddle and posterity;
not identified]. Trans. by G. Yarros. 30 Dnei (L.),
1936, No. 10, pp. 42-48. ZL 927.37 (s.)

DELL, Floyd
266. Alliluya, ya bosyak ("Hallelujah, I'm a bum!"). Trans.
by P. Khrapchenko. Kras. Nov (M.), 1933, No. 11,
pp. 41-54. ZL 4528.34 (sk.)
From Love in Greenwich village.
267. Beglets (Runaway). Trans. by L. S. Savelyev. Kniga,
L. & M., 1928. 242 p., 4200 c. KL 173.28 (n.)
268. Chudak (Moon-calf). Trans. and abridged by N. S.
Petrova-Shur. Gosizdat., M. & L., 1930. 208 p.,
4000 c. KL 20431.30 (n.)
269. Epton Sinkler (Upton Sinclair). Trans. by R. Rait.
Gosizdat., M. & L., 1928. 172 p., 7000 c. KL 159.28
(biog.)

DELL, Floyd (Continued)

270. Kholostoi otets (An unmarried father). Trans. by V. A. Barbasheva. Gosizdat., M. & L., 1929. 275 p., 4000 c. KL 1457.29 (n.)

271. Prichudy starika (An old man's folly). Trans. by A. V. Krivtsova. Gosizdat., M. & L., 1927. 343 p., 7000 c. KL 19307.27 (n.)

DOBIE, Charles Caldwell

272. Otkrytoye okno (Open window). Trans. by A. V. Krivtsova. Int. Lit. (M.), 1936, No. 3, pp. 81-92. (s.) From Golden Book, June, 1929, pp. 63-71.

DODD, Martha

273. Iz okna posolstva (Through embassy eyes). Foreword by A. Abramov. Int. Lit. (M.), 1941, No. 9-10, pp. 147-181. (Coll. sk.) An excerpt

274. Same. Goslitizdat., M., 1942. 96 p., 50,000 c. KL 4778.43 An excerpt

275. Same. G. A. Rokotov, editor of translation. Goslitizdat., M., 1942. 136 p., 25,000 c. KL 12194.42

276. Same. Foreword by A. Abramov. Sovetskaya Kolyma, Magadan, 1943. 122 p., 3000 c. KL 9904.43

DOOLITTLE, Hilda

Kormchi (The helmsman). See 22.

Ostrova (The islands). See 22.

Znoi (Heat). See 22.

DORET, Bernard (Bernard Dworetsky)

277. Zalozhnik (Hostage). Trans. by N. Man. Int. Lit. (M.), 1942, No. 6, pp. 5-12. (s.) From Scholastic Magazine, Nov. 2, 1942, pp. 25-26.

DOS PASSOS, John

278. Aktsionernoye obshchestvo "Vozdukh-put" (Airways, Inc.). Trans. by V. Toper. Int. Lit. (M.), 1933, No. 1, pp. 19-46. (pl.)

279. Amerikanskiye portrety (1919). Trans. by V. Stenich. Oktyabr (M. & L.), 1932, No. 10, pp. 3-24. (n.) An excerpt.

280. Ben Kompton (Ben Compton). Trans. by S. G. Zaslavski. Kras. Nov (M.), 1932, No. 8, pp. 56-72. An excerpt from 1919.

281. Same. Trans. by V. Stenich. Zhurn. Gaz. Obyed., M., 1932. 40 p., 20,000 c. KL 24294.32

282. Charli Andersen (Charley Anderson). Trans. by V. Stenich. Zvezda (L.), 1930, No. 8, pp. 27-54. An excerpt from The 42nd parallel.

283. Same. Trans. by Ye. Levenmal and I. Rentsa. Zhurn. Gaz. Obyed., M., 1932. 54 p., 20,000 c. KL 16921.32

284. Dochka (Daughter). Trans. by V. Stenich. Zvezda (L.), 1932, No. 7, pp. 3-66. An excerpt from 1919.

285. Dzho Vilyams (Joe Williams). Trans. by V. Stenich. Zvezda (L.), 1932, No. 4, pp. 16-37; No. 5, pp. 34-63. An excerpt from 1919.

286. Elinor Stoddard (Eleanor Stoddard). Trans. by V. Stenich. Zvezda (L.), 1931, No. 5, pp. 107-138. An excerpt from The 42nd parallel.

287. Evelain Khetchins (Eveline Hutchins). Trans. by V. Stenich. Zvezda (L.), 1932, No. 10-11, pp. 32-84. An excerpt from 1919.

288. Ispaniya na novoi puti (The republic of honest men). Trans. by N. Daruzes and N. Volzhina. Int. Lit. (M.), 1934, No. 1, pp. 66-83. (sk.) From In all countries.

289. Kharlan, pod dulom vintovki (Harlan, working under the gun). Trans. by O. Kholmskaya. Lit. Mir. Rev. (M.), 1932, No. 3, pp. 70-77. (sk.) From New Republic, Dec. 2, 1931, pp. 62-67.

290. Mankhetten (Manhattan transfer). Trans. by V. I. Smetanich; introd. by L. Vaisenberg. Mysl, L., 1927. 414 p., 5000 c. KL 4466.27 (n.)

291. Same. Trans. by V. Stenich. Proboi, L., 1930. 354. p., 5000 c. KL 9274.30

292. Same. 1931. 354 p., 5000 c. KL 11299.31

DOS PASSOS, John (Continued)

293. Oni ni odinoki [they are not alone]. Trans. by V.
     Stenich. Izvestiya (M.), 1934, No. 134, p. 3; No. 143,
     p. 3. ZL 652.34 (sk.)
     A section of the chapter "Views of Washington" from
     In all countries.

294. Richard Elsuers Sevedzh (Richard Ellsworth Savage).
     Trans. by V. Stenich. Zvezda (L.), 1932, No. 6, pp.
     30-64.
     An excerpt from 1919.

295. 42-aya parallel (The 42nd parallel). Trans. by V.
     Stenich. Goslitizdat., L. & M., 1931. 376 p., 10,140
     c. KL 29297.31 (n.)

296. Same. 1936. 451 p., 10,300 c. KL 31267.36

297. Same. Trans. by I. A. Kashkin, with an introd. by
     the translator. Goslitizdat., M., 1936. 507 p., 15,000
     c. KL 33884.36 (n.)

298. Sorvanets (Playboy). Trans. by S. G. Zaimovski. Lit.
     Mir. Rev. (M.), 1932, No. 5, pp. 65-67.
     An excerpt from 1919.

299. Strana bolshikh vulkanov (Land of great volcanos).
     Trans. by Ye. Kalashnikova. Int. Lit. (M.), 1934, No.
     6, pp. 80-88. (sk.)
     An excerpt from In all countries.

300. "Teper oni myortvy" (They are dead now). Trans. by
     T. Levish. Kras.Nov (M.), 1930, No. 11, pp. 93-94.
     (p.)
     From New Masses, Oct., 1927, p. 7.

301. Tri soldata (Three soldiers). Trans. by V. A. Azov.
     Gosizdat., L., 1924. 356 p., 3000 c. KL 5358.24. (n.)

302. 1919 (1919). Trans. by V. Stenich. Len. GIKHL., L.,
     1933. 375 p., 10,200 c. KL 12949.33 (n.)

303. Same. 1936. 493 p., 10,300 c. KL 30555.36

304. 1919-i god (1919). Trans. by S. Zaimovski. Lit. Mir.
     Rev. (M.), 1932, No. 7-8, pp. 3-45. (n.)
     An excerpt.

305. 1917 (One man's initiation — 1917). Trans. by I. K.
     Romanovich. Lit. Mir. Rev. (M.), 1932, No. 9-10,
     pp. 33-68. (n.)
     Excerpts.

306.　Ueslei Everest (Paul Bunyan). Trans. by V. Toper.
　　　Lit. Mir. Rev. (M.), 1932, No. 2, pp. 52-54.
　　　An excerpt from 1919.

　　　Same. See 14.

307.　Vershiny schastya (Fortune heights). Trans by M.
　　　Marushkevich. Int. Lit. (M.), 1933, No. 5, pp. 49-60.
　　　(pl.)
　　　An excerpt.

308.　Same. Trans. by V. Stenich. Zvezda (M. & L.), 1934,
　　　No. 1, pp. 39-114. ZL 19154.34

309.　Same. Goslitizdat., L., 1934. 135 p., 3250 c.
　　　KL 11031.34

310.　Vidy Vashingtona (Views of Washington). Trans. by
　　　V. Stenich. Kras. Nov (M., 1934, No. 8, pp. 3-23.
　　　ZL 47119.34 (sk.)
　　　From In all countries.

DREISER, Theodore

Collected Works

311.　Sobraniye sochineni [collected works]. Edited by S. S.
　　　Dinamov. ZIF, M. & L., 1928, 1929, 1930. 9 vols.

Separate publications

312.　Amerikanskaya tragediya (An American tragedy).
　　　Trans. by Z. A. Vershinina; introd. by S. Dinamov.
　　　ZIF, M. & L., 1928. 831 p., 5000 c. Sob. soch., Vol.
　　　VI. See 311. KL 9900.28 (n.)

313.　Same. With a critical essay by John Cowper Powys.
　　　1930. 831 p., 5000 c. KL 3064.30

314.　Same. Trans. by Z. A. Vershinina; introd. by A. A.
　　　Yelistratova. Goslitizdat., M., 1933. 558 p., 50,000
　　　c. KL 7470.34

315.　Same. Trans. by D. Gorfinkel and L. Domger.
　　　Goslitizdat., L., 1936. 441 p., 10,300 c. KL 1076.37

316.　Same. Trans. by D. Gorfinkel and L. Domger; introd.
　　　by O. Nemerovskaya. Goslitizdat., L., 1936. 618 p.,
　　　10,300 c. KL 41632.36

　　　Do groba (The lost Phoebe). See 1.

317.　Dvenadtsat amerikantsev (Twelve men). Trans. by
　　　M. Volosov; introd. by S. Dinamov. ZIF, M. & L.,

DREISER, Theodore (Continued)

1929. 435 p., 5000 c. Sob. soch., Vol. X. See 311.
KL 4449.29 (coll. sk.)

318. Dzhenni Gergardt (Jennie Gerhardt). Trans. by Mark
Volosov. Mysl, L., 1927. 324 p., 6200 c. KL 9384.27
(n.)

319. Same. Trans. by V. A. Barbasheva; introd. by I.
Anisimov. ZIF, M. & L., 1929. 495 p., 5000 c. Sob.
soch., Vol. XII. See 311. KL 11568.29

320. Same. 1930. 495 p., 10,000 c. KL 5324.30

321. Finansist (The financier). Trans. by M. Levina;
introd. by S. Dinamov. ZIF, M. & L., 1928. 656 p.,
5000 c. Sob. soch., Vol. II. See 311. KL 6318.28 (n.)

322. Same. 1929. 656 p., 5000 c. KL 6186.29

323. Gallereya zhenshchin. (A gallery of women). Trans.
by V. Stanevich and V. Barbasheva; introd. by S. S.
Dinamov. Goslitizdat., M. & L., 1933. 306 p., 5000 c.
KL 13376.33 (coll. sk.)

324. "Geni" (The "genius"). Trans. by M. Volosov; introd.
by S. Dinamov. ZIF, M. & L., 1928. 712 p., 5000 c.
Sob. soch., Vol. IV. See 311. KL 15487.28 (n.)

325. Same. 1930. 712 p., 10,000 c. KL 1180.30

326. Same. Trans. by M. Volosov; introd. by N. Gorin.
Goslitizdat., M., 1937. 782 p., 10,000 c. KL 36265.37

327. Kniga o samom sebe (A book about myself). Trans.
by G. Prokunina. Int. Lit. (M.), 1935, No. 7, pp. 76-85;
No. 8, pp. 120-125; No. 9, pp. 65-72; No. 10, pp. 99-
106; No. 11, pp. 79-84; No. 12, pp. 61-68. ZL 2015.36
(autobiog.)
Excerpts.

328. Kniga o sebe (A book about myself). Trans. by G.
Prokunina. Int. Lit. (M.), 1935, No. 2, pp. 104-110;
No. 3, pp. 67-72; No. 4, pp. 77-87; No. 5, pp. 83-93;
No. 6, pp. 88-95. ZL 23680.35 (autobiog.)
Excerpts.

329. Kommercheskoye predpriyatiye (The titan). Lit. Sov.
(L.), 1937, No. 12, pp. 214-219. ZL 4791.38 (n.)
An excerpt.

330. Kraski Nyu Iorka (The color of a great city). Trans.
by V. P. Steletski. Mysl, L., 1927. 280 p., 5000 c.
KL 13960.27 (coll. sk.)

331. Mukhi i sarancha [the flies and the grasshopper; not
identified]. Int. Lit. (M.), 1933, No. 5, pp. 124-126.
(sk.)

332. Neobyknovennaya istoriya i drugiye rasskazy (Free,
and other stories). Trans. by T. and V. Ravinski.
Mysl, L., 1927. 195 p., 6200 c. KL 14905.27 (coll. s.)

333. Nyu Iork (The color of a great city). Trans. by P.
Okhrimenko. Gosizdat., M. & L., 1927. 125 p., 7000
c. KL 17906.27 (coll. sk.)

334. Okhota na muzhchinu (Nigger Jeff). Trans. by Mark
Volosov. Seyatel, L., 1925. 96 p., 15,000 c.
KL 16563.25 (coll. s.)
From Free, and other stories. Other titles not listed
in KL.

335. Osvobozhdeniye (Free, and other stories). Trans. by
V. O. Stanevich. ZIF, M. & L., 1928. 294 p., 5000 c.
Sob. soch., Vol. V. See 311. KL 16265.28 (coll. s.)

336. Sestra Kerri (Sister Carrie). With an introd. by
Sherwood Anderson. Trans. by M. Volosov. Mysl, L.,
1927. 388 p., 6200 c. KL 13367.27 (n.)

337. Same. Trans. by M. Volosov; introd. by I. Anisimov.
ZIF, M. & L., 1930. 656 p., 10,000 c. Sob. soch.,
Vol. XI. See 311. KL 348.30

338. Same. Trans. by Mark Volosov; edited by D. Gorfinkel;
introd. by A. Yelistratova. Goslitizdat., M., 1941.
448 p., 50,000 c. KL 18117.41

339. Same. Trans. by M. Volosov. Goslitizdat., M., 1947.
504. p., [no. of copies omitted]. Sov. Knig., 1947,
No. 11, p. 126.

340. Sud lincha i drugiye rasskazy (Free, and other stories).
Trans. by Mark Volosov. Seyatel, L., 1925. 208 p.,
4000 c. KL 9663.25 (coll. s.)

341. Same. 1925. 64 p., 15,000 c. KL 17350.25
Contents not listed in KL.

342. Taunsend [Townsend; not identified]. Trans. by V.
Barbasheva. Int. Lit. (M.), 1933, No. 5, pp. 5-8.
(sk.)

DREISER, Theodore (Continued)

343. Titan (The titan). Trans. by Z. Vershinina; foreword
by S. S. Dinamov. ZIF, M. & L., 1928. 694 p., 5000 c.
Sob.soch., Vol. III. See 311. KL 19716.28 (n.)

344. Same. 1930. 694 p., [no. of copies omitted].
KL 13580.30

345. Same. Trans. by Z. Vershinina. Goslitizdat., M., 1938.
568 p., 50,000 c. KL 6209.38

346. Tsepi (Chains). Trans. by V. Barbasheva; foreword
by R. Kennel. ZIF, M. & L., 1928. 344 p., 5000 c.
Sob. soch., Vol. VII. See 311. KL 12090.28 (coll. s.)

347. Same. Trans. by V. Barbasheva. Zhurn. Gaz. Obyed.,
M. 1936. 48 p., 50,000 c. KL 8573.36 (s.)

348. Uinterton [Winterton; not identified]. Trans. by A. D.
Kislova. Int. Lit. (M.), 1934, No. 2, pp. 58-62. (sk.)

349. Vstupleniye v zhizn (A start in life.) Trans. by L.
Barkman. Zvezda (M. & L.), 1934, No. 12, pp. 142-
152. ZL 23731.35 (s.)
From Scribner's magazine, Oct., 1934, pp. 211-217.

DU BOIS, William E. B.

350. Za serebryanym runom (The quest of the silver fleece).
Trans. by A. S. Polotska; edited by A. G. Gornfeld.
Seyatel, L., 1925. 270 p., 4000 c. KL 1600.25 (n.)

EARHART, Amelia

351. Posledni polyot (Last flight). Trans. by M. Loriye.
Int. Lit. (M.), 1938, No. 10, pp. 133-156. (autobiog.)
An excerpt.

EASTMAN, Max

352. Vpechatleniya amerikantsa [impressions of an American; not identified]. Zhizn (M.), 1924, No. 1, pp. 76-
89. (sk.)

EDWARDS, Albert (Arthur Bullard)

353. Na poroge zhizni (A man's world). Ts.K.R.K.S.M.,
M., 1922. 130 p., 10,000 c. KL 7103.22 (n.)
Abridged.

354. Tovarishch Iyetta (Comrade Yetta). Trans. by M. A.

Dyakonov; foreword by Zin. Vengerova. Gosizdat., P., 1919. 268 p., [no. of copies omitted]. Kniga i Rev., 1920, No. 2, p. 53. (n.)

355. Same. Trans. and abridged by M. Ilina. V.Ts.S.P.S., M., 1925. 137 p., 10,000 c. KL 1644.25

356. Same. Trans. by M. A. Dyakonov. Mysl, L., 1927. 404 p., 6000 c. KL 11760.27

EHRLICII, Leonard

357. Dzhon Braun (God's angry man). Trans. and abridged by A. Gurevich. Int. Lit. (M.), 1938, No. 9, pp. 54-135 (n.)

358. Same. Trans. by A. D. Gurevich; foreword by P. Tuei; notes by Ye. D. Kantor. Goslitizdat., M., 1940. 336 p., 50,000 c. KL 1126.40

ELSER, Frank B.

359. Zhgucheye zhelaniye (The keen desire). Trans. by Ye. Fortunato; edited by L. L. Domger. Vremya, L., 1927. 278 p., 4150 c. KL 16401.27 (n.)

ENGSTRAND, Stuart D.

360. Vesnoi 1940 goda (Spring 1940). Trans. by N. Volzhina and L. Telesheva. Int. Lit. (M.), 1942, No. 12, pp. 3-92 (n.)

361. Same. Sovetskaya Kolyma, Magadan, 1944. 156 p., 5000 c. KL 9151.44 (n.)

FAULKNER, William

Kogda nastupayet noch. See 5.

362. Pisatel u sebya doma (Artist at home). Trans. by V. Stenich. Lit. Sov. (L.), 1935, No. 10, pp. 103-114. ZL 53387.35 (s.)
From Collected stories of William Faulkner (Random House, 1950).

FAUSET, Jessie

363. Chyornaya kozha (There is confusion). Trans. by M. Volosov. Gosizdat., L., 1927. 387 p., 5000 c. KL 15039.27 (n.)

FEARING, Kenneth

364. Kak vsegda delovoye (Business as usual). Trans. by
E. Gorlin. Lit. Sov. (L.), 1940, No. 7, p. 135.
ZL 44520.40 (p.)

FERBER, Edna

365. Miss Bobbi (Mother knows best). Trans. by M.
Volosov. Mysl, L., 1928. 224 p., 5100 c. KL 10382.28
(coll. s.)
366. Plovuchi teatr (Show boat). Trans. by M. G. Volosov
and M. Ye. Levberg; edited by A. N. Gorlin. Gosizdat.,
L., 1927. 339 p., 6000 c. KL 11752.27 (n.)
367. Takoi bolshoi (So big). Trans. by M. Ye. Abkina. Mysl,
L., 1926. 292 p., 6000 c. KL 6183.26 (n.)
368. Tri sharlotti (The girls). Trans. by L. L. Domger;
edited by D. M. Gorfinkel. Vremya, L., 1927. 238 p.,
4150 c. KL 10531.27 (n.)

FIELD, Ben

369. Dlinny Yakov [long Jacob; not identified]. Trans. by
T. Ozerskaya. Int. Lit. (M.), 1941, No. 11-12, pp. 149-
151. (s.)
370. Pokhorony petukha (The cock's funeral). Trans. by A.
Gurevich. Pravda, M., 1938. 40 p., 50,000 c.
KL 27090.38 (coll. s.)
From The cock's funeral. Other titles not listed in
KL.
371. Vozvrashcheniye (The return). Trans. by V. K. Int.
Lit. (M., 1937, No. 10, pp. 140-143. (s.)
From The cock's funeral.

FLETCHER, John Gould

Iz knigi "Izlucheniya." See 311.

FORD, Henry

372. Moya zhizn, moi dostizheniya (My life and work).
V. A. Zorgenfrei, editor of translation; foreword by
N. S. Lavrov. Vremya, L., 1924. 326 p., 10,000 c.
KL 3253.24 (autobiog.)
373. Same. 1924. 326 p., 5000 c. KL 7042.24

374. Same. 1924. 324 p., 10,000 c. KL 9525.24
375. Same. 1924. 324 p., 10,000 c. KL 13347.24

FRANK, Waldo

376. Perekryostok (City block). Trans. by Ye. E. and G. P.
Blok. Vremya, L., 1926. 107 p., 3500 c. KL 19659.26
(n.)
377. Prazdnik (Holiday). Trans. by A. V. Krivtsova. ZIF,
M. & L., 1926. 135 p., 5000 c. KL 19271.25 (n.)
378. Smert i rozhdeniye Davida Markenda (The death and
birth of David Markand). Trans. by Ye. Kalashnikova.
Int. Lit. (M.), 1935, No. 3, pp. 3-44. (n.)
An excerpt.
379. Same. Trans. by Ye. Kalashnikova; introd. by S. S.
Dinamov. Goslitizdat., M., 1936. 557 p., 10,000 c.
KL 15697.36
380. Same. Zhurn. Gaz. Obyed., M., 1936. 48 p., 50,000 c.
KL 11803.36
An excerpt.

FREEDMAN, David

381. Mendel Marants (Mendel Marantz). Trans. by P.
Okhrimenko. Puchina, M., 1926. 260 p., 7650 c.
KL 21345.26 (coll. s.)
382. Mendel Marants — domashnaya khozyaika (Mendel
Marantz — housewife). Trans. by P. Okhrimenko.
Biblioteka Zhurnala "Ogonyok," M., 1925. 302 p.,
9000 c. KL 18310.25 (coll. s.)
From Mendel Marantz. Other titles not listed in KL.
383. Same. 1926. 48 p., 15,000 c. KL 12209.26 (coll. s.)
Other titles not listed in KL.
384. Same. 1926. 56 p., 25,000 c. KL 16152.26
385. Same. 1926. 56 p., 15,000 c. KL 19356.26
386. Same. 1927. 56 p., 30,000 c. KL 10894.27
387. Mendel Marants menyayet kvartiru (Mendel Marantz
moves). Trans by P. Okhrimenko. Biblioteka Zhurnala
"Ogonyok," M., 1926. 56 p., 35,000 c. KL 9593.26
(coll. s.)
From Mendel Marantz. Other titles not listed in KL.

FREEDMAN, David (Continued)

388. Same. 1926. 56 p., 25,000 c. KL 16153.26
389. Same. 1926. 56 p., 15,000 c. KL 19357.26
390. Same. 1927. 56 p., 30,000 c. KL 10895.27
391. Nadelson i Shnaps (Nadelson and Shnaps). Trans. by P. Okhrimenko. Biblioteka Zhurnala "Ogonyok," M., 1926. 48 p., 15,000 c. KL 12209.26 (coll. s.)
From Mendel Marantz. Other titles not listed in KL.
392. Same. 1926. 48 p., 50,000 c. KL 14881.26
393. Same. 1926. 56 p., 25,000 c. KL 16154.26
394. Same. 1926. 56 p., 15,000 c. KL 19358.26
395. Same. 1927. 56 p., 30,000 c. KL 10896.27
396. Vozvrashcheniye Mendelya Marantsa (Mendel Marantz returns). Trans. by P. Okhrimenko. Biblioteka Zhurnala "Ogonyok," M., 1926. 46 p., 35,000 c. KL 9592.26 (coll. s.)
From Mendel Marantz. Other titles not listed in KL.
397. Same. 1926. 48 p., 25,000 c. KL 16151.26
398. Same. 1926. 48 p., 15,000 c. KL 19355.26
399. Same. 1927. 48 p., 30,000 c. KL 10893.27

FREEMAN, Joseph

Dzhentlmen iz Arkanzasa. See 14.
400. Zavet amerikantsa (An American testament). Trans. by Z. Gan. Int. Lit. (M.), 1937, No. 1, pp. 176-182; No. 2, pp. 140-152; No. 3, pp. 156-174. (autobiog.) Excerpts.

FROST, Robert

"Aut, Aut" ('Out, out —'). See 401.
Ogon i lyod (Fire and ice). See 401.
Pochinka steny (Mending wall). See 401.
Smert batraka (Death of the hired man). See 401.
401. Stikhi [poems]. Trans. by M. Zenkevich. Int. Lit. (M.), 1936, No. 4, pp. 62-65. (coll. p.)
Contents: "Aut, Aut" ('Out, out —'). Pochinka steny

(Mending wall). Ogon i lyod (Fire and ice). Smert batraka (Death of the hired man).
From Collected poems of Robert Frost.

GALE, Zona

402. Prolog k zhizni (Preface to a life). Trans. by Z. Vygodskaya; edited by D. M. Gorfinkel. Priboi, L., 1928. 285 p., 4000 c. KL 5411.28 (n.)

GARLAND, Hamlin

Pod lapoi lva (Under the lion's paw). See 4.

Vozvrashcheniye soldata (The return of a private). See 4.

GLASGOW, Ellen

403. Dorinda (Barren ground). Trans. by M. I. Ratner. Mysl, L., 1927. 323 p., 5200 c. KL 20355.27 (n.)

GLASPELL, Susan

404. Vernost (Fidelity). Trans. by A. S. Polotskaya. Mysl, L., 1928. 270 p., 5200 c. KL 21766.28 (n.)

GLASS, Montague

405. Nikogda ne imeite delo so lvami (Never begin with lions). Trans. by N. A. Kazmin. ZIF, M. & L., 1928. 29 p., 10,000 c. KL 10359.28 (s.)
From Y' understand!

406. Sami ponimayete (Y' understand!). Trans. by E. M. Katulski. Kras. Gaz., L., 1927. 47 p., 20,000 c. KL 6765.27 (coll. s.)
Contents not listed in KL.

GODCHAUX, Elma

407. Tsepi (Chains). Trans. by G. Yarros. 30 Dnei (L.). 1937, No. 10, pp. 54-61. ZL 43327.37 (s.)
From O'Brien, The best short stories, 1937.

GOLD, Michael

Dopros s pristrastiyem. See 14.

408. Dzhon Broun (Battle hymn). Trans. by V. M. Toper;

GOLD, Michael (Continued)

foreword by J. Kunitz. Goslitizdat., M., 1937. 133 p., 5000 c. KL 12935.37 (pl.)

409. Ist-Said (Jews without money). Mol. Gvard., M., 1932. 48 p., 25,300 c. KL 12823.32 (coll. sk.)
Excerpts.

410. Izmenim mir (Change the world). Trans. by M. Volosov. Kras. Nov (M.), 1937, No. 9, pp. 132-147. (coll. essays).
Excerpts.

411. Kak sdelatsya millionerom [how to become a millionaire; not identified]. Trans. by S. Berner. Mol. Gvard. (M.), 1930, No. 18, pp. 48-57. (s.)

412. Kommunist povis na zare [a communist hung at daybreak; not identified]. Trans. by T. Levish. Kras. Nov (M.), 1930, No. 11, p. 95. (p.)

413. Krasnyie negry Chikago [red Negroes of Chicago; not identified]. Trans. by M. Volosov. Lit. Mir. Rev. (M.), 1932, No. 9-10, pp. 75-85. (sk.)

414. Lyubovnoye pismo k Frantsii (A love letter for France). Int. Lit. (M.), 1935, No. 11, pp. 143-148. (essay)
From Change the world.

415. Malchik, kotory umer za Tammani (The boy who died for Tammany). Trans. by Ye. Kalashnikova. Lit. Mir. Rev. (M.), 1932, No. 3, pp. 46-53. (s.)
From New Masses, Jan., 1932, p. 18.

Same. See 5.

Pogonya za kuskom khleba. See 14.

416. Proklyaty agitator (A damned agitator). Foreword by V. D. Kheiwud [William D. Haywood]. Nedra, M., 1925. 185 p., 10,000 c. KL 4631.25 (coll. s.)

417. Same. Trans. by M. Volosov. Biblioteka Zhurnala "Ogonyok," M., 1931. 48 p., 20,000 c. KL 803.31 (coll. s.)
From A damned agitator. Other titles not listed in KL.

418. 120 millionov (120 million). Trans. by M. Volosov. ZIF, M. & L., 1930. 184 p., 5000 c. KL 16721.30 (sk.)

Svobodny. See 5.

419. Tom Muni vykhodit v polnoch (Tom Mooney walks at midnight). Trans. by A. Balbekov. Na rubezhe (M., Khabarovsk), 1934, No. 2, pp. 67-68. ZL 58716.34 (p.) From New Masses, Jan. 2, 1934. p. 19.

420. Yevreiskaya bednota (Jews without money). Trans. by M. Volosov. Goslitizdat., M. & L., 1931. 305 p., 10,000 c. KL 5853.31 (coll. sk.)

421. Same. 1932. 248 p., 5000 c. KL 13793.32

422. Same. Oktyabr (M. & L.), 1931, No. 2, pp. 3-52. An excerpt.

423. Same. Trans. and abridged by M. Volosov. Goslitizdat., M. & L., 1931. 215 p., 25,000 c. KL 31790.31

GORDON, David

424. Izdevatelstvo [mockery; not identified]. Trans. by V. Stanevich; foreword by S. Dinamov. Goslitizdat., M. & L., 1931. 85 p., 5000 c. KL 20411.31 (coll. sk.) According to KL, this is "sketches of American prisons."

GOW, James, and Arnaud D'Usseau

425. Glubokiye korni (Deep are the roots). Trans. by A. Mingulina. Zvezda (L.), 1947, No. 2, pp. 13-58. (pl.)

GREEN, Howard, Brown Holmes, and Sheridan Gibney

426. Ya — begly katorzhnik (I am a fugitive from the chain gang). Goskinoizdat, M., 1939. 128 p., 5000 c. KL 7888.40 (scenario)

GREY, Zane

427. Pogranichny legion (The border legion). Trans. by O. Tselkhert. Kras. Gaz., L., 1929. 253 p., 50,000 c. KL 22364.28 (n.)

428. V preriyakh Tekhasa (The thundering herd). Trans. by L. S. Savelyeva. Kniga, L. & M., 1928. 237 p., 4200 c. KL 12488.28 (n.)

429. Veliki rab (The great slave). Trans. by Yu. Rodnyan-skaya. ZIF, M. & L., 1927. 78 p., 5000 c. KL 7936.27 (coll. s.) From Tappan's burro, and other stories.

HALDEMAN-JULIUS, Emanuel, and Anna Marcet

430. Pyl (Dust). With a foreword to the Russian transla-
tion by Upton Sinclair. Trans. by P. Okhrimenko.
Gosizdat., M. & L., 1926. 192 p., 15,000 c.
KL 11213.26 (n.)

431. Same. Sov. Prob., M., 1924. 182 p., 5000 c.
KL 13644.24

HALE, Edward E. [Everett]

Chelovek bez rodiny (The man without a country).
See 4.

HALL, James Norman

432. Slava mistera Bitti (Fame for Mr. Beatty). Trans.
by A. V. Krivtsova. 30 Dnei (L.), 1935, No. 3, pp. 60-
65. ZL 25882.35 (s.)
From O'Brien, The best short stories of 1929.

HALPER, Albert

433. S doktorom po Chikago [with a doctor about Chicago;
not identified]. Trans. by Ye. Kalashnikova. Int. Lit.
(M.), 1935, No. 2, pp. 115-119. (sk.)

434. Slovolitnya (The foundry). Trans. by A. Gavrilova.
Kras. Nov (M.), 1936, No. 6, pp. 59-116; No. 7, pp.
39-83; No. 8, pp. 95-157; No. 9, pp. 116-170.
ZL 37298.36 (n.)

435. Same. Goslitizdat., M., 1937. 444 p., 10,000 c.
KL 11746.37

436. Vzmakh topora [stroke of the axe]. Trans. by N.
Volzhina. Int. Lit. (M.), 1935, No. 6, pp. 15-31.
An excerpt from The foundry.

HARRIMAN, Florence Jaffray

437. Missiya na Severe (Mission to the North). V. Toper,
editor of translation; introd. by Vl. Rubin. Int. Lit.
(M.), 1942, No. 3-4-5, pp. 157-181. (memoirs)
An excerpt.

HARRIS, Joel Chandler

438. Baratets krolik i yevo krolchata [brother rabbit and

little rabbits; not identified]. Trans. and adapted by
M. Gershenzon. Detizdat., M. & L., 1937. 31 p.,
100,300 c. KL 9123.37 (coll. s.)
A juvenile publication. Other titles not listed in KL.

439. Skazki dyadyushki Rimusa [tales of Uncle Remus].
Trans. and adapted by M. Gershenzon. Detizdat.,
M. & L., 1936. 142 p., 25,000 c. KL 23429.36 (coll.
s.)
A juvenile publication. Contents not listed in KL.

440. Same. 1937. 142 p., 50,300 c. KL 19523.37

441. Same. 1939. 104 p., 274,000 c. KL 10054.39

Same. See 4.

HARRISON, Charles

442. Generaly umirayut v posteli (Generals die in bed).
Trans. by M. Volosov; foreword by Joshua Kunitz.
Goslitizdat., M. & L., 1931. 175 p., 5000 c.
KL 17614.31 (n.)

443. Rebyonok rodilsya (A child is born). Trans. by M.
Volosov. Goslitizdat., M. & L., 1932. 154 p., 5000 c.
KL 20820.32 (n.)

444. Same. Oktyabr (M. & L.), 1932, No. 5-6, pp. 137-159.
(n.)
An excerpt.

HARTE, Bret

Collected works

445. Polnoye sobraniye sochineni [complete collected
works]. Introd. by L. Grossman. Kras. Gaz., L., 1928.
12 vols.

Separate publications

Bludny syn Mistera Tomsana (Mr. Thompson's
prodigal). See 462.

Braun iz Kalaverasa (Brown of Calaveras). See 462.

446. Devushka iz Kentukki (Cressy). Trans. by S. Ya.
Arefin. Puchina, L. & M., 1925. 201 p., 6000 c.
KL 12211.25 (n.)

Don Kikhot (A knight-errant of the foot-hills). See
457 and 445.

HARTE, Bret (Continued)

Durak (The fool of Five Forks). See 460 and 445.

Dzhentlmen iz Laporta (A tourist from "Injianny").
See 462.

447. Ekstselsior (The crusade of the Excelsior) and
Metsenat (A Maecenas of the Pacific slope). Kras.
Gaz., L., 1928. 216 p., 50,000 c. Pol. sob. soch., Vol.
V. See 445. KL 9887.28 (coll. n., s.)
"The crusade of the Excelsior" is from The crusade
of the Excelsior and other tales; "A Maecenas of the
Pacific slope" is from Cressy and other tales.

Flip (Flip: a California romance). See 459 and 445.

448. Gabriel Konroi (Gabriel Conroy). Kras. Gaz., L.,
1928. 2 vols., 259 p. and 274 p., 50,000 c. Pol. sob.
soch., Vols. XI and XII. See 445. KL 20677.28,
KL 2254.29 (n.)

Gornaya idilliya. See 460 and 445.

Idilliya Red-Gocha (The idyl of Red Gulch). See 456
and 445.

Iliada Sendi-Bara (The iliad of Sandy Bar). See 462.

449. Iskateli zolota [the gold seekers; not identified].
Trans. by N. A. Kazmin. Puchina, M., 1925. 139 p.,
5000 c. KL 2284.25

Izgnanniki (The outcasts of Poker Flat). See 458 and
445.

Izgnanniki Poker-fleta (The outcasts of Poker Flat).
See 462.

450. Kak Plunket domoi sezdil (A Monte Flat pastoral:
how old man Plunket went home) and Opekun [guardian;
not identified, but possibly A ward of the Golden Gate].
Kras. Gaz., L., 1928. 193 p., 50,000 c. Pol. sob.
soch., Vol. II. See 445. KL 3465.28 (coll. s.)

Kak Santa Klaus prishol v Simson-Bar (How Santa
Claus came to Simpson's Bar). See 462.

Same. See 4.

451. Kaliforniskiye povesti [California tales]. Trans. by N.
Volzhina and N. Daruzes; edited and with a foreword

by A. Startsev. Goslitizdat., M., 1939. 592 p., 20,000
c. KL 23009.39 (coll. s.)
Contents not listed in KL.

452. Kitaiski malchik (Wan Lee, the pagan). Trans. and
adapted by N. Gorvits and A. Slonimski. Gosizdat.,
M. & L., 1927. 30 p., 35,000 c. KL 17938.27 (s.)
A juvenile publication. From Tales of the Argonauts.

Kompanion Tenessi (Tennessee's partner). See 462.

Kompanyon Tenessi (Tennessee's partner). See 460
and 445.

Same. See 4.

Kompanyony (Three partners). See 455 and 445.

453. Malenki staratel (The youngest prospector in
Calaveras). Trans. by M. Gershenzon. Detizdat.,
M. & L., 1937. 30 p., 100,300 c. KL 32862.37 (s.)
A juvenile publication. From The ancestors of Peter
Atherly and other tales.

454. Mat pyaterykh (A mother of five). Trans. by M.
Gershenzon. Pioner (M.), 1938, No. 11, pp. 51-57.
ZL 2774.39 (s.)
From Stories of and for the young.

Metsenat (A Maecenas of the Pacific slope). See 447
and 445.

455. Miggls (Miggles) and Kompanyony (Three partners).
Kras. Gaz., L., 1928. 196 p., 50,000 c. Pol. sob. soch.,
Vol. I. See 445. KL 2148.28 (coll. s.)
"Miggles" is from The luck of Roaring camp; "Three
partners" is from Three partners and other tales.
Other titles not listed in KL.

Miggls (Miggles). See 462.

Millioner (A millionaire of Rough-and-Ready). See
459 and 445.

Mliss (M'liss: an idyl of Red Mountain). See 460 and
445.

Same. See 462.,

Monte-fletskaya pastoral (A Monte Flat pastoral).
See 462.

Naslednitsa (An heiress of Red Dog). See 459 and
445.

HARTE, Bret (Continued)

Same. See 462.

Opekun. See 450 and 445.

Pastukh iz Solano (The man from Solano). See 459 and 445.

Pokinutyie okalatki (Neighborhoods I have moved from). See 456 and 445.

Povest doliny Madronio (The romance of Madroño Hollow). See 458 and 445.

456. Rasskazy [short stories]. Kras. Gaz., L., 1928. 216 p., 50,000 c. Pol. sob. soch., Vol. IV. See 445. KL 8359.28 (coll. s.)

Contents: Safo (A Sappho of Green Springs). Zanesennyie snegom (Snowbound at Eagle's). Pokinutyie okalatki (Neighborhoods I have moved from). Idilliya Red-Gocha (The idyl of Red Gulch). "A Sappho of Green Springs" is from The crusade of the Excelsior; "Snowbound at Eagle's" is from Maruja and other tales; "Neighborhoods I have moved from" is from Gabriel Conroy: Bohemian papers of and for the young; "The idyl of Red Gulch" is from The luck of Roaring Camp and other tales.

457. Rasskazy [short stories]. Kras. Gaz., L., 1928. 158 p., 50,000 c. Pol. sob. soch., Vol. VI. See 445. KL 11260.28 (coll. s.)

Contents: Don Kikhot (A knight errant of the foothills). Tankfella Blossom (Thankful Blossom: a romance of the Jerseys). Tommi Islington (Mrs. Skagg's husbands). "A knight errant of the foot-hills" is from Maruja and other tales; "Thankful Blossom" is from Thankful Blossom and other Eastern tales and sketches; "Mrs. Skagg's husbands" is from Tales of the Argonauts.

458. Rasskazy [short stories]. Kras Gaz., L., 1928. 232 p., 50,000 c. Pol. sob. soch., Vol. VII. See 445. KL 12844.28 (coll. s.)

Contents: Izgnanniki (The outcasts of Poker Flat). V priiskovoi glushi (The story of a mine). Povest doliny Madronio (The romance of Madroño Hollow). "The outcasts of Poker Flat" is from The luck of

Roaring Camp; "The romance of Madroño Hollow" is
from Tales of the Argonauts; "The story of a mine"
is from The story of a mine and other tales.

459. Rasskazy [short stories]. Kras. Gaz., L., 1928. 220
p., 50,000 c. Pol. sob. soch., Vol. IX. See 445.
KL 15095.28 (coll. s.)
Contents: Flip (Flip: a California romance). Pastukh
iz Solano (The man from Solano). Zhenitba Mistera
Trotta [the marriage of Mister Trott; not identified].
Naslednitsa (An heiress of Red Dog). Millioner (A
millionaire of Rough-and-Ready).
"Flip" is from The story of a mine and other tales;
"The man from Solano" and "An heiress of Red Dog"
are from Tales of the Argonauts; "A millionaire
of Rough-and-Ready" is from Maruja and other tales.

460. Rasskazy [short stories]. Kras. Gaz., L., 1928. 210
p., 50,000 c. Pol. sob. soch., Vol. VIII. See 445.
KL 15095.28 (coll. s.)
Contents: Schastye revushchevo stana (The luck of
Roaring Camp). Mliss (M'liss: an idyl of Red Mountain). Kompanyon Tenessi (Tennessee's partner).
Durak (The fool of Five Forks). Gornaya idilliya
[mountain idyl; not identified].
"The luck of Roaring Camp" and "Tennessee's partner" are from The luck of Roaring Camp and other
tales; "M'liss" is from Earlier sketches; "The fool
of Five Forks" is from Tales of the Argonauts.

Safo (A Sappho of Green Springs). See 456 and 445.

Schastye revushchevo stana (The luck of Roaring
Camp). See 460 and 445.

461. Schastye revushchevo stana (The luck of Roaring
Camp and other tales). Foreword by V. S. Uzin. Mol.
Gvard., M., 1928. 341 p., 5000 c. KL 7396.28 (coll.
s.)
A juvenile publication.

462. Schastye revushchevo stana i drugiye rasskazy (The
luck of Roaring Camp and other tales). A. Startsev,
editor of translation. Goslitizdat., M., 1945. 303 p.,
25,000 c. (coll. s.)
Contents: Schastye revushchevo stana. Izgnanniki
Poker-fleta (The outcasts of Poker Flat). Mliss

HARTE, Bret (Continued)

(M'liss: an idyl of Red Mountain). Kompanion Tenessi
(Tennessee's partner). Miggls (Miggles). Braun iz
Kalaverasa (Brown of Calaveras). Iliada Sendi-Bara
(The liliad of Sandy Bar). Bludny syn Mistera
Tomsona (Mr. Thompson's prodigal). Kak Santa
Klaus prishol v Simson-Bar (How Santa Claus came
to Simpson's Bar). Monte-fletskaya pastoral (A
Monte Flat pastoral). Naslednitsa (An heiress of Red
Dog). Dzhentlmen iz Laporta (A tourist from
"Injianny"). Van-li — yazychnik (Wan Lee, the pagan).
Sluchai iz zhizni mistera Dzhona Okkhersta (a
passage in the life of Mr. John Oakhurst). Stikhi
[poems; titles not listed]. The volume also contains
a critical article, Chernyshevski o Bret-Garte
[Chernyshevski on Bret Harte], by A. Startsev.
All the stories are from The luck of Roaring Camp
and other tales, except "M'liss," which is from
Earlier sketches.

463. Shumny lager (The luck of Roaring Camp). M. O.
      Volf, P., 1918. 14 p., [no. of copies omitted].
      KL 4681.18 (s.)

      Sluchai iz zhizni Mistera Dzhona Okkhersta (A
      passage in the life of Mr. John Oakhurst). See 462.

464. Stepnoi naidenysh (A waif of the plains). D. Vygodski,
      editor of translation. Priboi, L., 1927. 111 p.,
      5000 c. KL 988.28 (coll. s.)
      A juvenile publication. From A waif of the plains and
      other tales. Other titles not listed in KL.

      Stikhi [poems]. See 462.

465. Sud lincha [lynch law]. Kras. Gaz., L., 1928. 225 p.,
      50,000 c. Pol. sob. soch., Vol. III. See 445.
      KL 5404.28 (coll. s.)
      Contents not listed in KL.

466. Suzi (Susy: a story of the plains). Kras. Gaz., L.,
      1928. 188 p., 50,000 c. Pol. sob. soch., Vol. X. See
      445. KL 17474.28 (n.)

      Tankfella Blossom (Thankful Blossom: a romance of
      the Jerseys). See 457 and 445.

      Tommi Islington (Mrs. Skagg's husbands). See 457
      and 445.

467. V gornoi kotlovine (In a hollow of the hills). ZIF,
      M., 1927. 92 p., 50,000 c. KL 13945.27 (s.)
      From In a hollow of the hills and other tales
      V priiskovoi glushi (The story of a mine). See 458
      and 445.
      Van-li — yazychnik (Wan Lee, the pagan). See 462.
      Zanesennyie snegom (Snowbound at Eagle's). See 455
      and 445.
      Zhenitba Mistera Trotta. See 459 and 445.

HARTMAN, Lee Foster

468. Mister Smit (Mister Smith). Trans. by P. Okhrimen-
      ko. 30 Dnei (L.), 1937, No. 3, pp. 66-76. ZL 18359.37
      (s.)
      From O. Henry memorial award prize stories of 1928.

HAWKINS, Everett

      Prometei. See 16.

HAWTHORNE, Nathaniel

      Gibel Mistera Khigginbotoma (Mr. Higginbothom's
      catastrophe). See 4.
      Molodoi Braun (Young Goodman Brown). See 4.
      Opyt doktora Kheideggera (Dr. Heidegger's experi-
      ment). See 4.
      Sedoi zastupnik (The gray champion). See 4

HEARN, Lafcadio

469. Kokoro (Kokoro: hints and echoes of Japanese inner
      life). Trans. by Ye. Maurin. E. A. Shpakovski, P.,
      1918. 281 p., 600 c. KL 2480.19 (coll. essays)
      Contents: Predisloviye (Preface). Konservator
      (A conservative). Dukh Yaponskoi tsivilizatsii (The
      genius of Japanese civilization). Na zhelezno-
      dorozhnoi stantsii (At a railway station). Ulichnaya
      pevitsa (A street singer). Iz putevo dnevnika (From a
      travelling diary). Monakhinya khrama Amidy (The
      nun of the temple of Amida). Posle voiny (After the
      war). Kharu (Haru). Puti progressa (A glimpse of
      tendencies). Vlast Karmy (By force of Karma).

HEARN, Lafcadio (Continued)

Sumerki bogov (In the twilight of the gods). Idyeya predsushchestvovaniya (The idea of pre-existence). V kholernoye vremya (In cholera time). Mysli o kulte predkov (Some thoughts about ancestor worship). Kimiko (Kimiko).

HECHT, Ben

470. Erik Dorn (Erik Dorn). Trans. by L. S. Savelyeva. Mysl, L., 1927. 356 p., 5000 c. KL 20389.27 (n.)

471. Geni naiznanku (Count Bruga). Trans. by N. N. Davydov. Nov. Vsemir. Lit., L., 1927. 263 p., 4000 c. KL 8486.27 (n.)

472. Greshnik (Broken necks). Trans. by L. Slonimskaya. Priboi, L., 1927. 176 p., 4000 c. KL 14018.27 (coll. s.)

473. Igra v zhizn (Humpty Dumpty). Trans. by R. Veller; edited by D. Gorfinkel; foreword by S. Dinamov. Gosizdat., L., 1927. 403 p., 5000 c. KL 13434.27 (n.)

474. Tysyacha i odin den v Chikago (A thousand and one afternoons in Chicago). Trans. by P. Okhrimenko. Gosizdat., M., 1928. 216 p., 4000 c. KL 4047.28 (coll. sk.)

HELLMAN, Lillian

475. Lisichki (The little foxes). Trans. by L. Bolshintsova. V.U.O.A.P., M., 1944. 63 p., 200 c. KL 1094.45 (pl.)

HEMINGWAY, Ernest

Alpiskaya idilliya (An Alpine idyll). See 5.

476. Amerikantsam, pavshim za Ispaniyu (On the American dead in Spain). Inter. Mayak. (M.), 1939, No. 7, p. 11. ZL 24775.39 (sk.)
From New Masses, Feb. 14, 1939, p. 3.

477. Chisto i svetlo (A clean, well-lighted place). Trans. by Ye. Romanova. 30 Dnei (L.), 1934, No. 10, pp. 46-47. ZL 54915.34 (s.)
From Winner take nothing.

478. Dostoprimechatelnosti Uaitkhed Strit (The sights of

Whitehead Street). Trans. by N. Daruzes. <u>30 Dnei</u>.
(L.), 1936, No. 4, pp. 66-68. ZL 23009.36 (sk.)
From <u>Esquire</u>, April, 1935.

479. Fiyesta (The sun also rises). Trans. by V. Toper;
foreword by N. Gorin. Goslitizdat., M., 1935. 224 p.,
10,000 c. KL 37580.35 (n.)

480. Same. <u>Int. Lit</u>. (M.), 1935, No. 1, pp. 3-44.
An excerpt.

481. Imet i ne imet (To have and have not). Trans. by Ye.
Kalashnikova; foreword by I. Anisimov. Goslitizdat.,
M., 1938. 240 p., 10,000 c. KL 2363.39 (n.)

482. Same. <u>Int. Lit</u>. (M.), 1938, No. 4, pp. 22-100.
An excerpt.

483. Indeiski posyolok (Indian camp). Trans. by O. Kholmskaya. <u>Int. Lit</u>. (M.), 1934, No. 1, pp. 57-58. (s.)
From <u>In our time</u>.

484. Ispanskaya zemlya (The Spanish earth). Trans. by R.
Rait. <u>Int. Lit</u>., (M.), 1938, No. 12, pp. 164-169.
Commentary and narration to accompany the film
"The Spanish earth."

485. Kakimi vy ne budete (A way you'll never be). Trans.
by I. Kashkin. <u>Znamya</u> (M.), 1938, No. 7, pp. 153-
162. ZL 37822.38 (s.)
From <u>Winner take nothing</u>.

Na Big-River (Big two-hearted river). See 12.

486. Na fronte [at the front]. Trans. by P. Okhrimenko.
Zhurn. Gaz. Obyed., M., 1937. 64 p., 50,000 c.
KL 22256.37
An excerpt from <u>A farewell to arms</u>.

487. Nedolgoye schastye Frensisa Mekombera (The short
happy life of Francis Macomber). Trans. by E. L.
Zhukhovinski and G. M. Svobodin. <u>Int. Lit</u>. (M.),
1937, No. 3, pp. 27-43. (s.)
From <u>The fifth column and the first forty-nine stories</u>.

488. Nepobedimy (The undefeated). Trans. by V. Toper.
<u>Int. Lit</u>. (M.), 1936, No. 3, pp. 34-49. (s.)
From <u>Men without women</u>.

489. O Shveitsarii (Homage to Switzerland). Trans. by Ye.

HEMINGWAY, Ernest (Continued)

Kalashnikova. 30 Dnei (L.), 1934, No. 9, pp. 43-49.
ZL 54914.34 (s.)
From Winner take nothing.

490. Oborona Madrida [defense of Madrid; not identified].
Trans. by V. Toper. Int. Lit. (M.), 1938, No. 11,
pp. 116-125. (sk.)

491. Ottsi i deti (Fathers and sons). Trans. by N. Daruzes.
30 Dnei (L.), 1937, No. 1, pp. 44-50. ZL 15345.37
(s.)
From Winner take nothing.

492. Ozhidaniye [expectation, or, waiting; not identified,
but possibly A day's wait from The fifth column and
the first forty-nine stories]. Trans. by R. Rait. Lit.
Sov. (L.), 1939, No. 5-6, pp. 128-130. ZL 39522.39
(s.)

493. Pamyati amerikantsev, pogibshikh v Ispanii (On the
American dead in Spain). Trans. by L. Nikitina and
I. Volevich. 30 Dnei (L.), 1939, No. 4, p. 7.
ZL 23648.39 (p.)
From New Masses, Feb. 14, 1939, p. 3.

494. Predisloviye k knige "Pyataya kolonna i pervyie 49
rasskazov" [preface to The fifth column and the first
forty-nine stories]. Int. Lit. (M.), 1939, No. 1, pp.
209-216.

495. Proshchai oruzhiye (A farewell to arms). Trans. by
Ye. Kalashnikova; foreword by S. Dinamov. Goslitizdat., M., 1936. 338 p., 10,000 c. KL 38381.36 (n.)

496. Same. Int. Lit. (M.), 1936, No. 7, pp. 6-138.

497. Same. Trans. by P. Okhrimenko. Znamya (M.), 1936,
No. 5, pp. 128-227; No. 6, pp. 111-221. ZL 29900.36.

498. Same. Trans. by Ye. Kalashnikova. Zhurn. Gaz.
Obyed., M., 1937. 364 p., 20,000 c. KL 29984.37

499. Same. Dalgiz., Khabarovsk, 1939. 216 p., 12,000 c.
KL 13408.39

500. Pyataya kolonna (The fifth column). Trans. by Yev.
Kalashnikova and V. Toper. Int. Lit. (M.), 1939, No.
1, pp. 99-138. (pl.)
From The fifth column and the first forty-nine stories.

501. Pyataya kolonna i pervyie tridtsat vosem rasskazov
      [the fifth column and the first thirty-eight stories].
      I. A. Kashkin, editor of translation. Goslitizdat.,
      M., 1939. 656 p., 10,000 c. KL 5005.39 (coll. pl., s.)
      From The fifth column and the first forty-nine stories.
      Contents not listed in KL.

502. Pyatdesyat tysyach (Fifty grand). Trans. by O. Kholm-
      skaya. Kras. Nov   (M.), 1938, No. 9, pp. 105-117.
      ZL 53146.38 (s.)
      From Men without women.

503. Reis k pobede [passage to victory; not identified].
      Trans. by Ye. Kalashnikova. Znamya (M.), 1944, No.
      9-10, pp. 178-182. (sk.)

504. Roga byka (The horns of the bull). Trans. by L.
      Nikitina. 30 Dnei (L.), 1937, No. 7, pp. 57-65.
      ZL 8362.37 (s.)
      From Esquire, June 1936, p. 37.

505. Smert posle poludnya (Death in the afternoon). Edited
      and with an introd. by I. Kashkin. Goslitizdat., M.,
      1934. 265 p., 8,000 c. KL 3624.34 (coll. essays)

506. Snega Kilimandzharo (The snows of Kilimanjaro).
      Trans. by G. Yarros and N. Daruzes. Znamya (M.),
      1937, No. 9, pp. 149-167. ZL 38939.37 (s.)
      From The fifth column and the first forty-nine stories.

507. Starik u mosta (Old man at the bridge). Trans. by T.
      Ozerskaya. Int. Lit. (M.), 1938, No. 8, pp. 99-100.
      (s.)
      From The fifth column and the first forty-nine stories.

508. Tsely den (A day's wait). Trans. by L. Nikitina and I.
      Volevich. Rezets (L.), 1939, No. 7, pp. 10-11.
      ZL 24776.39 (s.)
      From The fifth column and the first forty-nine stories.

509. Ubitsy (The killers). Trans. by G.K.Kh. Int. Lit. (M.),
      1934, No. 1, pp. 52-56. (s.)
      From Men without women.

HERBST, Josephine

510. Rasplata blizka (The executioner waits). Trans. by G.
      Prokunina; introd. by P. Balashov. Goslitizdat., M.),
      1938. 368 p., 10,000 c. KL 25353.38 (n.)

HERBST, Josephine (Continued)

511. Udachlivy chelovek (Very successful man). Trans.
      by A. Yeleonskaya. Int. Lit. (M.), 1933, No. 5,
      pp. 61-69. (s.)
      From American Mercury, June, 1933, p. 211.

512. Zhalosti nedostatochno (Pity is not enough). Trans.
      by I. Klyagina-Kondratyeva; introd. by A. Startsev.
      Goslitizdat., M., 1936. 376 p., 10,000 c. KL 38993.36
      (n.)

513. Zolotaya zhatva (Golden harvest). Trans. by N.
      Daruzes. Int. Lit. (M.), 1936, No. 5, pp. 129-134.
      (s.)
      From Partisan Review, March, 1936, p. 3.

HERGESHEIMER, Joseph

514. Belisend (Balisand). Trans. by A. Shchvyrov.
      Puchina, L. & M., 1926. 196 p., 4000 c. KL 8047.26
      (n.)

515. Goryachaya krov (Mountain blood). Trans. by Ye.
      Batkhon. Puchina, M., 1927. 210 p., 4150 c.
      KL 12010.27 (n.)

516. Kukla i zhenshchina (Cytherea). Trans. by D. Kormen;
      edited by N. Kazmin; introd. by M. Levidov. Puchina,
      L. & M., 1925. 222 p., 5000 c. KL 13658.24 (n.)

517. Same. 1927. 208 p., 4150 c. KL 2160.27

518. Linda (Linda Condon). Trans. by F. Rudin. Puchina,
      M., 1925. 191 p., 4000 c. KL 15330.25 (n.)

519. Tampiko (Tampico). Trans. by Mark Volosov. Vremya,
      L., 1927. 260 p., 5150 c. KL 13435.27 (n.)

520. Tri pokoleniya (The three black Pennys). Trans. by
      A. Shchvyrov; edited and with an introd. by S. Arefin.
      Puchina, L. & M., 1925. 192 p., 4000 c. KL 12227.25
      (n.)

521. Yarkaya shal (The bright shawl). Trans. by A.
      Shchvyrov. Puchina, L., 1926. 181 p., 4000 c.
      KL 13192.26 (n.)

522. Yavaiski pik (Java Head). Trans. by A. Shchvyrov.
      Puchina, M., 1926. 234 p., 4000 c. KL 2999.26 (n.)

HERNDON, Angelo

523. Ya budu zhit (Let me live). Trans. by M. B.
Astrakhan and Ye. Romanova; foreword by I.
Schneider. Goslitizdat., M., 1938. 344 p., 10,000 c.
KL 27093.38 (autobiog.)

524. Same. [no translator given]. Zhurn. Gaz., Obyed.,
M., 1938. 306 p., 25,000 c. KL 13366.38

525. Same. Trans. by M. B. Astrakhan and Ye. Romanova.
Mol. Gvard., M., 1938. 263 p., 25,000 c. KL 6773.38

526. Same. Mol. Gvard. (M.), 1938, No. 2, pp. 89-156.
ZL 14944.38
An excerpt.

527. Zhertvy burzhuaznovo pravosudiya [victims of
bourgeois justice]. Sputnik Agitatora (M.), 1938, No.
17, pp. 41-43. ZL 42586.38
An excerpt from Let me live.

HERRICK, Robert

528 Lavka uchyonosti (Chimes). Trans. by N. Volnin and
N. Chukovski. Gosizdat., M. & L., 1928. 294 p.,
4000 c. KL 4005.28 (n.)

529. Opustosheniye (Waste). Trans. by M. Volosov. ZIF,
M. & L., 1930. 389 p., 5000 c. KL 5757.30 (n.)

530. Same. Goslitizdat., M. & L., 1931. 344 p., 5000 c.
KL 3358.31

531. Yeshchyo ne pozdno (Homely Lilla). Trans. by L. L.
Domger; edited by D. M. Gorfinkel. Kniga, L. & M.,
1927. 208 p., 4200 c. KL 7935.27 (n.)

HERVEY, Harry Clay

532. Kongai (Congai). Trans. by T. O. Davydova. Mysl,
L., 1928. 247 p., 5200 c. KL 2152.28 (n.)

HETH, Edward Harris

533. Vilikiye dni vperedi (Big day's beginning). Trans. by
G. Yarros. 30 Dnei (L.), 1937, No. 4, pp. 57-66.
ZL 28974.37 (s.)
From Harper's Magazine, Feb., 1936, pp. 332-340.

HEYWARD, Du Bose

534. Pordzhi (Porgy). Trans. by V. A. Dilevskaya; edited
      by A. A. Smirnov. Vremya, L., 1930. 144 p., 3570 c.
      KL 20434.29 (n.)

HILL, Edwin C.

535. Zhelezny kon (The iron horse). Trans. by A. Matov;
      introd. by S. Dinamov. Mol. Gvard., M. & L., 1929.
      219 p., 5000 c. KL 19790.29 (n.)

HILL, Joe (Joseph Hillstrom)

536. Stikhi [poems]. Trans. by M. Zenkevich. Int. Lit.
      (M.), 1936, No. 2, pp. 47-51. ZL 13596.36 (coll. p.)
      Contents: Alliluya, ya bosyak (Hallelujah, I'm a bum).
      Keisi Dzhons-shtreikbrekher (Casey Jones — the union
      scab). Propovednik i rab (The preacher and the slave).
      Yesli ya soldatom budu (Should I ever be a soldier).
      Ne berite papu ot menya (Don't take my papa away
      from me). Zaveshchaniye Dzho Khilla (Joe Hill's last
      will).

HOWARD, Sydney

537. Zholty Dzhek (Yellow Jack). Trans. by P. Khatskelson.
      Teatr i dramaturgiya (M.), 1936, No. 10(43), pp. 616-
      639. ZL 58600.36 (pl.)

HUDSON, Alec (W. J. Holmes).

538. Protivnik obnaruzhen (Enemy sighted). Trans. by N.
      Daruzes. Int. Lit. (M.), 1942, No. 3-4-5, pp. 9-33.
      (s.)

HUGHES, Langston

539. Ballada o Lenine (Ballad of Lenin). Trans. by Yu.
      Anisimov. Int. Lit. (M.), 1936, No. 1, p. 27. (p.)
      From A new song.

      Ballada o Meri, lyubivshei dzhin (Ballad of Gin Mary).
      See 556.

540. Berri (Berry). Trans. by Ye. Romanova. Int. Lit.
      (M.), 1935, No. 9, pp. 61-64. (s.)
      From The ways of white folks.

541. "Blyustiteli zakona" stuchatsya v moyu dver ["guard-
ians of the law" are knocking at my door; not identi-
fied]. Trans. from the manuscript by Ester Ber. Int.
Lit. (M.), 1934, No. 6, pp. 96-98. (sk.)

Chyornaya sluzhanka (Negro servant). See 544.

Dom v mire (House in the world). See 16.

542. Doma (Home). Trans. by G. Yarros. Kras.Nov (M.),
1935, No. 11, pp. 46-51. ZL 55413.35 (s.)
From The ways of white folks.

543. Same. Trans. by Ye. Romanova. Int. Lit. (M.), 1935,
No. 9, pp. 55-60.

Doroga (Bound No'th blues). See 559.

544. Dva stikhotvoreniya [two poems]. Trans. by Yu.
Anisimov. Int. Lit. (M.), 1933, No. 1, p. 85. (coll. p.)
Contents: Otkrytoye pismo yugu (Open letter to the
South). Chyornaya sluzhanka (Negro servant).
"Open letter to the South" is from A new song; "Negro
servant" is from One way ticket.

Khozyayeva (Ballad of the landlord). See 555.

Kore ne stydno (Cora unashamed). See 558.

Mednyie plevatelnitsy (Brass spitoons). See 556.

Morskaya tish (Sea calm). See 555.

545. Moskva i ya [Moscow and I; not identified]. Trans. by
B. Boleslavskaya. Int. Lit. (M.), 1933, No. 5, pp. 78-
82. (sk.)

546. Nachalo zanyati (A good job gone). Trans. by Yu.
Aksel. 30 Dnei (L.), 1938, No. 11, pp. 89-90.
ZL 3926.39 (s.)
From Esquire, April, 1935, p. 46.

547. Same. Kostyor [place of publication not available],
1939, No. 4, pp. 60-61. ZL 24792.39

Nasha vesna (Our spring). See 559.

548. Nravy belykh (The ways of white folks). Trans. by N.
S. Nadezhdina; edited by M. A. Dyakonov. Goslitizdat.,
L., 1936. 268 p., 10,300 c. KL 10084.36 (coll. s.)

Otets i syn (Father and son). See 558.

Otkrytoye pismo yugu (Open letter to the South). See 544.

Pesn chyornoi devushki (Song for a dark girl). See 555.

HUGHES, Langston (Continued)

549. Pesn Ispanii (Song of Spain). Trans. by Yu. Anisimov.
      Int. Lit. (M.), 1937, No. 5, pp. 3-4. (p.)
      From A new song.

      Primorskiye ulitsy (Water-front streets). See 555.

550. "Prodan v rabstvo" (Slave on the block). Trans. by N.
      Daruzes. 30 Dnei (L.), 1934, No. 8, pp. 63-65.
      ZL 49572.34. (s.)
      From The ways of white folks.

551. Professor (Professor). Trans. by N. Nadezhdina. Lit.
      Sov. (L.), 1938, No. 6, pp. 101-105. ZL 30907.38 (s.)
      From Dorothy Brewster, A book of contemporary
      short stories.

      Rodina (Home). See 558.

552. Skottsboro (Scottsboro limited). Trans. and adapted
      by A. Grevs and A. Meier. Ts.K.Mopr., M., 1932.
      24 p., 10,000 c. KL 2973.32 (pl.)

553. Smekh skvoz slyozy (Not without laughter). Trans. by
      V. Stanevich. Goslitizdat., M. & L., 1932. 237 p.,
      5000 c. KL 20303.32 (n.)

      Smirennaya Kora (Cora unashamed). See 5.

554. Stikhi [poems]. Trans. by Yu. Anisimov. Lit. Mir.
      Rev. (M.), 1932, No. 9-10, pp. 69-71. (coll. p.)

555. Stikhi [poems]. Trans. by Yu. Anisimov. Kras. Nov
      (M.), 1933, No. 4, p. 106. ZL 24042.33 (coll. p.)
      Contents: Pesn chyornoi devushki (Song for a dark
      girl). Morskaya tish (Sea calm). Khozyayeva (Ballad
      of the landlord). Primorskiye ulitsy (Water-front
      streets).
      "Song for a dark girl" is from Fine clothes to the
      Jew; "Sea calm" and "Water-front streets" are from
      The weary blues; "Ballad of the landlord" is from
      Jim Crow's last stand.

556. Stikhi [poems]. Trans. by Yu. Anisimov. Int. Lit.
      (M.), 1934, No. 5, pp. 89-90. (Coll. p.)
      Contents: Vorovskaya pesn (Death of Do Dirty: a
      rounder's song). Ballada o Meri, lyubivshei dzhin (Ballad
      of Gin Mary). Mednyie plevatelnitsy (Brass spitoons).
      From Fine clothes to the Jew.

557. Syn Oistera (Oyster's son). Trans. by Yu. Smirnov.
30 Dnei (L.), 1938, No. 4, pp. 71-75. ZL 17294.38 (s.)

558. Tri rasskaza [three stories]. Trans. by N. Nadezhdina.
Lit. Sov. (L.), 1935, No. 10, pp. 115-150. ZL 53388.35
(coll. s.)
Contents: Otets i syn (Father and son). Rodina (Home).
Kore ne stydno (Cora unashamed).
From The ways of white folks.

559. Tri stikhotvoreniya [three poems]. Trans. by A.
Romm, Yu. Anisimov and L. Filatov. Int. Lit. (M.),
1933, No. 5, pp. 35-36. (coll. p.)
Contents: Nasha vesna (Our spring). Doroga (Bound
No'th blues). Vsyo ravno [it's all the same; not iden-
tified].
"Bound No'th blues" is from The dream keeper; the
source of "Our spring" could not be determined.

Vorovskaya pesn (Death of Do Dirty: a rounder's
song). See 556.

Same. See 15.

Vsyo ravno. See 559.

560. Vyslushaite menya, mister [listen to me, Mister; not
identified]. Trans. by Yu. Smirnov. Rabotnitsa (M.),
1939, No. 5, p. 17. ZL 14087.39 (s.)

561. Zdravstvui revolyutsiya (Good morning, revolution).
Selected and trans. by Yu. Anisimov. Goslitizdat.,
M. & L., 1933. 103 p., 3000 c. KL 22399.33 (coll. p.)
The title poem of this collection is from New Masses,
Sept., 1932, p. 5. Other contents not listed in KL.

HURST, Fannie

562. Mancken (Mannequin). Trans. by L. M. Gausman.
Mysl, L,, 1926. 212 p., 5000 c. KL 17528.26 (n.)

563. Same. 1927. 212 p., 5000 c. KL 9435.27

564. Pesn zhizni (Song of life). Trans. by A. M. Karnaukhova. Mysl, L., 1927. 192 p., 5200 c. KL 15608.27
(coll. s.)

565. T. V. S. (T.B.). Trans. by S. Gurevich. Biblioteka
Zhurnala "Ogonyok," M., 1930. 48 p., 20,000 c.
KL 25793.30 (s.)
From Every soul hath its song.

HURST, Fannie (Continued)

566. Vrazhda (Song of life). Trans. by T. O. Davydova. Mysl. L., 1927. 208 p., 5200 c. KL 15607.27 (coll. s.)

567. Zolotyie perezvony (Lummox). Trans. by Mariana Kuznets. Vremya, L., 1925, 285 p., 4100 c. KL 15481.25 (n.)

568. Same. Foreword by I. Neustroyev. 1927. 270 p., 4150 c. KL 8487.27

INGERSOLL, Ralph

569. Sovershenno sekretno (Top secret). Introd. by S. K. Bushuyev. Oktyabr (M. & L.), 1946, No. 9, pp. 149-181; No. 10-11, pp. 152-178; No. 12, pp. 121-148. (rep.) An excerpt.

INGLEWOOD, M.

570. Lyubov, zabastovka, dinamit i sobaka [love, a strike, dynamite, and a dog; not identified]. Trans. by Yu. Smirnov. Rezets (L.), 1939, No. 15-16, pp. 17-18. ZL 54223.39 (s.) This writer not identified.

IRVING, Washington

571. Rasskazy i legendy [stories and legends; not identified, but possibly selections from The sketch book]. Trans. by M. Gershenzon, with notes and a biographical sketch of Irving by the translator. Detizdat., M. & L., 1939. 192 p., 25,000 c. KL 2269.40 A juvenile publication.

572. Rip Van Vinkl (Rip Van Winkle). Trans. by M. Gershenzon. Detizdat., M. & L., 1937. 32 p., 100,300 c. KL 24850.37 (s.) A juvenile publication.

Same. See 4.

573. Zamechatelnyie deyaniya Pitera Tvyordogolovovo (The admirable exploits of Peter the headstrong). Trans. by M. Gershenzon, with a preface by the translator. Detizdat., M. & L., 1940. 16 p., 25,000 c. KL 26810.40 From A history of New York, Chapter VIII, Book VI.

574. Zhenikh-prizrak (The spectre bridgegroom.). Pioner (M.), 1938, No. 1, pp. 78-86. ZL 19419.38 (s.) From The sketch book.

IRWIN, Wallace

575. Rasskaz o sebe [story about myself; not identified]. Trans. by M. Urnov. Int. Lit. (M.), 1935, No. 4, pp. 90-92.

JACKSON, Aunt Molly
Golodnyie pesni (The hungry blues). See 17.

JAMES, Henry
Biografiya pisatelya. See 5.
Dezi Miller (Daisy Miller). See 4.

JENNINGS, Alphonso J.

576. O. Genri na dne (Through the shadows with O. Henry). Trans. by N. F. Davydova; edited by V. A. Azov. Gosizdat., L., 1926. 197 p., 4000 c. KL 3414.26 (memoirs).

577. Same. 1927. 310 p., 4000 c.

JOHN, William

578. Skvoz ad (Through hell). Trans. by P. Okhrimenko. 30 Dnei (L.), 1936, No. 12, pp. 73-80. ZL 8784.37 (s.) From Century Magazine, Sept., 1926, p. 577.

JOHNSON, Josephine

579. Medovy mesyats (Nigger honeymoon). Trans. by E. Ber. 30 Dnei (L.), 1939, No. 2, pp. 83-84. ZL 13084.39 (s.) From Winter orchard.

580. Teper v noyabre (Now in November). Trans. by Ester Ber. Zhurn. Gaz. Obyed., M., 1937. 157 p., 25,000 c. KL 37092.37 (n.)

581. Same. Trans. by E. Ber; edited by O. Kholmskaya. Goslitizdat., M., 1938. 188 p., 10,000 c. KL 8272.38

KALAR, Joseph
Syn shakhtera. See 14.

KAUFFMAN, Reginald

582. Na ostrove kalibrii ili krov korolei (The blood of kings). Trans. by D. M. Gorfinkel. Priboi, L., 1928. 180 p., 6000 c. KL 13629.28 (n.)

KEMP, Harry

583. Ispoved amerikantsa [confessions of an American; not
     identified, but possibly Tramping on life]. Trans. by
     M. V. Volosov; edited by V. A. Azov. Gosizdat., L.,
     1926. 315 p., 4000 c. KL 2036.26 (autobiog.)

KELLY, Edith

584. Sornaya trava (Weeds). With a foreword by Upton
     Sinclair. Trans. by M. Volosov. ZIF, M. & L., 1930.
     282 p., 5000 c. KL 5760.30 (n.)

585. Same. 1930. 282 p., 10,000 c. KL 25784.30

KERR, Sophie

586. Dikaya zemlya (Wild earth). Trans. by P. Okhrimenko.
     Biblioteka Zhurnala "Ogonyok," M., 1930. 56 p.,
     20,000 c. KL 5327.30 (s.)
     From O'Brien, Best American stories, 1919-1924,
     Vol. I.

KIMBALL, Paul

587. Missis Merivel (Mrs. Merivale). Trans. by Mark
     Volosov. Vremya, L., 1927. 264 p., 5150 c.
     KL 4145.27 (n.)

KINGSLEY, Sidney

588. Lyudi v belykh khalatakh (Men in white). Trans. by
     Ilya Rubinshtein. Oktyabr (M.), 1935, No. 2, pp. 35-
     73. ZL 17208.35 (pl.)

589. Same. Trans. and adapted by Ilya Rubinshtein.
     Tsedram., M., 1935. 63 p., 2150 c. KL 6576.35

590. Same. Iskusstvo, M., 1938. 83 p., 5000 c. KL 23433.38

591. Tupik (Dead end). Trans. by M. Volosov. Kras. Nov
     (M.), 1938, No. 4, pp. 71-127. ZL 24107.38 (pl.)

KNOWLES, Joseph

592. Dva mesyatsa v lesakh (Alone in the wilderness).
     Trans. and edited by L. Andruson. Gosizdat., M.,
     1922. 156 p., 3000 c. KL 5710.22 (autobiog.)

KOMROFF, Manuel

593. Zavtra! zavtra! (The great tomorrow). Trans. by N.
Volzhina. Int. Lit. (M.), 1941, No. 11-12, pp. 118-
123. (s.)
From Esquire, March 1935, p. 60.

KRETON [sic.], Anna Washington

594. Marka "B.V.D's" [a B.V.D. label; not identified].
Mol. Gvard. (M.), 1929, No. 9, pp. 50-53. (s.)
This writer not identified, but possibly Creighton or
Craton.

LANE, Tamar

595. Amerikanskiye kinostsenari (The new technique of
screen writing). Introd. by I. Trauberg. Goskinoizdat, M., 1940. 152 p., 3000 c. KL 25129.40 (coll.
scenarios)

LARDNER, Ring

596. Chelovek za bortom (Man not overboard) and Dvorets
svobodi (Liberty hall). Trans. by M. Urnov. Kras.
Nov (M.), 1936, No. 11, pp. 79-89. ZL 3460.37 (coll.
s.)
From Round up.

Chempion (Champion). See 5.

597. Chempion (Champion) and Den Konrada Grina (A day
with Conrad Green). Trans. by V. K. Zhitomirski.
Lecheniye solntsem (Sun cured) and Tainy pisatelskoi
kukhni [secrets of the writer's kitchen; not identified].
Trans. by M. Urnov. Int. Lit. (M.), 1934, No. 5, pp.
62-84. (coll. s.)
From The collected short stories of Ring Lardner.

Den Konrada Grina (A day with Conrad Green). See
597.

Dvorets svobdy (Liberty hall). See 596.

Lecheniye solntsem (Sun cured). See 597.

598. Ledi sfinks ("Zone of quiet"). Trans. by M. Urnov.
30 Dnei (L.), 1935, No. 10, pp. 56-62. ZL 53383.35 (s.)
From Round up.

LARDNER, Ring (Continued)

599. Novelly [short stories]. Trans. and edited by M.
Levidov. Goslitizdat., M., 1935. 157 p., 10,000 c.
KL 3936.36 (coll. s.)
Contents not listed in KL.
Tainy pisatelskoi kukhni. See 597.

LEMMON, Robert Stell

600. Bambukovaya lovushka (The bamboo trap). Trans. by
P. Okhrimenko. 30 Dnei (L.), 1937, No. 7, pp. 57-64.
ZL 35007.37 (s.)
From O'Brien, Best American stories, 1919-1924,
Vol. II.

LEWIS, Sinclair

Collected works

601. Sobraniye sochineni [collected works]. Gosizdat.,
M. & L., 1927. Only two volumes in this edition were
listed in KL. See 613 and 618.

Separate publications

602. Alleya pod ivami (The willow walk). Trans. by P.
Okhrimenko. Mol. Gvard. (M.), 1936, No. 5, pp.
112-130. ZL 29895.36 (s.)
From Selected short stories of Sinclair Lewis.

603. Anna Vikkers (Ann Vickers). Trans. by L. Barkman.
Zvezda (M.), 1934, No. 10, pp. 98-107. ZL 7603.35
(n.)
An excerpt.

604. Bebbit (Babbitt). Trans. by A. G. and G. A. Zukkau.
Mysl, L., 1928. 368 p., 6200 c. KL 534.28 (n.)

605. Dacha na stremnine (Mantrap). Trans. by S. G.
Zaimovski. Mysl, L., 1927. 242 p., 6200 c.
KL 13399.27 (n.)

606. Elmer Gantri (Elmer Gantry). Trans. by L. L. Domger and G. A. Zukkau; edited by D. M. Gorfinkel.
Vremya, L., 1927. 408., 4150 c. KL 8914.27 (n.)

607. Same. Trans. by M. A. Dyakonov. Priboi, L., 1927.
514 p., 7000 c. KL 19814.27

608. Same. Trans. and abridged by A. V. Krivtsova; foreword by P. S. Kogan. Bezbozhnik, M., 1929. 308 p., 20,000 c. KL 18465.29

609. Enn Vikkers (Ann Vickers). Trans. by I. K. Romanovich. Int. Lit. (M.), 1933, No. 5, pp. 9-25. (n.) An excerpt.

610. Same. Trans. by M. Volosov. Goslitizdat., M., 1936. 499 p., 10,000 c. KL 15694.36

611. Erousmit (Arrowsmith). Trans. by N. Volnin. Goslitizdat., M., 1936. 496 p., 10,000 c. KL 17084.36 (n.)

612. Glavnaya ulitsa (Main street). Trans. by D. M. Gorfinkel. Gosizdat., L., 1924. 401 p., 5000 c. KL 8699.24 (n.)

613. Same. Gosizdat., M. & L., 1927. 568 p., 7000 c. Sob. soch., Vol. III. See 601. KL 18561.27

614. Istoriya odnoi amerikanki (Main street). Trans. by T. Shchepkina-Kupernik. Sov. Prob., M., 1924. 287 p., 3000 c. KL 13076.24 (n.)

615. Same. 1927. 314 p., 4000 c.

616. Kapkan (Mantrap). Trans. by A. V. Krivtsova. Gosizdat., M. & L., 1927. 320 p., 15,000 c. KL 9408.27 (n.)

617. Martin Arrousmit (Arrowsmith). Trans. by M. P. Chekhov. Mysl, L., 1925. 542 p., 6000 c. KL 18278.25 (n.)

618. Martin Errousmit (Arrowsmith). Trans. by L. L. Domger; edited by D. M. Gorfinkel. Gosizdat., M., 1929. 551 p., 5000 c. Sob. soch., Vol. II. See 601. KL 15503.29

619. Mentrap (Mantrap). Trans. by A. B. Rozenbaum; edited by N. N. Shulgovski. Vremya, L., 1926. 264 p., 4150 c. KL 19344.26 (n.)

620. Mister Bebbit (Babbitt). Trans. by M. Prussak; edited and with an introd. by M. Levidov. Gosizdat., M. & P., 1924. 534 p., 5000 c. KL 2539.24 (n.)

621. Same. 1926. 413 p., 5000 c. KL 12183.26

622. Na volnom vozdukhe (Free air). Trans. by T. A. Bogdanovich. Mysl, L., 1924. 281 p., 3000 c. KL 12417.24 (n.)

LEWIS, Sinclair (<u>Continued</u>)

623. Nash Mister Renn: romanticheskoye puteshestviye odnovo dzhentelmena (Our Mr. Wrenn: the romantic adventures of a gentle man). Trans. by M. Matveyev. Seyatel, L., 1925. 318 p., 4000 c. KL 13077.24 (n.)

624. Same. 1927. 310 p., 5000 c. KL 15579.27

625. Polyot sokola (The trail of the hawk). Trans. by A. M. Karnaukhova. Mysl, L., 1925. 304 p., 8000 c. KL 13078.24 (n.)

626. Same. 1927. 316 p., 5000 c. KL 11735.27

627. Proizvedeniye iskusstva (Work of art). Trans. by N. Daruzes. <u>Int. Lit</u>. (M.), 1934, No. 3-4, pp. 171-179. (n.)
An excerpt.

628. Prostaki (The innocents). Trans. by N. Soifer. Gosizdat., M. & L., 1928. 152 p., 7000 c. KL 14305.28 (n.)

629. U nas eto nevozmozhno (It can't happen here). Trans. by Z. S. Vygodskaya; foreword by S. S. Dinamov. Zhurn. Gaz. Obyed., M., 1937. 480 p., 20,000 c. KL 17721.37 (n.)

630. Same. Trans. by Z. S. Vygodskaya. <u>Int. Lit</u>. (M.), 1937, No. 2, pp. 29-127; No. 3, pp. 44-127. Abridged.

631. Una Golden (The job). Trans. by E. K. Pimenova and T. A. Bogdanovich. Mysl, L., 1926. 223 p., 5100 c. KL 16459.26 (n.)

632. Ya znakom s samim prezidentom (The man who knew Coolidge). Trans. by M. Volosov. Kras. Gaz., L., 1928. 59 p., 25,000 c. KL 9915.28 (n.)
An excerpt.

LINDSAY, Vachel

Dzhon Braun (John Brown). See 17.

Kongo (The Congo). See 17.

Prolog k stikham "V obmen na khleb." See 633.

633. Simon Legri: negrityanskaya propoved (Simon Legree: a negro sermon) and Prolog k stikham "V obmen na

khleb" [prologue to Rhymes to be traded for bread].
Znamya (M.), 1936, No. 8, pp. 135-138. ZL 49789.36
(coll. p.)
"Simon Legree" is from The Booker Washington
trilogy, Part I.

LONDON, Charmian

Zhizn Dzheka Londona (The book of Jack London). See
710.

634. O moyem muzhe [about my husband]. With an introductory note by D. Gorbov. 30 Dnei (L.), 1926, No. 9,
pp. 20-29. (biog.)
An excerpt from The book of Jack London.

LONDON, Jack

Collected Works

635. Sobraniye sochineni [collected works]. A. N. Kudryat-
seva, editor of translation; introd. by Leonid Andreyev.
Gosizdat., M., 1922.
Only five volumes in this edition were listed in KL,
but there are probably more.

636. Polnoye sobraniye sochineni [complete collected
works]. Edited by Yev. Kavalyer. ZIF, M. & L., 1924-
1927. 41 vols.

637. Sobraniye sochineni [collected works]. Edited by V.
A. Azov and A. N. Gorlin. Gosizdat., L., 1925-1926.
12 vols.

638. Polnoye sobraniye sochineni [complete collected works].
Mysl, L., 1925. 8 vols.
There are many other London titles published by Mysl
in this period which are probably part of this edition,
but they were not so listed in KL.

639. Polnoye sobraniye sochineni [complete collected
works]. Introd. by Prof. P. S. Kogan; biographical
sketch by Charmian London. ZIF, M. & L., 1928-1930.
24 vols.

Separate publications

A-cho (The Chinago). See 865.

LONDON, Jack (Continued)

640. Same. Introd. by L. Nedal. Gosizdat., M. & L., 1927.
32 p., 20,000 c. KL 12031.27 (s.)
From When God laughs.

641. Alaya chuma (The scarlet plague). Trans. by M.
Likiardopulo. Univ. Bib., M., 1917. 96 p., 1500 c.
KL 6698.17 (n.)

642. Same. 1918. 96 p., 10,000 c. KL 1354.18

643. Same. Gosizdat., M., 1922. 90 p., 5000 c. KL 5644.22

644. Same. Trans. by A. S. Urvich. Mysl, L., 1925. 80 p.,
8000 c. KL 16591.25

Same. See 696 and 636.

Same. See 650 and 637.

Same. See 818 and 639.

645. Bely klyk (White fang). Trans. by L. A. Kutukova. 5th
ed. Univ. Bib., M., 1917. 320 p., 20,000 c.
KL 11777.17 (n.)

646. Same. Trans. by R. Rubinova. Yunaya Rossiya, M.,
1918. 192 p., 4000 c. KL 1024.18

647. Same. Trans. by Ye. A. Barot. Gosizdat., M., 1922.
231 p., 5100 c. Sob. soch. See 635. KL 5646.22

648. Same. Trans. by Ye. A. Barot and Zin. Lvovski. Mysl,
L., 1925. 193 p., 10,000 c. KL 1100.25

649. Same. 1926. 193 p., 4000 c. KL 7451.26

650. Bely klyk (White fang). Trans. by N. S. Kaufman. Do
Adama (Before Adam). Trans. by E. I. Nelius. Alaya
chuma (The scarlet plague). Trans. by V. K.
Zagorskaya. Gosizdat., M. & L., 1926. 348 p., 5000 c.
Sob. soch., Vol. IX. See 637. KL 14422.26 (coll. n.)

651. Same. 1927. 348 p., 2500 c. KL 9406.27

652. Same. 1927. 348 p., 2500 c. KL 10514.27

653. Bely klyk (White fang). Trans. by Z. Lvovski.
Seyatel, L., 1926. 292 p., 15,250 c. KL 10248.26 (n.)

Same. See 1033 and 636.

Same. See 735.

654.   Same. [no translator given]. Ts.K.S.T., M., 1927.
       119 p., 75,000 c. KL 20371.27

655.   Same. 1927. 119 p., 30,000 c. KL 21951.27

656.   Same. 1928. 119 p., 20,000 c. KL 5422.28

       Same. See 1034 and 639.

       Same. See 941.

657.   Same. Trans. by N. Volzhina. Detizdat., M. & L.,
       1936. 286 p., 25,000 c. KL 24102.36
       A juvenile publication.

658.   Same. 1937. 276 p., 50,300 c. KL 17176.37

659.   Same. 1937. 207 p., 74,000 c. KL 871.38

660.   Bely klyk (White fang) and Zov predkov (The call of the
       wild). Trans. by D. M. Gordinkel; introd. by M.
       Gutner. Mol. Gvard., M., 1938. 284 p., 25,000 c.
       KL 7967.38 (coll. n.)

661.   Belyic bogi (Jerry of the islands). Trans. by E. K.
       Brodersen. Mysl, L., 1924. 216 p., 6000 c. Pol. sob.
       soch., Vol. VI. See 638. KL 8070.24 (n.)

662.   Same. 1925. 189 p., 5000 c. KL 5547.25

663.   Berega Sakramento (The banks of the Sacramento).
       Gosizdat., M. & L., 1927. 77 p., 7000 c. KL 3862.27
       (coll. s.)
       A juvenile publication. From Dutch courage and
       other stories. Other titles not listed in KL.

664.   Same. 1929. 23 p., 50,000 c. KL 19807.29 (s.)

       Bog yevo ottsov (The God of his fathers and other
       stories). See 879 and 635.

665.   Same. Trans. by N. M. Tsymovich. Mysl, L., 1924.
       184 p., 8000 c. KL 13060.24 (coll. s.)

666.   Same. Trans. by Zin. Lvovski. ZIF, M. & L., 1925.
       188 p., 10,000 c. Pol. sob. soch., Vol. XII, Book 2.
       See 636. KL 4685.25

       Same. See 690 and 639.

667.   Bog yevo ottsov (The God of his fathers). Trans. by
       Zin. Lvovski. Univ. Bib., M., 1917. 94 p., 15,000 c.
       KL 7660.17 (coll. s.)
       From The God of his fathers and other stories. Other
       titles not listed in KL.

LONDON, Jack (Continued)

668. Same. Gosizdat., M. & P., 1923. 92 p., 10,000 c.
KL 3579.23
Other titles not listed in KL

Bolezn pokinutovo vozhdya (The sickness of Lone
Chief). See 784.

669. Borba klassov (War of the classes). Nevskaya
Tipografiya, P., 1918. 77 p., 300 c. KL 88.18 (coll.
essays)
Contents not listed in KL.

670. Same. Trans. by D. Ye. Deikhtenberg; edited and with
an introd. by D. O. Zaslovski. Mysl, L., 1924. 152 p.,
6000 c. KL 10629.24
Contents not listed in KL.

671. Brodyagi, puteshestvuyushchiye nochyu (Hoboes that
pass in the night). Priboi, L., 1926. 31 p., 15,000 c.
KL 12735.26 (sk.)
From The road.

672. Buk — pochtovaya sobaka (The call of the wild). Trans.
by Manaseina. G. F. Mirimanov, M., 1925. 60 p.,
10,000 c. KL 22016.27 (n.)
A juvenile publication. Probably abridged.

673. Same. 1928. 60 p., 10,000 c. KL 19291.25

674. Bunt na "Elsinore" (The mutiny of the Elsinore).
Trans. by S. Matveyev and Ye. Speranskaya. Gosizdat.,
M. & P., 1924. 399 p., 5000 c. KL 401.24 (n.)

Bury volk (Brown wolf). See 894.

675. Same. Trans. by S. G. Zaimovski. G. F. Mirimanov,
M., 1926. 20 p., 10,000 c. KL 16166.26 (s.)
A juvenile publication. From Love of life and other
stories.

676. Same. 1927. 23 p., 15,000 c. KL 16079.27

677. "Byki" (Bulls). Novaya Moskva, M., 1924. 29 p., 8000
c. KL 3772.25 (sk.)
From The road.

678. Byvaly [there once was; not identified] and Zolotaya
zorka (Burning Daylight). Trans. by S. Tsederbaum
and B. Tsemlin. Gosizdat., M. & P., 1923. 230 p.,
10,000 c. KL 3580.23 (coll. n.)

679. Byvaly [there once was; not identified]. Uralskaya
     Kniga, Yekaterinburg, 1924. 168 p., 3000 c.
     KL 405.24 (n.)

680. Charodei [the magician; not identified]. Gomelski
     Rabochi, Gomel, 1926. 19 p., 5000 c. KL 4471.26 (s.)

681. Chelovek on byl [he was a real man; not identified].
     Trans. by V. Aleksandrov; edited by V. A. Azov.
     Kniga, M. & L., 1924. 230 p., 6000 c. KL 8686.24
     (coll. s.)

682. Same. 1925. 230 p., 4000 c. KL 1623.25

     Chelovek s shramom (The man with the gash). See
     843.

683. Chelovek so shramom (The man with the gash).
     Ts.K.S.T., M., 1928. 112 p., 150,000 c. KL 15117.28
     (coll. s.)
     From The God of his fathers. Other titles not listed
     in KL.

684. Cherepakhi Tasmana (The turtles of Tasman).
     Trans. by Ye. G. Guro; edited by Yev. Lann. ZIF,
     M. & L., 1925. 138 p., 10,000 c. Pol. sob. soch., Vol.
     XIII, Book 3. See 636. KL 5546.25 (coll. s.)

     Cherepakhi Tesmana (The turtles of Tasman). See
     797 and 639.

     Cheri. See 723 and 639.

     Cherri. See 921 and 636.

685. Den plameneyet (Burning Daylight). Trans. by A. V.
     Krivtsova and V. Zhitomirski; edited by Yev. Lann.
     ZIF, L., 1925. 301 p., 10,000 c. Pol. sob. soch., Vol.
     11, Book 2. See 636. KL 13890.24 (n.)

686. Same. 1927. 302 p., 6000 c. KL 0455.27

687. Same. Trans. by A. V. Krivtsova. ZIF, M. & L., 1929.
     In two parts, published separately: Part 1, pp. 1-128;
     Part 2, pp. 129-250; 80,000 c. each. Pol. sob. soch.,
     Vol. XX, Books 39 and 40. See 639. KL 16548.29,
     KL 19769.29

     Derzhite kurs na zapad (Make westing). See 865.

688. Deti moroza (Children of the frost). Trans. by M. M.

LONDON, Jack (Continued)

Birinski. Mysl, L., 1925. 160 p., 8000 c. Pol. sob. soch., Vol. XXVI. See 638. KL 10420.25 (coll. s.)

689. Same. Trans. by L. Brodskaya. ZIF, M. & L., 1926. 144 p., 6000 c. Pol. sob. soch., Vol. VIII, Book 2. See 636. KL 22291.26

690. Deti moroza (Children of the frost). Trans. by L. Brodskaya. Bog yevo ottsov (The God of his fathers). Trans. by Z. Lvovski. ZIF, M. & L., 1929. In two parts, published separately: Part I, pp. 1-128; Part 2, pp. 129-272; 90,000 c. each. Pol. sob. soch., Vol. XIV, Books 27 and 28. See 639. KL 5257.29, KL 5762.29 (coll. s.)

691. Deti snegov (Children of the frost). Trans. by A. Tarasova. 4th ed. Univ. Bib., M., 1917. 170 p., 15,000 c. KL 2992.17 (coll. s.)

692. Same. Gosizdat., M. & P., 1923. 168 p., 10,000 c. KL 3035.23

693. Dikaya sila [wild strength; not identified]. Trans. by R. Rubinova. Gosizdat., M., 1922. 122 p., 5000 c. KL 9267.22

694. Do Adama (Before Adam). Trans. by E. Pimenova. 4th ed. Univ. Bib., M., 1917. 184 p., 15,000 c. KL 3672.17 (n.)

695. Same. Gosizdat., M. & P., 1923. 186 p., 10,000 c. KL 3036.23

696. Do Adama (Before Adam) and Alaya chuma (The scarlet plague). Trans. by L. Lanskaya; edited by Yev. Lann. ZIF, M. & L., 1925. 149 p., 10,000 c. Pol. sob. soch., Vol. XVIII, Book 1. See 636. KL 7587.25 (coll. n.)

697. Do Adama (Before Adam). Trans. by Zin. Lvovski. Mysl, L., 1925. 164 p., 10,000 c. KL 13887.24

698. Same. 1926. 164 p., 5000 c. KL 671.26

Same. See 650 and 637.

Same. See 1034 and 639.

699. Doch snegov (A daughter of the snows). Trans. by Zin. Lvovski. Mysl, L., 1924. 204 p., 10,000 c. KL 13057.24 (n.)

700. Same. Trans. by D. Zinev. Novella, L. & M., 1924. 204 p., 7000 c. KL 4856.24

701. Doch snegov (A daughter of the snows). Trans. by N. F. Davydova and N. F. Rachinskaya. Priklyuchiniya rybachyevo patrulya (Tales of the fish patrol). Trans. by N. F. Davydova. Gosizdat., M. & L., 1926. 406 p., 5000 c. Sob. soch., Vol. XII. See 637. KL 17517.26 (coll. n., s.)
This volume also contains a biographical sketch of London by P. Guber.

702. Same. 1927. 407 p., 2500 c. KL 11181.27

703. Doch snegov (A daughter of the snows). Trans. by V. I. Smetanich. ZIF, M. & L., 1926. 248 p., 5000 c. Pol. sob. soch., Vol. VII, Book 2. See 636. KL 3424.26

704. Same. Trans. by N. F. Davydova and N. F. Rachinskaya. Gosizdat., M. & L., 1927. 355 p., 2500 c. KL 17517.26

705. Doch snegov (A daughter of the snows). Trans. by V. I. Smetanich. Severnaya odisseya (An odyssey of the North). Trans. by Ye. G. Guro and B. Ya. Pod. ZIF, M. & L., 1928. In three parts, published separately: Part I, pp. 1-56; Part 2, pp. 57-184; Part 3, pp. 185-335; 50,000 c. each. Pol. sob. soch., Vol. IV, Books 6, 7, and 8. See 639. KL 5914.28, KL 7615.28, KL 8374.28 (coll. n., s.)
"An odyssey of the North" is from The son of the wolf. Other titles not listed in KL.

706. Same. 1929. In three parts; pp. 1-56; 57-184; 185-335; 36,000 c. each. KL 5762.29, KL 7173.29, KL 7633.29

707. Dom gordosti (The house of pride). Trans. by D. Ye. Deikhtenberg. Mysl, L., 1924. 136 p., 6000 c. KL 8008.24 (coll. s.)

708. Doroga (The road). Trans. by S. A. Adrianov. Mysl, L., 1924. 160 p., 7000 c. KL 9282.24 (coll. sk.)

709. Same. Trans. by S. G. Zaimovski. ZIF, M. & L., 1927. 376 p., 6000 c. Pol. sob. soch., Vol. I. See 636. KL 275.27
This volume also contains a biographical sketch of London by Charmian London.

LONDON, Jack (Continued)

710. Same. ZIF, M. & L., 1928. In two parts, published separately: Part 1, pp. 1-128; Part 2, pp. 129-256; 50,000 c. each. Pol. sob. soch., Vol. I, Books 1 and 2. See 639. KL 2541.28, KL 2542.28 (coll. sk., biog.) This volume also includes Zhizn Dzheka Londona (The book of Jack London) by Charmian London.

711. Same. 1929. In two parts: pp. 1-128; pp. 129-256; 40,000 c. each. KL 1841.29, KL 2719.29

712. Dorozhnyie parni i vesyolyie koty (Road-kids and gay-cats). Priboi, L., 1926. 74 p., 15,000 c. KL 21329.26 (sk.) From The road.

713. Drama na more [drama at sea, not identified]. Nevskoye Izdatelstvo, P., 1922. 16 p., 10,000 c. KL 9268.22

714. Dve tysyachi "stiffov" (Two thousand stiffs). Priboi, L., 1926. 27 p., 15,000 c. KL 12736.26 (sk.) From The road.

715. Dvoistvennaya lichnost [dual personality; not identified]. Trans. by Zin. Lvovski. Seyatel, L., 1926. 48 p., 15,000 c. KL 234.26 (coll. s.)

Same. See 736 and 635.

Dzhek London o sebe. See 723 and 639.

716. Dzherri (Jerry of the islands). Trans. by Ya. I. Yasinski. Nauchnoye Knigoizdatelstvo, L., 1924. 127 p., 5000 c. KL 5510.24 (n.)

717. Dzherri ostrovityanin (Jerry of the islands). Trans. by A. V. Krivtsova; edited by Yev. Lann. ZIF, M. & L., 1925. 186 p., 10,000 c. Pol. sob. soch., Vol. XI, Book 1. See 636. KL 3080.25

718. Dzherri ostrovityanin (Jerry of the islands). Trans. by A. V. Krivtsova. Maikel brat Dzherri (Michael brother of Jerry). Trans. by L. Brodskaya. ZIF, M. & L., 1928. In three parts, published separately: Part 1, pp. 1-128; Part 2, pp. 129-288; Part 3, pp. 289-368; 70,000 c. each. Pol. sob. soch., Vol. IX, Books 16, 17 and 18. See 639. KL 15497.28 (coll. n.)

719. Same. 1929. In three parts: pp. 1-128; pp. 129-288; pp. 289-368; 30,000 c. each. KL 17893.29, KL 18463.29, KL 19196.29

720. Dzherri s Solomonovykh Ostrovov (Jerry of the islands). Trans. by V. Onegin. Petrograd, L. & M., 1924. 224 p., 6000 c. KL 11309.24

721. Dzho u piratov (The cruise of the Dazzler). Trans. by N. Yu. Zhukovskaya. Mysl, L., 1925. 142. p., 3000 c. Pol. sob. soch., Vol. XIX. See 638. KL 1626.25 (n.)

722. Dzhon Yachmennoye zerno (John Barleycorn). Trans. by V. Azov. ZIF, M. & L., 1925. 192 p., 5000 c. Pol. sob. soch., Vol. XXII, Book I. See 636. KL 15402.25

723. Dzhon Yachmennoye zerno (John Barleycorn), Pisma Kempton-Uesu (The Kempton-Wace Letters), Cheri [not identified], and Dzhek London o sebe [Jack London about himself; not identified]. ZIF, M. & L., 1930. In two parts, published separately; Part 1, pp. 1-112; Part 2, pp. 113-312; 70,000 c. each. Pol. sob. soch., Vol. XXIV, Books 47 and 48. See 639. KL 3543.30, KL 7309.30 (coll. n., autobiog.)

724. Dzhon Yachmennoye zerno ili alkogolnyie vospominaniya (John Barleycorn). V. Onegin, editor of translation; foreword by D. Nezhdanov. Petrograd., L. & M., 1925. 198 p., 8000 c. KL 1622.25 (n.)

725. Eskimosik Kish (The story of Keesh). Gosizdat., M. & L., 1928. 22 p., 25,000 c. KL 8917.28 (s.) A juvenile publication. From Love of life.

726. Same. 1930. 14 p., 25,000 c. KL 27682.30

Frensis Speit (The "Francis Spaight"). See 869.

727. Gavaiskiye rasskazy [Hawaiian stories; not identified, but possibly On the Makaloa mat or House of pride]. Trans. by A. A. Davydova. Mysl, L., 1925. 180 p., 8000 c. Pol. sob. soch., Vol. XXXVII. See 638. KL 10420.25 (coll. s.) On the Makaloa mat was published in England (London, Mills & Boon, Ltd., 1920) under the title "Island tales."

728. Same. 1925. 180 p., 8000 c. KL 11204.25

LONDON, Jack (Continued)

729. Same. Trans. by A. Ostrogorskaya-Malkina. Petrograd, L. & M., 1925. 151 p., 8000 c. KL 1621.25

730. Glaza Azii [the eyes of Asia; not identified, but
possibly The yellow peril]. Trans. by V. Vilyams;
introd. by F. Sologub. Kolos, L., 1925. 111 p.,
10,000 c. KL 15401.25 (coll. essays)
Contents: Glaza Azii. Kak ya ponimayu zhizn (What
life means to me).
"The yellow peril" and "What life means to me" are
from Revolution and other essays.

731. Goliaf (Goliah). Gosizdat., M. & L., 1926. 64 p.,
15,000 c. KL 20385.26 (coll. essays)
From Revolution, and other essays. Other titles not
listed in KL.

732. Gollandskaya doblest (Dutch courage and other
stories). With an introd. by Charmian London. Trans.
by A. V. Krivtsova and V. Zhitomirski; edited by
Yev. Lann. ZIF, M. & L., 1924. 108 p., 10,000 c.
Pol. sob. soch., Vol. XI, Book 1. See 636. (coll. s.)

Same. See 899 and 639.

733. Gollandskoye muzhestvo (Dutch courage and other
stories). Mysl, L., 1924. 144 p., 5000 c. KL 3722.24
(coll. s.)

734. Same. With an introd. by Charmian London. 1926.
128 p., 5000 c. KL 2044.26

Golos krovi (The call of the wild). See 961 and 637.

735. Golos krovi (The call of the wild) and Bely klyk
(White fang). Gudok, M., 1927. 128 p., 50,000 c.
KL 4152.27 (coll. n.)

736. Golos krovi i drugiye rasskazy [the call of the wild
and other stories]. Trans. by Zin. Lvovski and
others. Gosizdat., M., 1922. 222 p., 3000 c. Sob. soch.
See 635. KL 6652.22 (coll. n., s.)
Contents: Golos krovi. Konets rasskaza (The end of
the story). Dvoistvennaya lichnost [dual personality;
not identified]. Obichai belovo cheloveka (The white
man's way). Mest [vengeance; not identified]. Zhan
neraskayavshisya (Jan, the unrepentant).

"The end of the story" is from The turtles of Tasman;
"The white man's way" is from Love of life; "Jan,
the unrepentant" is from The God of his fathers.

737. Same. 1923. 218 p., 7000 c. KL 5407.23

738. Igra (The game) and Pervobytny zver (The abysmal
brute). Trans. by N. Utkina and L. Brodskaya; edited
by Yev. Lann. ZIF, M. & L., 1925. 115 p., 10,000 c.
Pol. sob. soch., Vol. XIII, Book 1. See 636.
KL 13777.25 (coll. n.)

739. Igra (The game). Trans. by V. I. Smetanich. Puti
zhenshchiny (Scorn of women). Trans. by Zin. Lvovski and N. V. Lanina. Mysl, L., 1925. 192 p., 8000 c.
KL 3076.25 (coll. n., pl.)

Igra (The game). See 917 and 637.

740. Igra (The game). Trans. by N. Utkina and L.
Brodskaya. Sila silnykh (The strength of the strong).
Trans. by S. S. Zayaitski. Pervobytny zver (The
abysmal brute). Trans. by N. Utkina and L. Brodskaya.
ZIF, M. & L., 1928. In two parts, published separately:
Part 1, pp. 1-64; Part 2, pp. 65-191; 50,000 c. each.
Pol. sob. soch., Vol. VI, Books 10 and 11. See 639.
KL 10372.28 (coll. n., s.)

741. Same. 1929. In two parts: pp. 1-64; 65-191; 36,000
c. each. KL 10493.29, KL 11977.29

742. Ischeznoveniye Markusa O'Braiyena (The passing of
Marcus O'Brien). Seyatel, L., 1925. 96 p., 15,000 c.
KL 13776.25 (coll. s.)
From Lost face. Other titles not listed in KL.

743. Ischeznoveniye Markusa O'Briyena (The passing of
Marcus O'Brien), Trans. by Gart. Mezhrabpom., M. &
Berlin, 1924. 63 p., 35,000 c. KL 12410.24 (coll. s.)
Other titles not listed in KL.

744. Izbrannyie rasskazy [selected short stories]. Uchpedgiz.,
M., 1945. 32 p., 10,000 c. KL 4371.45 (coll. s.)
Contents: Zakon zhizni (The law of life). Nos korolya
(A nose for the king). Nem-bok lgun (Nam-Bok the
unveracious). Volki [the wolves; not identified].
"The law of life" and "Nam-Bok the unveracious"
are from Children of the frost; "A nose for the king"
is from When God laughs.

LONDON, Jack (Continued)

745. Izmennik [the traitor; not identified]. Ts.K.S.T., M., 1926. 16 p., 30,000 c. KL 19649.26 (s.)

746. Same. D. Gorfinkel, editor of translation; introd. by M. Gershenzon. Detizdat., M. & L., 1938. 32 p., 100,300 c. KL 716.39
A juvenile publication.

Kak ya ponimayu zhizn (What life means to me). See 730.

747. Kak ya stal sotsialistom (How I became a socialist). Trans. by R. V. Musselyuss. Nevskaya Tipografiya, P.,1918. 80 p., 3000 c. KL 742.18 (coll. essays)
From War of the classes. Other titles not listed in KL.

748. Same. Trans. by P. Okhrimenko. Gosizdat., M.& L., 1922. 84 p., 7000 c. KL 9269.22 (coll. essays)
Other titles not listed in KL.

749. Same. 2nd revised ed., 1925. 123 p., 4200 c. KL 13886.24

750. Khodya (The Chinago). Trans. by S. G. Zaimovski. G. F. Mirimanov, M., 1926. 20 p., 10,000 c. KL 17994.26 (s.)
A juvenile publication. From When God laughs.

751. Same. 1928. 24 p., 16,000 c. KL 17995.26

752. Khram gordyni (The house of pride). Trans. by A. V. Krivtsova; edited by Yev. Lann. ZIF, M. & L., 1925. 91 p., 10,000 c. Pol. sob. soch., Vol. XIV, Book 2. See 636. KL 8534.25 (coll. s.)

Same. See 868 and 639.

753. Khvat Bellyu: khvat i malysh (Smoke Bellew). Trans. by N. and L. Chukovski. Goslitizdat., M., 1937. 294 p., 25,000 c. KL 29979.37 (coll. s.)

754. Kogda bogi smeyutsya (When God laughs and other stories). Trans. by Zin. Lvovski. Mysl, L., 1924. 180 p., 8000 c. KL 13061.24 (coll. s.)

755. Same. Yev. Lann, editor of translation. ZIF, M. & L., 1925. 155 p., 10,000 c. Pol. sob. soch., Vol. XII, Book 1. See 636. KL 11205.25

Same. See 917 and 637.

Same. See 926 and 639.

756. Kogda bogi smeyutsya (When God laughs). V.Ts.I.K.,
M., 1918. 88 p., 28,000 c. KL 631.19 (coll. s.)
Contents: Kogda bogi smeyutsya. Zabastoval (The
apostate). Kusok myasa (A piece of steak).
From When God laughs and other stories.

757. Kogda ya byl brodyagoi (The road). Trans. by D. Ye.
Deikhtenberg. Kniga, L. & M., 1924. 140 p., 3000 c.
KL 9283.24 (coll. sk.)

Konets rasskaza (The end of the story). See 730.

758. Krasavitsa Li-Van (Li Wan, the fair). Trans. by A.
Tarasova and Zin. Lvovski. 4th ed. Univ. Bib., M.,
1918. 102 p., 25,000 c. KL 4749.18 (coll. s.)
Contents: Krasavitsa Li-Van. Soyuz starikov (The
league of old men). Yakh! Yakh! Yakh! (Yah! Yah!
Yah!). Vezdesushchi bely chelovek (The inevitable
white man).
"Li Wan, the fair" and "The league of old men" are
from Children of the frost; "Yah! Yah! Yah!" and
"The inevitable white man" are from South sea tales.

759. Same. 1918. 102 p., 15,000 c. KL 632.19

760. Same. Gosizdat., M. & P., 1923. 96 p., 10,000 c.
KL 1669.23 (coll. s.)
Other titles not listed in KL.

761. Krasnoye bozhestvo (The red one). Trans. by M.
Kuznets and N. M. Tsymovich. Mysl, L., 1924. 192
p., 8000 c. KL 8687.24 (coll. s.)

762. Krasnoye solnyshko (Burning Daylight). Trans. by Zin.
Lvovski. Mysl, L., 1925. 325 p., 6000 c. KL 10419.25
(n.)

763. Same. Trans. by M. V. Volosov. Gosizdat., L., 1925.
346 p., 10,000 c. Sob. soch., Vol. III. See 637.
KL 13774.25

764. Kris Farrington, matros pervoi stati (Chris Farrington, able seaman). D. Gorfinkel, editor of translation.
Detizdat., M. & L., 1939. 32 p., 100,000 c. KL 15784.39
(s.)
A juvenile publication. From Dutch courage, and
other stories.

LONDON, Jack (Continued)

Krovnaya mest. See 843.

765. Kulo — prokazhonny (Koolau the leper). Trans. by F. D. Gardt. Gosudarstvennaya Tipografiya v Ryazani, M., 1924. 159 p., 3000 c. KL 4252.24 (coll. s.) From The house of pride. Other titles not listed in KL.

Kusok myasa (A piece of steak). See 756.

766. Same. Trans. by Zin. Lvovski. Seyatel, L., 1925. 48 p., 15,000 c. KL 16588.25 (coll. s.) From When God laughs. Other titles not listed in KL.

767. Legenda o ruke tkacha (A curious fragment). Ts.K.S.T., M., 1926. 14 p., 30,000 c. KL 19649.26 (s.) From When God laughs.

768. Londonskiye trushchoby (The people of the abyss). Trans. by L. N. Rizhova-Gerst and M. I. Brusyanina; edited by V. Azov. Petrograd, L. & M., 1924. 197 p., 10,000 c. KL 7498.24 (coll. sk.)

769. Same. With an introd. by Ellen Wilkinson. Rabochaya Moskva, M., 1926. 55 p., 11,000 c. KL 15183.26. An excerpt.

770. Lunnaya dolina (The valley of the moon). Trans. by Z. A. Rogozina. Knizhny Ugol, L. & M., 1924. 319 p., 8000 c. KL 5511.24 (n.)

771. Same. Trans. by N. K. Chukovski and Yu. S. Kaufman. Gosizdat., L., 1925. 377 p., 10,000 c. Sob. soch., Vol. I. See 637. KL 10416.25

772. Same. Trans. by V. Stanevich and L. Brodskaya; edited by Yev. Lann. ZIF, M. & L., 1925. 482 p., 10,000 c. Pol. sob. soch., Vol. V. See 636. KL 16592.25

773. Same. 1927. 479 p., 10,000 c. KL 7107.27

774. Same. Trans. by V. Stanevich and L. Brodskaya; introd. by A. Belayev. ZIF, M. & L., 1929. In four parts, published separately: Part 1, pp. 1-64; Part 2, pp. 65-224; Part 3, pp. 225-368; Part 4, pp. 369-381; 85,000 c. each. Pol. sob. soch., Vol. XVIII, Books 35 and 36. See 639. KL 11977.29, KL 12976.29, KL 14511.29, KL 15000.29

775. Lunny lik (Moon-face and other stories). Trans. by Zin. Lvovski. Mysl, L., 1925. 128 p., 8000 c. Pol. sob. soch., Vol. XXXVI. See 638. KL 2320.25 (coll. s.)

776. Same. Trans. by Z. A. Vershinina. ZIF, M. & L., 1926. 151 p., 6000 c. Pol. sob. soch., Vol. IV, Book 3. See 636. KL 20996.26

    Same. See 996 and 639.

777. Lunny lik (Moon-face: a story of mortal antipathy). Trans. by Ye. Broido. Gosizdat., M. & P., 1923. 96 p., 10,000 c. KL 3038.23 (coll. s.)
    From Moon-face and other stories. Other titles not listed in KL.

778. Lyubimtsy Midasa (The minions of Midas), Ten i blesk (The shadow and the flash), and Ushchelye sploshnovo zolota (All Gold Canyon). Trans. by Ye. Kudasheva. Gosizdat., M. & P., 1923. 80 p., 10,000 c. KL 3582.23 (coll. s.)
    From Moon-face and other stories.

779. Lyubov k zhizni i drugiye rasskazy (Love of life and other stories). Trans. by Ye. Broido; edited by Yev. Zamyatin. Vsemir. Lit., P., 1922. 124 p., 3500 c. KL 9270.22 (coll. s.)
    Contains a bibliography of Russian editions of London.

780. Lyubov k zhizni (Love of life and other stories). Yev. Lann, editor of translation. ZIF, M. & L., 1925. 127 p., 10,000 c. Pol. sob. soch., Vol. X, Book 1. See 636. KL 3774.25 (coll. s.)

    Same. See 868 and 639.

781. Lyubov k zhizni (Love of life). Trans. by N. A. Almedingen. Nachatki Znanii, P., 1919. 142 p., 10,000 c. KL 6477.19 (coll. s.)
    Contents: Dzhek London: biograficheski ocherk [Jack London: a biographical sketch]. Lyubov k zhizni. Potomak Mak-koya (The seed of McCoy). Yazychnik (The heathen). Ryzhi volk (Brown wolf).
    "Love of life" and "Brown wolf" are from Love of life and other stories; "The seed of McCoy" and "The heathen" are from South Sea tales.

782. Same. Trans. by N. A. Almedingen, with a biographical sketch of London by the translator. Gosizdat., M. & P.,

LONDON, Jack (Continued)

1923. 104 p., 5000 c. KL 12940.23 (coll. s.) From Love of life and other stories. Other titles not listed in KL.

Same. See 5.

783. Same. Trans. by L. Vaisenberg. Detizdat., M., 1937. 30 p., 100,300 c. KL 18330.37 (s.)
A juvenile publication.

784. Same. Voyenizdat., M., 1945. 66 p., [no. of copies omitted]. KL 15870.45 (coll. s.)
Contents: Lyubov k zhizni. Skazaniye o Kishe (The story of Keesh). Bolezn pokinutovo vozhdya (The sickness of Lone Chief).
"Love of life" and "The story of Keesh" are from Love of life and other stories; "The sickness of Lone Chief" is from Children of the frost.

785. Same. Introd. by L. Gorbatov. Oblastnoye Knizhnoye Izdatelstvo (Stalingrad), Stalingrad, 1947. 81 p., 10,000 c. KL 10368.47 (coll. s.)
Other titles not listed in KL.

786. Lyudi bezdny (The people of the abyss). V. Azov, editor of translation. ZIF, M. & L., 1925. 183 p., 10,000 c. Pol. sob. soch., Vol. XXII, Book 2. See 636. KL 17363.25 (coll. sk.)

Same. See 1026 and 639.

787. Maikel brat Dzherri (Michael, brother of Jerry). Trans. by L. Brodskaya; edited by Yev. Lann. ZIF, M. & L., 1925. 269 p., 10,000 c. Pol. sob. soch., Vol. XX, Book 2. See 636. KL 9690.25 (n.)

Same. See 718 and 639.

788. Maikl, brat Dzherri (Michael, brother of Jerry). Trans. by M. Matveyev and T. Bogdanovich. Petrograd, L. & M., 1925. 283 p., 5000 c. KL 16590.25

789. Malenkaya khozyaika bolshovo doma (The little lady of the big house). Trans. by Z. A. Ragozina. Knizhny Ugol, P., 1923. 333 p., 3000 c. KL 12292.23 (n.)

790. Same. 1924. 333 p., 4000 c. KL 3063.24.

791. Same. Trans. by M. K. Grinvald. Mysl, L., 1925. 328 p., 8000 c. KL 3077.25

792. Same. 1925. 328 p., 10,000 c. KL 18276.25

793. Same. Trans. by Z. A. Ragozina; edited by M. Kuzmin. Seyatel, L., 1926. 266 p., 15,000 c. KL 4468.26

794. Same. [no translator given]. Knizh. Nov., L., 1926. 298 p., 8000 c. KL 14423.26

795. Same. Trans. by V. O. Stanevich; edited by Z. A. Vershinina. ZIF, M. & L., 1926. 288 p., 6000 c. Pol. sob. soch., Vol. VI. See 636. KL 18668.26

796. Same. 1929. 362 p., 10,000 c. KL 14999.29

797. Malenkaya khozyaika bolshovo doma (The little lady of the big house). Trans. by V. O. Stanevich; edited by Z. A. Vershinina. Cherepakhi Tesmana (The turtles of Tasman). Trans. by Yev. Lann. ZIF, M. & L., 1929. In two parts, published separately: Part 1, pp. 1-176; Part 2, pp. 177-336; 80,000 c. each. Pol. sob. soch., Vol. XXII, Books 43 and 44. See 639. KL 22293.29, KL 22813.29 (coll. n., s.)

798. Malenkaya khozyaika iz bolshovo doma (The little lady of the big house). Trans. by Ye. Shteinberg. Sov. Prob., M., 1917. 408 p., 5000 c. KL 8797.17

799. Malenkaya oshibka [a little mistake; not identified]. Trans. by Zin. Lvovski. Seyatel, L., 1926. 75 p., 15,250 c. KL 13216.26 (coll. s.)

Malenkaya samarityanka. See 873.

800. Martin Iden (Martin Eden). Trans. by E. Pimenova. 5th ed. Univ. Bib., M., 1917. 273 p., 20,000 c. KL 3673.17 (n.)

801. Same. 1918. 2 vols., 279 p., and 273 p. 15,000c. KL 1025.18

802. Same. Kniga, L. & M., 1924. 373 p., 6000 c. KL 5512.24

803. Same. 1925. 373 p., 4000 c. KL 2316.25

804. Same. Trans. by S. S. Zayaitski; edited by Ye. Kavaleria. ZIF, M. & L., 1924. 365 p., 10,000 c. Pol. sob. soch., Vol. III. See 636. KL 13062.24

805. Same. 1927. 366 p., 6000 c. KL 8456.27

806. Same. Trans by V. A. Aleksandrov. Gosizdat., L., 1925. 413 p., 10,000 c. Sob. soch., Vol. V. See 637. KL 19226.25

126

LONDON, Jack (Continued)

807. Same. Trans. by A. P. Kolmonovski. Trud i Kniga, M., 1925. 293 p., 10,000 c. KL 1624.25

808. Same. Mysl, L., 1925. 299 p., 5000 c. KL 2318.25

809. Same. Trans. by E. K. Pimenova. Priboi, L., 1927. 2 Vols., 306 p. and 312 p., 15,000 c. KL 11733.27, KL 13397.27

810. Same. Trans. by S. S. Zayaitski. ZIF, M. & L., 1929. In two parts, published separately: Part 1, pp. 1-160; Part 2, pp. 161-311; 85,000 c. each. Pol. sob. soch., Vol. XIII, Books 25 and 26. See 639. KL 3625.29, KL 4814.29

811. Same. Trans. by E. K. Pimenova; introd. by B. Gimelfarb. Gosizdat., M. & L., 1929. 445 p., 50,000 c. KL 9624.29

812. Same. Trans. by V. A. Aleksandrov; edited by D. M. Gorfinkel. Mol. Gvard., L., 1935. 418 p., 15,000 c. KL 28649.35

813. Matros pervoi stati (Chris Farrington, able seaman). Gosizdat., M. & L., 1930. 24 p., 75,000 c. KL 405.30 (s.)
A juvenile publication. From Dutch courage.

814. Meksikanets (The Mexican). V. A. Azov, editor of translation. Atenei, L., 1924. 213 p., 6000 c. KL 13056.24 (coll. s.)
From The night born. Other titles not listed in KL.

815. Same. [no translator given]. Nizhegorodskaya Kommuna, N.N., 1927. 32 p., 5600 c. KL 274.27 (s.)

816. Same. Trans. by D. M. Gorfinkel. Detizdat., M. & L., 1937. 47 p., 100,300 c. KL 31326.27
A juvenile publication.

Mest. See 736.

817. Mezhzvyozdny skitalets (The star rover). Trans. by S. Zaimovski. ZIF, M. & L., 1926. 283 p., 5000 c. Pol. sob. soch., Vol. XVIII, Book 2. See 636. KL 4964.26 (n.)

818. Mezhzvyozdny skitalets (The star rover). Trans. by S.

Zaimovski. Alaya chuma (The scarlet plague). Trans.
by Yev. Lann. Vechnyie formy i drugiye rasskazy
[the eternity of forms and other stories]. Trans.
by Z. Vershinina and Yev. Lann. ZIF, M. & L.,
1928. In three parts, published separately: Part 1,
pp. 1-64; Part 2, pp. 65-192; Part 3, pp. 193-320;
70,000 c. each. Pol. sob. soch., Vol. XII, Books 22,
23, and 24. See 639. KL 20282.28, KL 21779.28,
KL 167.29 (coll. n., s.)
"The eternity of forms" is from The turtles of Tasman.
Titles of the "other stories" not listed in KL.

819. Same. 1929. In three parts; pp. 1-64; pp. 65-192;
pp. 193-320; 30,000 c. each. KL 20411.29, KL 21023.29

820. Mikael, brat Dzherri (Michael, brother of Jerry).
Trans. by A. I. Yasinski. Nauchnoye Knigoizdatelstvo.
L., 1924. 126 p., 5000 c. KL 13058.24 (n.)

821. Moi skitaniya (The road). Gosizdat., M., 1922. 204 p.,
3200 c. See 635. KL 5647.22 (coll. sk.)

822. Same. Gosizdat., M. & P., 1923. 180 p., 10,000 c.
KL 1170.23

823. Same. Priboi, L., 1926. 64 p., 15,000 c. KL 6804.26
Probably excerpts or an abridgement.

824. Morskoi volk (The sea-wolf). Trans. by Ye. A. Barot
and Z. Lvovski; preface by Leonid Andreyev. Gosizdat., M., 1922. 321 p., 3000 c. Sob. soch. See 635.
KL 6653.22 (n.)

825. Same. Trans. by D. M. Gorfinkel. Novella, L. & M.,
1924. 272 p., 5000 c. KL 8685.24

826. Same. Trans. by Zin. Lvovski and Ye. A. Barot. Mysl,
L. & M., 1925. 293 p., 10,000 c. KL 1625.25

827. Same. 1927. 293 p., 5000 c. KL 4845.27

828. Same. Trans. by D. M. Gorfinkel. Gosizdat., L., 1925.
277 p., 10,000 c. Sob. soch., Vol. IV. See 637.
KL 19225.25

829. Same. Trans. by Z. A. Vershinina. ZIF, M. & L., 1926.
280 p., 6000 c. Pol. sob. soch., Vol. IV. See 636.
KL 17137.26

830. Same. Trans. and abridged by E. K. Pimenova. Gosizdat., M. & L., 1926. 96 p., 4000 c. KL 10780.26

LONDON, Jack (Continued)

831. Morskoi volk (The sea-wolf) and Rasskazy rybachyevo patrulya (Tales of the fish patrol). Z. A. Vershinina, editor of translation. ZIF, M. & L., 1928. In two parts, published separately: Part 1, pp. 1-160; Part 2, pp. 161-309; 50,000 c. each. Pol. sob. soch., Vol. II, Books 3 and 4. See 639. KL 3492.28, KL 5914.28 (coll. n., s.)

832. Same. 1929. Part 1, pp. 1-160, 36,000 c. KL 10493.29

833. Morskoi volk (The sea-wolf) and Poyezdka na "Oslepitelnom" (The cruise of the Dazzler). Trans. and abridged by D. M. Gorfinkel. Detizdat., M. & L., 1941. 360 p., 25,000 c. KL 3529.41 (coll. n.)

834. Muzhskaya vernost (The faith of men). Trans. by V. Koshevich. Gosizdat., M. & P., 1923. 96 p., 10,000 c. KL 4793.23 (coll. s.)
From The faith of men and other stories. Other titles not listed in KL.

835. Same. 1927. 96 p., 15,000 c. KL 10173.27

836. Myatezh (The mutiny of the Elsinore). Trans. by Zin. Lvovski and L. Golovchinskaya. Mysl, P., 1923. 360 p., 4000 c. KL 9174.23 (n.)

837. Same. 1925. 370 p., 5000 c. KL 3078.25

838. Myatezh na "Elsinore" (The mutiny of the Elsinore). Trans. by M. A. Shishmareva. ZIF, M. & L., 1926. 328 p., 6000 c. Pol. sob. soch., Vol. XVI. See 636. KL 19010.26

839. Same. 1929. In two parts, published separately: Part 1, pp. 1-128; Part 2, pp. 129-279; 90,000 c. each. Pol. sob. soch., Vol. XV, Books 29 and 30. See 639. KL 6193.29, KL 6633.29

Na abordazh. See 873.

840. Na dne (The people of the abyss). Trans. by S. A. Adrianov. Mysl, L., 1925. 228 p., 8000 c. Pol. sob. soch., Vol. XXVII. See 638. KL 10420.25 (coll. sk.)

841. Same. Trud i Kniga, M., 1925. 228 p., 8000 c. KL 3079.25

842. Na dne Londona (The people of the abyss). Knizh. Nov., L., 1926. 176 p., 8000 c. KL 13653.26

843. Na kontse radugi (At the rainbow's end). Trans. by
R. Tyutryumova. 4th ed. Univ. Bib., M., 1918. 91 p.,
10,000 c. KL 3285.18 (coll. s.)
Contents: Na kontse radugi. Krovnaya mest [blood
vengeance; not identified, but possibly Which make
men remember]. Chelovek s shramom (The man
with the gash). Sivashka (Siwash).
From The God of his fathers.

844. Same. Gosizdat., M. & P., 1923. 86 p., 10,000 c.
KL 2536.23 (coll. s.) Other titles not listed in KL.

Na stoyanke (A day's lodging). See 894.

845. Na svobodu [release to freedom; not identified].
Gosizdat., M. & L., 1926. 32 p., 15,000 c. KL 2590.26
(s.)

846. Same. 1929. 28 p., 20,000 c. KL 3624.29

847. Na tsynovke Makaloa (On the Makaloa mat). Trans.
by S. G. Zaimovski. ZIF, M. & L., 1926. 148 p.,
6000 c. Pol. sob. soch., Vol. XIV, Book 3. See 636.
KL 19650.26 (coll. s.)

Same. See 901 and 639.

848. Nakazanny sudya [a judge punished; not identified, but
possibly The passing of Marcus O'Brien from Lost
face]. ZIF, M. & L., 1926. 32 p., 15,000 c.
KL 8062.26 (s.)

Negore trus (Negore, the coward). See 865.

Nem-bok lgun (Nam-Bok the unveracious). See 744.

849. Neozhidannoye (The unexpected). Trans. by A. M.
Karnaukhova. Mysl, L., 1924. 165 p., 8000 c.
KL 10630.24 (coll. s.)
From Love of life and other stories. Other titles not
listed in KL.

850. Same. Seyatel, L., 1925. 48 p., 15,000 c. KL 12270.25
Other titles not listed in KL.

Nos korolya (A nose for the king). See 744.

Obichai belovo cheloveka (The white man's way). See
736.

851. Oshibka [the mistake; not identified]. Trans. by V.
Minina; edited by I. V. Zhilkin. Gosizdat., M. & L.,
1930. 32 p., 50,000 c. KL 9784.30

LONDON, Jack (Continued)

852. Ostrovityanin (Jerry of the islands). Trans. by D. M. Gorfinkel. Novella, L. & M., 1924. 197 p., 4000 c. KL 8069.24 (n.)

853. Ot smerti k zhizni [from death to life; not identified]. Yunaya Rossiya, M., 1918. 16 p., 3000 c. KL 89.18 (s.)

854. Pakhar morya (The sea-farmer). Trans. by S. Zaimovski. Mol. Gvard., P. & M., 1924. 144 p., 10,000 c. KL 865.24 (coll. s.)
   From The strength of the strong. Other titles not listed in KL.

   Perezhitok pliotsenovoi epokhi (A relic of the Pliocene). See 748.

   Pervobytny zver (The abysmal brute). See 738 and 636.

   Same. See 740 and 639.

   Pisma Kempton-Uesa (The Kempton-Wace letters). See 921 and 636.

   Pisma Kempton-Uesu (The Kempton-Wace letters). See 723 and 639.

855. Pisma o lyubvi (The Kempton-Wace Letters). Trans. by D. P. Nosovich. Mysl, L., 1924. 176 p., 8000 c. KL 13059.24 (n.)

856. Po tu storonu cherty [on the other side of the line; not identified, but possibly South of the slot from The strength of the strong]. Nizhegorodskaya Kommuna, N. N., 1925. 32 p., 8400 c. KL 2042.26 (s.)

857. Same. Kras. Prolet., M. & L., 1926. 59 p., 15,000 c. KL 7450.26 (coll. s.)
   Other titles not listed in KL.

858. Same. 1927. 60 p., 15,000 c. KL 12333.27

859. Po tu storonu "shcheli" [on the other side of the crevice; not identified, but possibly South of the slot from The strength of the strong]. Novaya Moskva, M., 1924. 44 p., 8000 c. KL 403.24 (s.)

860. Same. Trud, Kharkov, 1923. 35 p., 5000 c. KL 2532.24 (coll. s.)

861. Pod gnyotom (The people of the abyss). S. S. Mikhailova-Shtern, editor of translation; introd. by B. Barotov-Ulanski. Doloi Negramotnost, M. & L., 1927. 140 p., 15,000 c. KL 14534.27 (coll. sk.)

862. Podvig lyubvi [exploit of love; not identified]. Trans. by V. I. Smetanich. Seyatel, L., 1925. 93 p., 15,000 c. KL 15400.25 (coll. s.)

863. Porucheniye [mission; not identified]. Trans. by N. M. Tsymovich. Mysl, L. & M., 1924. 168 p., 8000 c. KL 9284.24 (coll. s.)

864. Same. Mysl, L., 1926. 183 p., 4000 c. KL 19227.25

865. Poslednyaya borba [the last struggle; not identified]. Trans. by L. Kutukova. 5th ed. Univ. Bib., M., 1919. 96 p., 40,000 c. KL 1179.19 (coll. s.)
Contents: Poslednyaya borba. Derzhite kurs na zapad (Make westing). Trans. by L. Kutukova. A-cho (The Chinago). Trans. by M. Likiardopulo. Negore trus (Negore, the coward). Trans. by E. Pimenova. "Make westing" and "The Chinago" are from When God laughs; "Negore, the coward" is from Love of life.

866. Poteryannoye litso (Lost face). Trans. by E. K. Pimenova. Petrograd, L. & M., 1925. 152 p., 8000 c. KL 2317.25 (coll. s.)

867. Poteryanny lik (Lost face). Yev. Lann, editor of translation. ZIF, M. & L., 1925. 115 p., 10,000 c. Pol. sob. soch., Vol. VIII, Book 3, See 636. KL 6493.25 (coll. s.)

868. Poteryanny lik (Lost face), Lyubov k zhizni (Love of life and other stories), and Khram gordyni (The house of pride). Yev. Lann, editor of translation. ZIF, M. & L., 1929. In two parts, published separately: Part 1, pp. 1-128; Part 2, pp. 129-276; 85,000 c. each. Pol. sob. soch., Vol. XIX, Books 37 and 38. See 639. KL 15000.29, KL 16548.29 (coll. s.)

869. Potomok Mak-koya (The seed of McCoy). Trans. by A. Tarasova. 5th ed., Univ. Bib., M., 1918. 94 p., 10,000 c. KL 4240.18 (coll. s.)
Contents: Potomok Mak-koya. Frensis Speit (The "Francis Spaight"). Slishkom mnogo zolota (Too much gold).

LONDON, Jack (Continued)

"The seed of McCoy" is from South Sea tales; "The Francis Spaight" is from When God laughs; "Too much gold" is from The faith of men.

Same. See 781.

870. Same. Trans. by A. Tarasova. Gosizdat., M. & L., 1923. 89 p., 10,000 c. KL 1670.23 (coll. s.)
Other titles not listed in KL.

871. Povest o Kishe (The story of Keesh). Trans. by S. Zaimovski. G. F. Mirimanov, M., 1927. 12 p., 10,000 c. KL 20401.27 (s.)
A juvenile publication. From Love of life.

872. Povesti i rasskazy [short stories]. Vol. I. Trans. by B. Pegelau and F. D. Putevodny Ogonyok, M., 1918. 32 p., 11,500 c. KL 1356.18 (coll. s.)
Contents: Taina [the secret; not identified]. Ushchelye zolota (All Gold Canyon)
"All Gold Canyon" is from Moon-face and other stories.

873. Same. Vol. II. Putevodny Ogonyok, M., 1918. 64 p., 12,050 c. KL 1355.18 (coll. s.)
Contents: Na abordazh [not identified]. Sever i yug [North and south; not identified]. Malenkaya samarityanka [the little samaritan; not identified]. Velikaya sila [great strength; not identified].

Poyezdka na "Oslepitelnom" (The cruise of the Dazzler). See 833.

874. Priboi Kanaka (The Kanaka surf). Trans. by A. V. Luchinskaya and N. L. Kutukova. Gosizdat., M. & L., 1926. 60 p., 15,000 c. KL 18666.26 (coll. s.)
From On the Makaloa mat. Other titles not listed in KL.

875. Priklyucheniya (Adventure). Trans. by M. M. Klechkovski. ZIF, M. & L., 1928. In two parts, published separately: Part 1, pp. 1-128; Part 2, pp. 129-200. 55,000 c. each. Pol. sob. soch., Vol. III, Books 5 and 6. See 639. KL 5914.28 (n.)

876. Same. 1929. In two parts: pp. 1-128; pp. 129-200; 36,000 c. each. KL 1463.29, KL 5762.29

877. Priklyucheniya rybachyevo patrulya (Tales of the fish
     patrol). Trans. by M. Rozenfeld. 3rd ed. Univ. Bib.,
     M., 1917. 150 p., 15,000 c. KL 3675.17 (coll. s.)

878. Same. 1918. 150 p., 10,000 c. KL 4241.18

879. Priklyucheniya rybachyevo patrulya (Tales of the fish
     patrol). Trans. by P. L. Polyakov. Bov yevo ottsov
     (The God of his fathers and other stories). Trans. by
     M. A. Kasminski. Gosizdat., M., 1922. 246 p., 3000
     c. Sob. soch. See 635. KL 6654.22 (coll. s.)

880. Same. Trans. by M. M. Birinski. Mysl, L., 1924.
     118 p., 8000 c. KL 13063.24
     Same. See 701 and 637.

881. Same. [no translator given]. Voyenmorizdat., M. & L.,
     1944. 156 p., [no. of copies omitted]. KL 1478.44

882. Same. Trans. by Ye. I. Patterson. Detizdat., M. & L.,
     1947. 108 p., 50,000 c. KL 2742.47
     A juvenile publication.

883. Priklyucheniye (Adventure). Trans. by M. Rozenfeld.
     3rd ed. Univ. Bib., M., 1917. 337 p., 10,000 c.
     KL 3674.17 (n.)

884. Same. Gosizdat., M. & P., 1923. 326 p., 10,000 c.
     KL 4226.23

885. Same. Trans. by A. N. Kudryavtseva and A. G.
     Movshenson. Novella, L. & M., 1924. 237 p., 4000 c.
     KL 2533.24

886. Same. Trans. by A. G. Movshenson. Mysl, L., 1925.
     220 p., 8000 c. KL 10423.25

887. Same. Trans. by M. M. Klechkovski. ZIF, M. & L.,
     1926. 236 p., 6000 c. Pol. sob. soch., Vol. IX. See
     636. KL 16788.26

888. Printsessa (The princess). Trans. by Z. A. Vershinina.
     ZIF, M. & L., 1926. 104 p., 6000 c. Pol. sob. soch.,
     Vol. II, Book 3. See 636. KL 21753.26 (coll. s.)
     From The red one. Other titles not listed in KL.
     Same. See 982 and 639.

889. Priznaniye (Confession). Priboi, L., 1926. 29 p.,
     15,000 c. KL 12737.26 (sk.)
     From The road.

LONDON, Jack (Continued)

890. Prokazhonny (Koolau the leper). Gosizdat., M. & L., 1926. 32 p., 15,000 c. KL 2591.26 (s.)
From The house of pride.

891. Same. 1927. 30 p., 15,000 c. KL 20893.27

892. Proshchai, Dzhek (Good-by, Jack). Trans. by M. Matveyeva and others. Seyatel, L., 1925. 48 p., 15,000 c. KL 16589.25 (coll. s.)
From The house of pride. Other titles not listed in KL.

893. Same. [no translator given]. Novaya Moskva, M., 1925. 89 p., 6000 c. KL 2315.25 (coll. s.)

894. Put lozhnykh solnts (The sun-dog trail). Trans. by N. Pusheshnikov. 4th ed. Univ. Bib. M., 1918. 92 p., 10,000 c. KL 3286.18 (coll. s.)
Contents: Put lozhnykh solnts. Na stoyanke (A day's lodging). Bury volk (Brown wolf). Skazaniye o Kishe (The story of Keesh).
From Love of life.

895. Same. Gosizdat., M. & P., 1923. 88 p., 10,000 c. KL 2081.23 (coll. s.)
Other titles not listed in KL.

896. Put moroznykh solnts (The sun-dog trail). Trans. by N. Pusheshnikov; edited by Ye. Zamyatin. Gosizdat., P., 1920. 102 p., [no. of copies omitted]. KL 01905.20 (coll. s.)
This volume also contains a bibliography of the most important articles in Russian about Jack London and a bibliography of the collected works of London in Russian.
From Love of life. Other titles not listed in KL.

897. Puteshestviye na "Oslepitelnom" (The cruise of the Dazzler). Trans. by V. Romanov. Knizhny Ugol, L. & M., 1924. 162 p., 5000 c. KL 7499.24 (n.)

898. Same. Trans. by M. M. Klechkovski. ZIF, M. & L., 1926. 119 p., 5000 c. Pol. sob. soch., Vol. XI, Book 3. See 636. KL 6805.26

899. Puteshestviye na "Oslepitelnom" (The cruise of the Dazzler). Trans. by M. M. Klechkovski. Gollandskaya

doblest (Dutch courage and other stories). Trans. by
A. V. Krivtsova and V. Zhitomirski. Skazki yuzhnykh
morei (South Sea tales). Trans. by Ye. Utkina. ZIF,
M. & L., 1929. In two parts, published separately:
Part 1, pp. 1-160; Part 2, pp. 161-296; 85,000 c.
each. Pol. sob. soch., Vol. XVI, Books 31 and 32.
See 639. KL 8155.29, KL 8520.29 (coll. n., s.)

900. Puteshestviye na "Snarke" (The cruise of the Snark).
Trans. by Ye. G. Guro; edited by Z. A. Vershinina.
ZIF, M. & L., 1927. 196 p., 6000 c. Pol. sob. soch.,
Vol. XV, Book 1. See 636. KL 2179.27 (coll. sk.)

901. Puteshestviye na "Snarke" (The cruise of the Snark).
Trans. by Z. A. Vershinina. Na tsynovke Makaloa
(On the Makaloa mat). Trans. by S. G. Zaimovski.
ZIF, M. & L., 1928. In two parts, published separate-
ly: Part 1, pp. 1-159; Part 2, pp. 161-280; 70,000 c.
each. Pol. sob. soch., Vol. VII, Books 12 and 13.
See 639. KL 12103.28, KL 14511.29 (coll. sk., s.)

902. Same. 1929. In two parts: pp. 1-159; pp. 161-280;
36,000 c. each. KL 10493.29

Puti zhenshchiny (Scorn of women). See 739.

903. Pytka (The star rover). Trans. by E. K. Pimenova.
Petrograd, P. & M., 1923. 312 p., 6000 c. KL 9173.23
(n.)

904. Same. Trans. by E. K. Pimenova. Mysl, L., 1925.
347 p., 8000 c. KL 320.25

905. Rasskazy [short stories]. Trans. by Zin. Lvovski.
5th ed. Univ. Bib., M., 1918. 98 p., 10,000 c.
KL 425.18 (coll. s.)
Contents: Velikoye chudo [a great miracle; not iden-
tified]. Yazychnik (The heathen). U cherti [at the line;
not identified].
"The heathen" is from South Sea tales.

Same. See 1024 and 637.

906. Same. [no translator given]. Gudok, M., 1926. 61 p.,
26,000 c. KL 17950.26
Contents not listed in KL.

907. Same. V. Stenich, editor of translation; foreword by

LONDON, Jack (Continued)

N. Rykova. Mol. Gvard., M. & L., 1932. 202 p.,
20,000 c. KL 8108.32
Contents not listed in KL.

908. Same. Goslitizdat., M., 1935. 60 p., [no. of copies
omitted]. KL 24811.35
Contents not listed in KL.

909. Same. D. M. Gorfinkel, editor of translation. Mol.
Gvard., L., 1935. 288 p., 3000 c. KL 2367.36
Contents not listed in KL.

910. Same. 1936. 228 p., 20,000 c. KL 914.35

911. Same. Selected and adapted by O. Reznik, with a foreword by the translator. Goslitizdat., M., 1937. 64 p.,
150,000 c. KL 33361.37
Contents not listed in KL.

912. Same. D. M. Gorfinkel, editor of translation. Goslitizdat., 1937. 422 p., 10,300 c. KL 27811.37
Contents not listed in KL.

913. Same. Detizdat., M. & L., 1938. 88 p., 129,000 c.
KL 25749.35
A juvenile publication. Contents not listed in KL.

914. Same. 1939. 296 p., 25,000 c. KL 3516.40

915. Rasskazy o dalnem severe [tales of the far North].
Trans. by Ye. N. Blagobeshchenskaya, L. M.
Vaisenberg, N. S. Kaufman, Yu. A. Nelidov and B. K.
Ryndy-Alekseyev. Gosizdat., M. & L., 1926. 420 p.,
5000 c. Sob. soch., Vol. VIII. See 637. KL 10781.26
(coll. s.)
Contents not listed in KL.

916. Same. 1927. 420 p., 2500 c. KL 9405.27

917. Rasskazy o Sandvichevykh Ostrovakh (South Sea tales).
Trans. by A. V. Aleksandrov. Kogda bogi smeyutsya
(When God laughs and other stories). Trans. by O.
Zolkind. Igra (The game). Trans. by B. K. Ryndy-
Alekseyev. Gosizdat., M. & L., 1926. 343 p., 5000
c. Sob. soch., Vol. XI. See 637. KL 16458.26 (coll.
s., n.)

918. Same. 1927. 343 p., 2500 c. KL 10174.27

919. Rasskazy o smelchakakh [stories about the dare-
devils; not identified]. Trans. by V. A. Azov and A.
N. Gorlin. Gosizdat., L., 1924. 116 p., 7000 c.
KL 8683.24 (coll. s.)

920. Rasskazy ob Amerikanskoi rabochei molodyozhi [tales
of young American workers]. Gudok, M., 1925. 31 p.,
40,000 c. KL 10415.25 (coll. s.)
Contents not listed in KL.

921. Rasskazy rybachyevo patrulya (Tales of the fish patrol), Pisma Kempton-Uesa (The Kempton-Wace
letters), and Cherri [not identified]. Z. Vershinina,
editor of translation. ZIF, M. & L., 1927. 267 p.,
6000 c. Pol. sob. soch., Vol. XI, Book 2. See 636.
KL 4473.27 (coll. s., n.)

    Same. See 831 and 639.

922. Revolyutsiya (Revolution and other essays). Trans.
by A. V. Luchinskaya. Mysl, L., 1924. 153 p., 7000 c.
KL 10632.24 (coll. essays).

923. Revolyutsiya [revolution; not identified, but possibly
Revolution from Revolution and other essays, or The
tears of Ah Kim from On the Makaloa mat]. Mezhrabpom, M., 1924. 52 p., 35,000 c. KL 10628.24
The KL entries for this item are ambiguous.

924. Same. 1925. 59 p., 20,000 c. KL 11203.25

925. Rozhdennaya v nochi (The night-born). Trans. by A.
M. Abramova; edited by S. G. Zaimovski. ZIF, M. &
L., 1925. 157 p., 10,000 c. Pol. sob. soch., Vol. X,
Book 2. See 636. KL 9690.25 (coll. s.)

926. Rozhdennaya v nochi (The night-born). Trans. by A.
M. Abramova. Kogda bogi smeyutsya (When God
laughs and other stories). Trans. by Yev. Lann. ZIF,
M. & L., 1929. In two parts published separately:
Part 1, pp. 1-128; Part 2, pp. 129-156; 80,000 c. each.
Pol. sob. soch., Vol. XXI, Books 41 and 42. See 639.
KL 20411.29 (coll. s.)

    Ryzhi volk (Brown wolf). See 781.

927. Same. Trans. by N. A. Almedingen. Redaktsionno-
Izdatelski Otdel Tsentralnovo Komiteta, M., 1927.
111 p., 50,000 c. KL 14535.27 (coll. s.)
From Love of life. Other titles not listed in KL.

CHECKLIST

LONDON, Jack (Continued)

928. Samuel (Samuel). Trans. by Vl. Yurev and L.
Kutukova. Kras. Prolet., M. & L., 1926. 64 p.,
15,000 c. KL 235.26 (coll. s.)
From The strength of the strong. Other titles not
listed in KL.

929. Sandvichevy ostrova (South Sea tales). Trans. by A.
V. Aleksandrov, O. I. Zolkind, B. K. Ryndy-Alekseyev.
Gosizdat., M. & L., 1927. 343 p., 2500 c. KL 10515.27
(coll. s.)

Semper idem (Semper idem). See 948.

930. Serdtsa tryokh (Hearts of three). Trans. by A. d'Aktil.
L. D. Frenkel, M. & L., 1923. 400 p., 5000 c.
KL 6021.23 (n.)

931. Same. 1923. 400 p., 5000 c. KL 11206.23

932. Same. 1924. 400 p., 5000 c. KL 3720.24

933. Same. Trans. by M. M. Birinski. Mysl, L., 1925.
405 p., 8000 c. KL 13778.25

934. Same. Trans. by N. F. Davydova, edited by V. A.
Azov. ZIF, M. & L., 1925. 344 p., 5000 c. Pol. sob.
soch., Vol. XVII. See 636. KL 21217.25

935. Same. 1927. 352 p., 6000 c. KL 6776.27

936. Same. Trans. by A. d'Aktil. Mysl, L., 1927. 368
p., 6200 c. KL 11734.27

937. Same. Trans. by N. F. Davydova. ZIF, M. & L.,
1929. In three parts, published separately: Part 1,
pp. 1-32; Part 2, pp. 33-160; Part 3, pp. 161-287;
35,000 c. each. Pol. sob. soch., Vol. VIII, Books 14
and 15. See 639. KL 14511.29, KL 13963.28
KL 15116.28 (n.)

938. Same. D. M. Gorfinkel, editor of translation. Mol.
Gvard., M., 1937. 378 p., 20,000 c. KL 16437.37

Sever i yug. See 873.

939. Severnaya odisseya (An odyssey of the North). Trans.
by Ye. G. Guro and B. Ya.; edited by Yev. Lann. ZIF,
M. & L., 1924. 145 p., 10,000 c. Pol. sob. soch., Vol.
VIII, Book 1. See 636. KL 13062.24 (coll. s.)
From The son of the wolf. Other titles not listed in

KL. The Son of the wolf, however, was published in England under the title An odyssey of the North (London, Mills & Boon, Ltd., 1915). It seems probable that the Russian translation was made from the English edition and that this volume contains the other stories from The son of the wolf.

940. Same. Trans. by Ye. N. Blagoveshchenskaya, L. M. Vaisenberg and N. S. Kaufman. Gosizdat., M. & L., 1927. 420 p., 2500 c. KL 10516.27 (coll. s.) Other titles not listed in KL.

Same. See 705 and 639.

941. Severnyie povesti [tales of the north]. Goslitizdat., M., 1935. 358 p., 50,000 c. KL 29346.35 (coll. s.) Contents: Bely klyk, i drugiye rasskazy [White fang, and other stories]. Titles other than White fang, not listed in KL.

942. Shabash (The apostate). Trans. by S. G. Zaimovski. G. F. Mirimanov, M., 1926. 22 p., 10,000 c. KL 17995.26 (s.) A juvenile publication. From When God laughs.

943. Shutka Porportuka (The wit of Porportuk). Trans. by N. M. Tsymovich. Seyatel, L., 1925. 96 p., 15,000 c. KL 13775.25 (coll. s.) From Lost face. Other titles not listed in KL.

944. Sila silnykh (The strength of the strong). Trans. by N. Yu. Zhukovskaya. Mysl, L., 1925. 123 p., 8000 c. Pol. sob. soch., Vol. XLIV. See 638. KL 5548.25 (coll. s.)

945. Same. Trans. by S. S. Zayaitski. ZIF, M. & L., 1927. 128 p., 6000 c. Pol. sob. soch., Vol. X, Book 3. See 636. KL 944.27 (coll. s.)

Same. See 740 and 639.

946. Sila silnykh (The strength of the strong). Trans. by F. Nyuton; edited and with a preface by A. N. Gorlin. Gosizdat., M. & L., 1923. 94 p., 4000 c. KL 12291.23 (coll. s.) From The strength of the strong. Other titles not listed in KL.

LONDON, Jack (Continued)

947. Same. [no translator given]. Gosizdat., M. & L.,
1926. 31 p., 35,000 c. KL 2043.26 (s.)
From The strength of the strong.

948. Sila zhenshchiny (Grit of women). Trans. by Z.
Lvovski. Perezhitok pliotsenovoi epokhi (A relic of
the Pliocene). Trans. by V. Koshevich. Semper
idem (Semper idem). Trans. by M. Likiardopulo.
Silnoye sredstvo i skvernaya zhenshchina (A wicked
woman). Trans. by Ye. Broido. 5th ed., Univ. Bib.,
M., 1919. 90 p., 15,000 c. KL 4154.19 (coll. s.)
"Grit of women" is from God of his fathers; "A
relic of the Pliocene" is from The faith of men;
"Semper idem" and "A wicked woman" are from
When God laughs.

949. Same. Gosizdat., M. & L., 1923. 93 p., 10,000 c.
KL 4225.23

950. Sila zhenshchiny (Grit of women). Trans. by Z.
Lvovski. Gosizdat., M. & L., 1927. 94 p., 15,000 c.
KL 14536.27 (coll. s.)
Other titles not listed in KL.

Silnoye sredstvo i skvernaya zhenshchina (A wicked
woman). See 948.

Sivashka (Siwash). See 843.

Skazaniye o Kishe (The story of Keesh). See 894.

951. Same. Trans. by V. Stenich. Mol. Gvard., M., 1933.
24 p., 50,000 c. KL 345.34 (s.)
From Love of life.

952. Same. Detizdat., M., 1936. 16 p., 100,000 c.
KL 13557.36 (s.)
A juvenile publication.

953. Same. 1936. 16 p., 100,000 c. KL 41802.36

Same. See 784.

954. Skazki yuzhnykh morei (South Sea tales). Trans. by
Zin. Lvovski. Mysl, L., 1925. 144 p., 5000 c. Pol.
sob. soch., Vol. XXX. See 638. KL 13064.24 (coll. s.)

955. Same. 1926. 144 p., 5000 c. KL 2319.25

956. Same. Trans. by Ye. Utkina; edited by Yev. Lann.
ZIF, M. & L., 1925. 141 p., 10,000 c. Pol. sob. soch.,
Vol. XIV, Book 1. See 636. KL 9690.25

Same. See 899 and 639.

Slishkom mnogo zolota (Too much gold). See 869.

957. Sluchainy priyut (A day's lodging). Trans. by A. M.
Karnaukhova. Seyatel, L., 1925. 47 p., 15,000 c.
KL 12271.25 (coll. s.)
From Love of life. Other contents not listed in KL.

958. Smiritelnaya kurtka (The star rover). Trans. by D.
P. Nosovich. Gosizdat., L., 1925. 299 p., 10,000 c.
Sob. soch., Vol. II. See 637. KL 12272.25 (n.)

959. Smok Bellyu (Smoke Bellew). Trans. by Zin Lvovski.
Mysl, L., 1924. 168 p., 5000 c. KL 867.24 (coll. s.)
Contents not listed in KL.

960. Same. 1924. 177 p., 8000 c. KL 12413.24

961. Smok Bellyu (Smoke Bellew) and Smok i kutsy
[Smoke and Shorty]. Trans. by L. and N. Chukovski.
Golos krovi (The call of the wild). Trans. by L. I.
Kartuzhanski. Gosizdat., M. & L., 1926. 352 p.,
5000 c. Sob. soch., Vol. X. See 637. KL 16138.26
(coll. s., n.)
Smok Bellew was published in England in two volumes
entitled "Smoke Bellew" and "Smoke and Shorty"
(London, Mills & Boon, Ltd., 1913 and 1920). It
seems probable that the Russians made their trans-
lation from this English edition. Contents of the two
Russian titles not listed in KL.

962. Same. 1927. 352 p., 2500 c. KL 9407.27

963. Same. 1927. 352 p., 2500 c. KL 10517.27

964. Smok Bellyu (Smoke Bellew). Trans. by N. F. Davydova. ZIF, M. & L., 1926. 144 p., 5000 c. Pol. sob.
soch., Vol. IV, Book 1. See 636. KL 13217.26 (coll.
s.)
Contents not listed in Kl.

965. Smok Bellyu (Smoke Bellew) and Smok i malysh
[Smoke and Shorty]. Trans. by N. F. Davydova and
V. N. Orechkina. ZIF, M. & L., 1928. In two parts,
published separately: Part 1, pp. 1-160; Part 2, pp.

LONDON, Jack (Continued)

161-239; 70,000 c. each. Pol. sob. soch., Vol. V, Book 9. See 639 KL 9401.28 (coll. s.) Contents not listed in KL. See note, item 961.

966. Same. 1929. In two parts: pp. 1-160; pp. 161-239. 36,000 c. each. KL 8155.29, KL 10493.29

Smok i kutsy. See 961 and 637.

967. Smok i malenki [Smoke and Shorty]. Trans. by V. I. Smetanich. Mysl, L., 1924. 190 p., 8000 c. KL KL 10061.24 (coll. s.) Stories from Smoke Bellew. Contents not listed in KL. See note, item 961.

968. Smok i malysh [Smoke and Shorty]. Trans. by V. N. Orechkina. ZIF, M. & L., 1926. 157 p., 6000 c. Pol. sob. soch., Vol. IX, Book 2. See 636. KL 14424.26 (coll. s.) Stories from Smoke Bellew. Contents not listed in KL. See note, item 961.

Smok i malysh. See 965 and 639.

969. Snark (The cruise of the Snark). Trans. by A. G. Movshenson. Mysl, L., 1925. 239 p., 8000 c. KL 4659.25 (coll. sk.)

970. Soperniki [the rivals; not identified]. Trans. by Zin. Lvovski. Seyatel, L., 1925. 48 p., 15,000 c. KL 12273.25 (coll. s.)

971. Sovremenny Argonavt [a modern Argonaut; not identified]. Mezhrabpom and Mospoligraf, M. & Berlin, 1924. 52 p., 20,000 c. KL 8684.24 (coll. s.)

Soyuz starikov (The league of old men). See 758.

972. Stachka [the strike; not identified]. V.Ts.S.P.S., M., 1926. 48 p., 5000 c. KL 12182.26 (s.)

973. Strashnyie Solomonovy ostrova (The terrible Solomons). Trans. by Zin. Lvovski. 4th ed. Univ. Bib., M., 1917. 106 p., 15,000 c. KL 4255.17 (coll. s.) From South Sea tales. Other titles not listed in KL.

974. Same. 1918. 106 p., 10,000 c. KL 4242.18

975. Same. Gosizdat., M. & P., 1923. 104 p., 10,000 c. KL 2082.23 (coll. s.) Other titles not listed in KL.

976. Same. 1927. 104 p., 15,000 c. KL 13398.27
977. Syn solntsa (A son of the sun). Trans. by V. Koshchevich. Gosizdat., M., 1922. 273 p., 5000 c. KL 5645.22 (coll. s.)
978. Same. 1927. 274 p., 15,000 c. KL 9842.27
979. Same. Trans. by Z. Lvovski. Novella, L. & M., 1924. 350 p., 9000 c. KL 3721.24
980. Same. Trans. by V. O. Smetanich. Gosizdat., L., 1926. 336 p., 10,000 c. Sob. soch., Vol. VII. See 637. KL 4470.26
981. Same. Trans. by M. V. Kovolenskaya. ZIF, M. & L., 1927. 181 p., 6000 c. Pol. sob. soch., Vol. XV, Book 2. See 636. KL 276.27
982. Syn solntsa (A son of the sun). Trans. by M. V. Kovalevskaya. Printsessa (The princess). Trans. by Z. A. Vershinina. ZIF, M. & L., 1928. In two parts, published separately: Part 1, pp. 1-80; Part 2, pp. 81-232; 70,000 c. each. Pol. sob. soch., Vol. X, Books 18 and 19. See 639. KL 16653.28 (coll. s.) "The princess" is from The Red one. Other titles not listed in KL.
983. Same. 1929. In two parts: pp. 1-80; pp. 81-232; 30,000 c. each. KL 19196.23, KL 20411.29
984. Syn volka (The son of the wolf). Trans. by M. M. Birinski. Mysl, L., 1924. 160 p., 8000 c. KL 12414.24 (coll. s.) From The son of the wolf. Other titles not listed in KL.
985. Same. Trans. by E. K. Pimenova. Seyatel, L., 1926. 96 p., 15,000 c. KL 3916.26 (coll. s.) Other titles not listed in KL.

Taina. See 872.

Ten i blesk (The shadow and the flash). See 778.

986. Torzhestvo pravosudiya [triumph of justice; not identified]. Trans. by S. G. Zaimovski; introd. by P. S. Kogan. Mol. Gvard., M. & L., 1924. 155 p., 8000 c. KL 4857.24 (coll. s.)
987. Trus (Negore, the coward). Trans. by A. V. Luchin-

LONDON, Jack (Continued)

skaya and L. Kutukova. Gosizdat., M. & L., 1926.
60 p., 15,000 c. KL 18666.26 (coll. s.)
From Love of life. Other titles not listed in KL.

Tysyacha dyuzhin (The one thousand dozen). See 1031.

988. Tysyacha zhiznei (The star rover). Knizh. Nov., L.,
1926. 231 p., 8000 c. KL 14035.26 (n.)

989. Tyurma (The pen). Novaya Moskva, M., 1924. 30 p.,
8000 c. KL 404.24 (sk.)
From The road.

Ublyudok (The story of Jees Uck). See 1031.

U cherti. See 905.

Ushchelye sploshnovo zolota (All Gold Canyon). See 778.

Ushchelye zolota (All Gold Canyon). See 872.

990. V plenu (Martin Eden). V.Ts.S.P.S., M., 1926. 187
p., 5000 c. KL 18278.26 (n.)
Abridged.

Vechnyie formy i drugiye rasskazy [the eternity of
forms and other stories]. See 818 and 639.

Velikaya sila. See 873.

991. Velikoye chudo [a great miracle; not identified].
Trans. by Zin. Lvovski. Gosizdat., M. & P., 1923.
97 p., 10,000 c. KL 3581.23 (coll. s.)

992. Same. 1927. 98 p., 15,000 c. KL 12332.27

Same. See 905.

993. Vera v cheloveka (The faith of men and other stories).
Trans. by N. M. Tsymovich. Mysl, L., 1925. 168
p., 8000 c. KL 10418.25 (coll. s.)

994. Same. 1925. 168 p., 4000 c. KL 20279.25

995. Same. Trans. by M. P. Chekhov; edited by Z. A.
Vershinina. ZIF, M. & L., 1927. 184 p., 6000 c. Pol.
sob. soch., Vol. XIII, Book 2. See 636. KL 4846.27

996. Vera v cheloveka (The faith of men and other stories).
Trans. by M. P. Chekhov. Lunny lik (Moon-face and
other stories). Trans. by Z. A. Vershinina. ZIF,

M. & L., 1929. In two parts, published separately: Part 1, pp. 1-160; Part 2, pp. 161-248; 85,000 c. each. Pol. sob. soch., Vol. XVII, Books 33 and 34. See 639. KL 9625.29, KL 11972.29 (coll. s.)

Vezdesushchi bely chelovek (The inevitable white man). See 758.

997. Vlastelin yuzhnykh morei [master of the southern seas; not identified, but possibly The sea-wolf]. Trans. by A. Movshenson. Novella, L. & M., 1925. 218 p., 6000 c. KL 13055.24 (n.)

998. Volchi dushi [wolf souls; not identified, but possibly Theft]. Trans. by Zin. Lvovski and N. V. Lapina. Mysl, P., 1922. 103 p., 3000 c. KL 9266.22 (pl.)

999. Same. 1923. 95 p., 5000 c. KL 2080.23

1000. Volk [wolf; not identified]. Trans. by V. Stenich. Detizdat., M. & L., 1936. 32 p., 100,000 c. KL 19688.36 (s.) A juvenile publication.

1001. Same. 1936. 32 p., 100,000 c. KL 42773.36

1002. Same. 1937. 32 p., 200,300 c. KL 19518.37

1003. Same. [no translator given]. Uchpedgiz., M., 1938. 28 p., 200 c. KL 11675.38

Volki. See 744.

1004. Vrag vsevo mira (The enemy of all the world). Trans. by Vl. Yurev. Gosizdat., M. & L., 1924. 164 p., 4000 c. KL 1934.24 (coll. s.) From The strength of the strong. Other contents not listed in KL.

1005. Vstrecha [the encounter; not identified]. Biblioteka Zhurnala "Ogonyok," M., 1926. 48 p., 12,500 c. KL 14860.26 (coll. s.)

Yakh! Yakh! Yakh! (Yah! Yah! Yah!). See 758.

Yazychnik (The heathen). See 781.

Same. See 905.

1006. Yukonskiye rasskazy [Yukon stories]. Trans. by M. Matveyeva. Prometei, M., 1924. 119 p., 5000 c. KL 866.24 (coll. s.) Contents not listed in KL

LONDON, Jack (Continued)

1007. Za kulisami tsirka (Michael, brother of Jerry). Trans. by N. Yu. Zhukovskaya. Mysl, L., 1924. 264 p., 8000 c. KL 8071.24 (n.)

Zabastoval (The apostate). See 756.

1008. Zabastoval i drugiye rasskazy iz zhizni rabochei molodyozhi [The apostate and other stories from the lives of young workers]. Edited by Yu. Danilin. Znaniye, M., 1924. 63 p., 5000 c. KL 3719.24 (coll. s.) "The apostate" is from When God laughs. This volume also contains stories by I. Danilin and Leonid Andreyev.

1009. Same. 1925. 32 p., 5000 c.

1010. Zabastoval (The apostate). Trans. and adapted by M. Pollat. Gosizdat., M. & L., 1928. 35 p., 20,000 c. KL 8916.28 (s.)

1011. Zakon belovo cheloveka (The white man's way). Gosudarstvenny Institut Zhurnalistiki, M., 1925. 84 p., 2000 c. KL 13772.25 (coll. s.) From Love of life. Other titles not listed in KL.

Zakon zhizni (The law of life). See 744.

1012. Zelyony zmi (John Barleycorn). Trans. by N. M. Tsymovich. Mysl, L., 1925. 232 p., 8000 c. KL 10417.25 (n.)

1013. Zemlya obetovannaya (The valley of the moon). Trans. by E. K. Brodersen. Mysl, L., 1924. 262. p., 8000 c. KL 12412.24 (n.)

Zhan neraskayavshisya (Jan, the unrepentant). See 736.

1014. Zheleznaya pyata (The iron heel). Trans. by Ye. Broido. 3rd ed. Univ. Bib., M., 1917. 398 p., 20,000 c. KL 1778.17 (n.)

1015. Same. [no translator given]. V.Ts.I.K., M., 1918. 398 p., 20,000 c. KL 3284.18

1016. Same. Trans. by I. A. Mayevski. I. A. Mayevski [pub.], M., 1918. 264 p., 5000 c. KL 2809.18

1017. Same. Trans. by Ye. Broido. Gosizdat., M., 1922. 372 p., 5000 c. KL 4616.22

1018. Same. 1927. 372 p., 15,000 c. KL 9841.27

1019. Same. Trans. by V. P. V.; edited by E. G. Lundberg.
Gosizdat., P., 1922. 260 p., 2000 c. KL 6651.22

1020. Same. Trans. by P. G. Guber. Krasnaya Nov, M.,
1923. 112 p., 20,000 c. KL 2585.23
Abridged

1021. Same. Trans. by Zin. Lvovski. Novella, L. & M.,
1924. 230 p., 8000 c. KL 5509.24

1022. Same. Mysl, L., 1924. 230 p., 10,000 c. KL 12411.24

1023. Same. 1927. 232 p., 5000 c. KL 943.27

1024. Zheleznaya pyata (The iron heel). Trans. by M. N.
Matveyev. Rasskazy [short stories]. Trans. by A.
V. Aleksandrov. Gosizdat., L., 1926. 401 p.,
10,000 c. Sob. soch., Vol. VI. See 637. KL 4469.26
(coll. n., s.)
Titles of "Rasskazy" not listed in KL.

1025. Zheleznaya pyata (The iron heel). Trans. by Ye. G.
Guro; edited by Z. A. Vershinina. ZIF, M. & L., 1927.
262 p., 6000 c. Pol. sob. soch., Vol. XXI, See 636.
KL 3829.27

1026. Zheleznaya pyata (The iron heel). Trans. by Z.
Vershinina. Lyudi bezdny (The people of the abyss).
Trans. by V. A. Azov. ZIF, M. & L., 1930. In three
parts, published separately: Part 1, pp. 1-144; Part
2, pp. 145-288; Part 3, pp. 289-368; 72,000 c. each.
Pol. sob. soch., Vol. XXIII, Books, 45, 46 and 47.
See 639. KL 1187.30, KL 3543.30 (coll. n., sk.)

1027. Zheleznaya pyata (The iron heel). Trans. by Ye.
G. Guro; edited by Z. A. Vershinina; introd. by
Karl Radek. ZIF, M. & L., 1930. 300 p., 50,000 c.
KL 12526.30

1028. Zheleznodorozhnyie zaitsi [railroad rabbits; not
identified, but possibly a chapter from The road].
Novaya Moskva, M., 1924. 36 p., 8000 c. KL 402.24 (s.)

1029. Zhemchug Parleya (A son of the sun). Trans. by Ye.
Patterson. Mysl, L., 1925. 246 p., 10,000 c.
KL 13888.24 (coll. s.)

1030. Same. 1926. 246 p., 4000 c. KL 21216.25

Zolotaya zorka (Burning Daylight). See 678.

LONDON, Jack (Continued)

1031. Zov predkov (The call of the wild). Trans. by M.
Likiardopulo and V. Koshevich. Univ. Bib., M., 1918.
198 p., 10,000 c. KL 2810.18 (coll. n., s.)
Contents: Zov predokov. Ublyudok (The story of Jees
Uck). Tysyacha dyuzhin (The one thousand dozen).
"The story of Jees Uck" and "The one thousand dozen"
are from The faith of men.

1032. Same. 1923. 193 p., 10,000 c. KL 3037.23

1033. Zov predkov (The call of the wild). Trans. by M. P.
Chekhov; edited by Z. Vershinina. Bely klyk (White
fang). Trans. by I. G. Bakhmetyev; edited by Z.
Vershinina. ZIF, M. & L., 1927. 291 p., 6000 c. Pol.
sob. soch., Vol. XIX. See 636. KL 4847.27 (coll. n.)

1034. Zov predkov (The call of the wild). Trans. by Z.
Vershinina. Bely klyk (White fang). Trans. by Z.
Vershinina. Do Adama (Before Adam). Trans. by L.
Lanskaya. ZIF, M. & L., 1928. In three parts, pub-
lished separately: Part 1, pp. 1-128; Part 2, pp. 129-
256; Part 3, pp. 257-320; 70,000 c. each. Pol. sob.
soch., Vol. XI, Books, 20, 21 and 22. See 639.
KL 18493.28, KL 19016.28, KL 20282.28 (coll. n.)

1035. Same. 1929. In three parts; pp. 1-128; pp. 129-256;
pp. 257-320; 30,000 c. each. KL 19769.29, KL 18463.29
KL 20411.29

Zov predkov (The call of the wild). See 660.

1036. Zov pustyni (The call of the wild). Trans. by Zin.
Lvovski. Mysl, L., 1925. 160 p., 10,000 c.
KL 13889.24 (n.)

1037. Same. 1926. 160 p., 4000 c. KL 1135.26

1038. Zver iz bezdny (The abysmal brute). Trans. by Zin.
Lvovski. Mysl, L. & M., 1924. 175 p., 5000 c.
KL 3062.24 (n.)

1039. Same. Mysl, L., 1925. 160 p., 8000 c. KL 319.25

1040. Same. Trans. by N. Gorvits. Seyatel, L., 1925. 96
p., 15,000 c. KL 13733.25

LONGFELLOW, Henry Wadsworth

1041. Khagenauski sapozhnik (The cobbler of Hagenau).

Trans. by D. M. Gorfinkel. Zvezda (M. & L.), 1939,
No. 2, pp. 120-122. ZL 16328.39 (p.)
From Tales of a wayside inn.

Monakh iz Kazalmadzhore (The monk of Casal-
Maggiore). See 1051.

Nevolnik v proklyatom bolote (The slave in the dismal
swamp). See 11.

Osen (Autumn). See 1051.

1042. Pesn o Gaiavate (The song of Hiawatha). Trans. by
I. Bunin. M. and S. Sabashnikov, M., 1918. 192 p.,
10,000 c. KL 4239.18 (p.)

1043. Same. Gosizdat., M. & L., 1928. 272 p., 7000 c.
KL 14305.28

1044. Same. 1931. Introd. by K. Derzhavin. 272 p., 6500
c. KL 17942.31

1045. Same. 1933. 184 p., 20,325 c. KL 2011.34

1046. Same. 1935. 174 p., 50,000 c. KL 21054.35

1047. Same. [no translator given]. Radioizdat., M., 1936.
8 p., 600 c. KL 38401.36.
Selection adapted for radio.

1048. Same. Trans. by I. A. Bunin; introd. by K. Derzhavin.
Detizdat., M. & L., 1941. 180 p., 70,000 c. KL 3528.41
A juvenile publication

1049. Pesni nevoli (Poems on slavery). Introd. by S. Nonin.
Nonin, P., 1919. 16 p., 10,000 c. KL 7314.19 (coll. p.)

Rassvet v gorakh (Sunrise on the hills). See 1051.

1050. Sokol sinora Federigo (The falcon of Ser Federigo).
M. O. Volf [pub.], P., 1918. 14 p., [no. of copies
omitted]. KL 4748.18 (p.)
From Tales of a wayside inn.

1051. Stikhi [poems]. Trans. by D. M. Gorfinkel. Zvezda
(M.), 1940, No. 5-6, pp. 140-145. ZL 41459.40 (coll.
p.)
Contents: Valter von der Fogelveide (Walter von der
Vogelweid). Strela i pesnya (The arrow and the song).
Rassvet v gorakh (Sunrise on the hills). Osen
(Autumn). Monakh iz Kazalmadzhore (The monk of
Casal-Maggiore).

LONGFELLOW, Henry Wadsworth (Continued)

"Walter von der Vogelweid," "The arrow and the song," and "Autumn" are from The belfry of Bruges and other poems; "The monk of Casal-Maggiore" is from Tales of a Wayside inn; "Sunrise on the hills" is from Earlier poems.

Strela i pesnya (The arrow and the song). See 1051.

1052. Svyatovstvo Mailza Stendisha (The courtship of Miles Standish). Trans. by D. M. Gorfinkel. Zvezda (M. & L.), 1940, No. 8-9, pp. 234-251. ZL 62723.40 (p.)

Valter fon der Fogelveide (Walter von der Vogelwcid). See 1051.

LOOMIS, Charles

1053. Za chayem [at tea; not identified]. Trans. by P. Okhrimenko. 30 Dnei (L.), 1940, No. 5-6, pp. 68-70. ZL 43312.40 (s.)

LOOS, Anita

1054. Dzhentelmeny predpochitayut blondinok (Gentlemen prefer blondes). Trans. by T. Shchepkina-Kupernik; foreword by A. Kollontai. Sov. Prob., M., 1927. 189 p., 5000 c. KL 18560.27 (n.)

LUMPKIN, Grace

1055. Radi khleba (To make my bread). Trans. by Ye. Romanova. Int. Lit. (M.), 1933, No. 5, pp. 37-48. (n.) An excerpt.

1056. Ya dobyvayu svoi khleb (To make my bread). Trans. by Mark Volosov. Goslitizdat., M., 1934. 337 p., 7000 c. KL 27753.34 (n.)

LUNDBERG, Ferdinand

1057. 60 semeistv Ameriki (America's 60 families). Trans. and with a foreword by S. K. Bushuyev. Oktyabr (M. & L.), 1947, No. 2, pp. 161-171. (coll. essays) An excerpt

McCULLEY, Johnston

1058. Znak Zorro (The mark of Zorro). Trans. by A. B.

Rozenbaum; edited by N. N. Shulgovski. Vremya, L.,
1926. 247 p., 4150 c. KL 21754.26 (n.)

1059. Same. 1927. 247 p., 4150 c. KL 5280.27

McKAY, Claude

1060. Bandzho (Banjo: a story without plot). Trans. by Z.
Vershinina. Gosizdat., M. & L., 1930. 325 p., 4000
c. KL 24196.30 (n.)

1061. Domoi v Garlem (Home to Harlem). Trans. by Mark
Volosov. ZIF, M. & L., 1929. 240 p., 5000 c.
KL 6196.29 (n.)

1062. Proklyatiye porabashchennovo [curses of the enslaved; not identified]. Trans. by V. Bryusov.
Sovremenny Zapad (L.), 1923, No. 2, p. 112. (p.)

Same. See 11.

1063. Sudom lincha [lynch law; not identified]. Trans. by
A. M. and P. Okhrimenko. Biblioteka Zhurnala
"Ogonyok," M., 1925. 45 p., 50,000 c. KL 9695.25

V plenu. See 11.

MacLEISH, Archibald

Slovo k tem, kto govorit tovarishch (Speech to those
who say comrade). See 1064.

1064. Vam, Endryu Marvell (You, Andrew Marvell). Slovo
k tem, kto govorit tovarishch (Speech to those who
say comrade). Znamya (M.), 1936, No. 8, pp. 127-129.
ZL 49790.36 (coll. p.)
"You, Andrew Marvell" is from Poems, 1924-1933;
"Speech to those who say comrade" is from Public
speech.

MacLEOD, Norman

Ovechye stado. See 14.

1065. Rybaki San-Pedro [the fishermen of San Pedro; not
identified]. Trans. by Ye. Romanova. Int. Lit. (M.),
1933, No. 1, pp. 89-90. (p.)

MAGIL, A. B.

Tak on umer. See 14.

MALTZ, Albert

1066. Chelovek na doroge (Man on a road). Trans. by M. Urnov. Int. Lit. (M.), 1935, No. 4, pp. 72-76. (s.) From The way things are.

Same. See 8.

1067. Same. Trans. by N. Volzhina; foreword by P. Balashov. Goslitizdat., M., 1941. 212 p., 25,000 c. KL 9327.41 (coll. s.) Other titles not listed in KL.

1068. Kanun novovo goda (New Year's eve). Trans. by N. Volzhina. Int. Lit. (M.), 1938, No. 12, pp. 100-127. (s.) From The way things are.

1069. Klochok bumagi (The piece of paper). Trans. by N. Volzhina. Int. Lit. (M.), 1941, No. 11-12, pp. 162-168. (s.) From Direction, Vol. 4, No. 5, 1941, p. 5.

1070. Poryadok veshchei (The way things are). Trans. by Yu. Smirnov. Mol. Gvard. (M.), 1940, No. 9, pp. 62-73, No. 10, pp. 39-52. ZL 55943.40 (s.) From The way things are.

1071. Proshchai (Goodbye). Trans. by N. Volzhina. 30 Dnei (L.), 1939, No. 7, pp. 49-55. ZL 46503.39 (s.) From The way things are.

1072. Ryadovoi Khiks (Private Hicks). Trans. by Yu. Smirnov; adapted by P. Furmanski. Krestyanskaya Gazeta, M., 1938. 20 p., 19,330 c. KL 12257.38 (pl.). From Kozlenko, The best short plays of the social theatre.

1073. Samy schastlivy chelovek na svete (The happiest man on earth). Trans. by G. Yarros. 30 Dnei (L.), 1939, No. 1, pp. 79-85. ZL 8369.39 (s.) From O'Brien, The best short stories: 1939.

1074. "Samy schastilivy chelovek v mire" (The happiest man on earth). Trans. by M. Levina. Industriya sotsializma (M.), 1939, No. 2, pp. 50-52. ZL 20314.39 (s.)

1075. Same. Trans. and abridged by V. Golant. Rezets (L.), 1939, No. 13-14, pp. 11-13. ZL 46504.39

1076. Takova zhizn (The way things are). Pravda, M.,
      1947. 47 p., [no. of copies omitted]. MLRA, Vol. 1,
      No. 2, p. 27. (coll. s.)
      From The way things are. Other contents not listed.

1077. V pervy raz (The game). Trans. by Yu. Smirnov.
      Rezets (L.), 1938, No. 20, pp. 18-20. ZL 55725.38
      (s.)
      From Scribner's Magazine, Dec., 1936, p. 6.

MASTERS, Edgar Lee

1078. Iz "Antologii Spun River" (Spoon river anthology).
      Trans. by Ivan Kashkin. Int. Lit. (M.), 1936, No. 3,
      pp. 77-80. (p.)
      An excerpt.

1079. Stikhi kitaitsa (Lichee nut poems). Trans. by I.
      Kashkin. Zapad i Vostok [place of publication not
      available], 1926, No. 1-2, pp. 94-98. (coll. p.)
      From American Mercury, Jan. 1925, pp. 61-62; June,
      1925, pp. 238-239.

MATHEUS, John F.

1080. Bolotny mokkasin [swamp moccasin; not identified].
      Trans. by I. Srednik; edited by Ye. G. Lundberg.
      Oktyabr (M. & L.), 1927, No. 3, pp. 7-11. ZL 9152.27
      (s.)

MELVILLE, Herman

1081. Taipi (Typee). Trans. by L. G. Shpet; edited by N. I.
      Ignatova. Gosizdat., M. & L., 1929. 208 p., 7000 c.
      KL 9667.29 (n.)
      A juvenile publication.

MERRILL, Irene

1082. Cherepakha [the turtle; not identified]. Trans. by Yu.
      Smirnov. Mol. Gvard. (M.), 1937, No. 10-11, pp. 22-
      53. ZL 45527.37 (s.)

MILBURN, George

1083. Deshovaya Amerika (Catalogue). Trans. by M. Urnov.
      Int. Lit. (M.), 1937, No. 6, pp. 6-90. (n.)
      Excerpts.

MILBURN, George (Continued)

Kabluk, nosok, i raz-dva-tri (Heel, toe and a 1, 2, 3, 4). See 5.

1084. Konets muzyke (No more trumpets). Trans. by A. Yeleonskaya. Int. Lit. (M.), 1935, No. 6, pp. 75-82. (s.)
From No more trumpets.

1085. Otmetka za semestr (A student in economics). Trans. by A. Yeleonskaya. Int. Lit. (M.), 1934, No. 3-4, pp. 191-201. (s.)
From Harper's Magazine, Feb., 1933, p. 265.

1086. Preiskurant (Catalogue). Trans. by M. Urnov. Goslitizdat., M., 1937. 248 p., 10,000 c. KL 4009.37 (n.)

MILHOLLAND, Ray

1087. Zavodski gudok (Six o'clock whistle). Trans. by M. Levina. Int. Lit. (M.), 1941, No. 11-12, pp. 152-161. (s.)
From Saturday Evening Post, Aug. 23, 1941, p. 20

MOLL, Elick

1088. On poluchil obratno svoyu rabotu (To those who wait). Trans. by Yu. Smirnov. Rezets (L.), 1939, No. 8, pp. 10-12. ZL 27314.39 (s.)
From O'Brien, The best short stories, 1938.

MORANG, Alfred

1089. Vozvrashcheniye domoi (Homecoming). Trans. by Yu. Smirnov. Rezets (L.), 1938, No. 21, pp. 21-22. ZL 58235.38 (s.)
From Partisan Review, April, 1936, p. 22.

MULLIN, Glen

1090. Khobo (Adventures of a scholar tramp). Trans. by O. P. Cherbonski. Gosizdat., M. & L., 1927. 292 p., 4000 c. KL 2512.27 (autobiog.)

NEWHOUSE, Edward

1091. Spat zdes ne razreshayetsya (You can't sleep here).

Trans. by N. Daruzes. Zhurn. Gaz. Obyed., M., 1938.
228 p., 25,000 c. KL 5763.38 (n.)

NIGGLI, Josephine

Byka otravili (This bull ate nutmeg). See 9.

NORRIS, Charles

1092. Filipp Bolduin (Brass). Trans. by A. A. Davydova.
Mysl, L., 1927. 341 p., 6200 c. KL 13995.27 (n.)

1093. Kusok khleba (Bread). Trans. by Mark Volosov. Mysl,
L., 1926. 304 p., 4000 c. KL 20391.26 (n.)

1094. Sol zemli (Salt). Trans. by T. A. Timiryazeva. Mysl,
L., 1929. 378 p., 5100 c. KL 2724.29 (n.)

1095. Zelda Marsh (Zelda Marsh). Trans. by M. Ye. Abkina.
Mysl, L., 1929. 464 p., 5100 c. KL 2274.29 (n.)

NORRIS, Frank

1096. Bliks (Blix). Trans. by Ye. I. Fortunato, Mysl, L.,
1927. 196 p., 5000 c. KL 13994.27 (n.)

1097. Omut (The pit). Trans. by A. G. Mysl, L., 1925.
373 p., 5000 c. KL 19246.25
Sdelka s pshenitsei (A deal in wheat). See 4.

1098. Silnaya dukhom (A man's woman). Trans. by Ye.
Fortunato. Mysl, L., 1928. 270 p., 5200 c.
KL 21185.28 (n.)

1099. Sprut (The octopus). Trans. by A. G.; edited by A.
M. Karnaukhova. Mysl, L., 1925. 351 p., 8000 c.
KL 8544.25 (n.)

1100. Same. Trans. by P. Okhrimenko; edited by M.
Levidov. Proletari, Simferopol, 1925. 267 p.,
10,000 c. KL 20291.25 (n.)

1101. Same. Trans. and abridged by E. K. Pimonova,
Gosizdat., M. & L., 1926. 111 p., 5000 c. KL 13656.26

1102. Toppan (Toppan). Trans. by M. Matveyeva. Seyatel,
L., 1926. 45 p., 15,000 c. KL 3928.26 (coll. s.)
From The third circle. Other titles not listed in KL.

NORRIS, Kathleen

1103. Chaika (The sea gull). Trans. by M. Ye. Abkina.
Mysl, L., 1928. 293 p., 5100 c. KL 9921.28 (n.)

O'CONNOR, Edward

Nikto ne proidyot (Nobody knows). See 17.

ODETS, Clifford

1104. "Edna i Dzho" [Edna and Joe]. Adapted by G. Vechor
from the translation by B. E. Gombard. Tsedram., M.,
1935. 5 p., 340 c. KL 29366.35 (pl.)
An excerpt from Waiting for Lefty.

1105. V ozhidanii Lefti (Waiting for Lefty). Trans. by
Nina Mints. Tsedram, M., 1935. 22 p., 125 c.
KL 36405.35 (pl.)

1106. Zhdut Lefti (Waiting for Lefty). Adapted by G. Vechor
from the trans. by B. Gombard. Tsedram, M., 1935.
29 p., 140 c. KL 28684.35 (pl.)

1107. Same. 1936. 30 p., 140 c. KL 7194.36

1108. Zolotoi malchik (Golden boy). Trans. by R. Rait.
Lit. Sov. (L.), 1940, No. 8-9, pp. 113-164. (pl.)

1109. Same. Trans. by R. Rait; edited by N. Otten. Iskusstvo,
M. & L., 1940. 84 p., 2000 c. KL 26790.40

O. HENRY (William Sydney Porter)

Collected works

1110. Sobraniye sochineni [collected works]. Edited by V.
A. Azov and A. N. Gorlin. Gosizdat., L., 1925, 1926.
4 vols.

1111. Sobraniye sochineni [collected works]. Mysl, M. & L.,
1925. 4 vols.
Other titles published by Mysl during this period are
probably a part of this collected works, but they were
not so listed in KL.

Separate publications

1112. Amerikanskiye rasskazy [American stories]. Trans.
by V. A. Azov, with a foreword by the translator.

Gosizdat., M. & L., 1923. 200 p., 10,000 c.
KL 6556.23 (coll. s.)
Contents not listed in KL.

1113. Avantyuristy [the adventurers; not identified]. Trans.
by V. A. Azov. Gosizdat., L., 1926. 278 p., 10,000
c. Sob. soch., Vol. III. See 1110. KL 1124.26

Babye leto (The Indian summer of Dry Valley Johnson).
See 1148.

1114. Binkli i yevo shkola prakticheskovo zhurnalisma
(Binkley's practical school of journalism). Trans.
by G. Svobodin. 30 Dnei (L.), 1937, No. 4, pp. 51-56.
ZL 28969.37 (s.)
From Mary S. Harrell, O. Henry encore.

1115. Blagorodny vor (The gentle grafter). Mezhrabpom.,
M., 1924. 56 p., 15,000 c. KL 7346.24 (coll. s.)
A selection. Contents not listed in KL.

1116. Same. 1925. 64 p., 20,000 c. KL 3755.25

1117. Blagorodny zhulik i drugiye rasskazy [The gentle
grafter and other stories]. Trans. by N. Bryanski,
L. Gausman, S. Marshak, O. Poddyacha, K. Chukovski; edited and with a foreword by Yev. Zamyatin and
K. Chukovski. Gosizdat., M. & L., 1924. 354 p.,
5150 c. KL 9652.25 (coll. s.)
This volume probably contains all of The gentle
grafter along with selected stories from other volumes. Titles not listed in KL.

Blagorodny zhulik (The gentle grafter). See 1143 and
1110.

1118. Same. Trans. by M. L. Lozinski. Seyatel, L., 1926.
78 p., 15,000 c. KL 11214.26 (coll. s.)
Titles not listed in KL.

1119. Blinchiki (The Pimienta pancakes). Voyenizdat., M.,
1943. 66 p., [no. of copies omitted]. KL 13578.43
(coll. s.)
From Heart of the West. Other titles not listed in KL.

1120. Chetyre milliona (The four million). Trans. by Zin.
Lvovski. Mysl, L., 1925. 186 p., 8000 c. Sob. Soch.,
Vol. VII. See 1111. KL 11187.25 (coll. s.)

O. HENRY (William Sydney Porter) (Continued)

1121. 4,000,000 (The four million). Trans. by V. A. Azov.
Gosizdat., L. & M., 1925. 298 p., 10,000 c. Sob.
soch., Vol. I, See 1110. KL 4629.25

1122. 4 rasskaza [four short stories]. Vkhutein., M., 1928.
43 p., 100 c. KL 3186.29 (coll. s.)
Contents not listed in KL.

1123. Chorny Bill (The hiding of Black Bill). Trans. by
Zin. Lvovski. Mysl, L., 1924. 181 p., 8000 c.
KL 10486.24 (coll. s.)
From Options. Other titles not listed in KL.

1124. Same. Seyatel, L., 1925. 48 p., 15,000 c. KL 12224.25
(coll. s.)
Other titles not listed in KL.

1125. Chto govorit gorod (Voice of the city). Trans. by
N. Yu. Zhukovski. Mysl, L., 1925. 200 p., 6000 c.
KL 307.25 (coll. s.)

1126. Dary volkhov (The gift of the Magi). Trans. by Z.
Lvovski. Seyatel, L., 1925. 45 p., 15,000 c.
KL 16547.25 (coll. s.)
From The four million. Other titles not listed in KL.

1127. Same. [no translator given]. Kras. Prolet., M. & L.,
1926. 64 p., 15,000 c. KL 3411.26 (coll. s.)
Other titles not listed in KL.

1128. Same. 1927. 64 p., 10,000 c. KL 12318.27

Same. See 1174.

Drug Telemak (Telemachus, friend). See 1174.

Durnoye pravilo (A poor rule). See 1174.

1129. Dusha Tekhasa (Heart of the West). Trans. by K.
Zhikhareva. Mysl, P., 1923. 278 p., 4000 c.
KL 5280.23 (coll. s.)

1130. Same. Trans. by E. K. Brodersen. Mysl, L., 1925.
297 p., 8000 c. KL 306.25

Dzheff Piters — kak lichny magnit (Jeff Peters as a
personal magnet). See 1177.

1131. Elsi v Nyu-Iorke (Elsie in New York). Trans. by N.

F. Davydova. Priboi, L., 1926. 46 p., 15,000 c.
KL 14833.26 (coll. s.)
From The trimmed lamp. Other titles not listed in
KL.

1132. Familny retsept [a family recipe or prescription;
not identified]. Trans. by K. Zhikhareva. Seyatel,
L., 1926. 80 p., 12,200 c. KL 19639.26

Gorod bez proisshestvi. See 5.

1133. Goryashchi svetilnik (The trimmed lamp). Trans. by
E. K. Brodersen. Mysl, L., 1924. 208 p., 8000 c.
Sob. soch., Vol. II. See 1111. KL 9123.24 (coll. s.)

1134. Same. 1925. 183 p., 7000 c. KL 3756.25

1135. Gromila i Tommi (Tommy's burglar). Trans. by N.
Daruzes. 30 Dnei (L.), 1937, No. 8, pp. 61-66.
ZL 38935.37 (coll. s.)
From Whirligigs.

1136. Igrushechka-pastushechka (Whirligigs). Trans. by V.
Aleksandrov; edited by V. A. Azov. Kniga, M. & L.,
1924. 182 p., 4000 c. KL 9124.24 (coll. s.)

1137. Izbrannyie novelly [selected short stories]. Edited
by A. N. Gorlin. Goslitizdat., L. & M., 1932. 270
p., 10,140 c. KL 12329.32 (coll. s.)
Contents not listed in KL.

Kafedra filantromatematiki (The chair of Philanthro-
mathematics). See 1177.

Klad (Buried treasure). See 1174.

1138. Koroleva zmei (An afternoon miracle). Trans. by K.
Zhikhareva. Seyatel, L., 1925. 45 p., 15,000 c.
KL 20256.25 (coll. s.)
From Heart of the West. Other titles not listed in
KL.

1139. Koroli i kapusta (Cabbages and kings). Trans. by K.
Chukovski. Sovremenny zapad (L.), 1922, No. 1,
pp. 17-52; 1923, No. 2, pp. 31-64; No. 3, pp. 7-61 (n.)

1140. Same. Trans. by K. Chukovski, with an introd. by the
translator. Vsemir. Lit., M. & L., 1923. 244 p.,
5250 c. KL 4644.23

1141. Same. 2nd revised ed., 1924. 207 p., 4000 c. KL 9890.24

O. HENRY (William Sydney Porter) (Continued)

1142. Same. Trans. by E. K. Pimenova. Mysl, L., 1925.
224 p., 8000 c. Sob. soch., Vol. VIII. See 1111.
KL 2291.25

1143. Koroli i kapusta (Cabbages and kings) and Blagorodny
zhulik (The gentle grafter). Trans. by K. Chukovski
and V. A. Azov. Gosizdat., L., 1925. 347 p., 10,000
c. Sob. soch., Vol. II. See 1110. KL 13,721.25 (coll.
n., s.)

1144. Koroli i kapusta (Cabbages and kings). Trans. by K.
Chukovski, with an introd. by the translator. Kras.
Prolet., M. & L., 1926. 256 p., 15,000 c. KL 6154.26

1145. Same. M. F. Lariye, editor of translation; foreword
by T. Silman. Goslitizdat., M., 1946. 471 p.,
100,000 c.

1146. Kotory iz dvukh [which of the two; not identified, but
possibly Thimble, thimble from Options]. Trans. by
Z. Lvovski. Seyatel, L., 1925. 48 p., 15,000 c.
KL 16548.25

1147. Kovboi (Heart of the West). Trans. by V. Azov and V.
Aleksandrov; introd. by B. M. Eikhenbaum. Gosizdat.,
M. & L., 1926. 238 p., 10,000 c. Sob. soch., Vol. IV.
See 1110. KL 16133.26 (coll. s.)

1148. Krasnyie rozy (The red roses of Tonia), Pozdno [late;
not identified], Babye leto (The Indian summer of Dry
Valley Johnson),Vykup [ransom; not identified, but
probably either The ransom of Mack, or The ransom
of Red Chief], and Krugovorot (Whirligig of life).
Trans. by Ye. Tolkacheva. Krasnaya Zvezda, M.,
1925. 64 p., 10,000 c. KL 2289.25 (coll. s.)
"The red roses of Tonia" is from Waifs and strays;
"The Indian summer of Dry Valley Johnson" is from
Heart of the West; "Whirligig of life" is from
Whirligigs; "The ransom of Mack" is from Heart of
the West; "The ransom of Red Chief" is from
Whirligigs.

1149. Kroshechnyie rasskazy (Postscripts). Trans. by A.
d'Aktil. Kras. Gaz., L., 1926. 40 p., 20,000 c.
KL 1295.27 (coll. s.)
Contents not listed in KL

Krugovorot (Whirligig of life). See 1148.

1150. Lan i ruchei [deer and brook; not identified]. Trans.
by V. A. Azov. Gosizdat., L., 1927. 266 p., 7000 c.

1151. Marionetki (The marionettes). Trans. by E. K.
Brodersen. Mysl, L., 1924. 176 p., 8000 c.
KL 12255.24 (coll. s.)
From Rolling stones. Other titles not listed in KL.
Mayatnik (The pendulum). See 1174.

1152. Mily zhulik (The gentle grafter). Trans. by S. A.
Adrianov. Mysl, L., 1924. 156 p., 8000 c.
KL 11793.24 (coll. s.)

1153. Mir i dver (The world and the door). Trans. by Zin.
Lvovski. Seyatel, L., 1925. 47 p., 15,000 c.
KL 18236.25 (coll. s.)
From Whirligigs. Other titles not listed in KL.

1154. Nalyot na poyezd (Holding up a train). Trans. by Zin.
Lvovski. Seyatel, L., 1926. 79 p., 15,250 c.
KL 9131.26 (coll. s.)
From Sixes and sevens. Other titles not listed in KL.

1155. Napadeniye na pochtu (A chaparral prince). Trans.
and adapted by P. Gorvits. Gosizdat., M. & L., 1927.
23 p., 35,000 c. KL 19346.27 (s.)
From Heart of the West.

1156. Novelly [short stories]. Selected and trans. by A. N.
Gorlin; introd. by O. Nemorovskaya. Mol. Gvard.,
M., 1938. 367 p., 25,000 c. KL 1863.38 (coll. s.)
Contents not listed in KL.

1157. Novy Bagdad (Strictly business). Trans. by E. K.
Brodersen and A. M. Karnaukhova. Mysl, L., 1925.
208 p., 8000 c. KL 13655.24 (coll. s.)

1158. Nyu-Iorkskiye rasskazy [New York stories; not iden-
tified, but possibly stories from The four million or
The voice of the city]. Trans. and with a foreword by
V. Dadonov. Puchina, M. & P., 1923. 101 p., 4000 c.
KL 11246.23 (coll. s.)

1159. O starom negre, bolshikh karmannykh chasakh i
voprose, kotory ostalsya otkrytym (Thimble, thimble).

O. HENRY (William Sydney Porter) (Continued)

> V. A. Azov, editor of translation. Atenei, L., 1924.
> 245 p., 6000 c. KL 11113.24 (coll. s.)
> From Options. Other titles not listed in KL.

> Pimiyentskiye blinchiki (The Pimienta pancakes).
> See 1174.

1160. Porosyachya etika (The ethics of pig). Trans. by K.
Chukovski, L. M. Gausman. O. Poddyacha. Gosizdat.,
M. & L., 1926. 62 p., 15,000 c. KL 11692.26 (coll.
s.)
From The gentle grafter. Other titles not listed in
KL.

1161. Same. 1927. 62 p., 15,000 c.

1162. Posledni list (The last leaf). Introd. by M. Urnov.
Detizdat., M. & L., 1939. 32 p., 50,000 c.
KL 12842.39 (coll. s.)
From The trimmed lamp. Other titles not listed in KL.
A juvenile publication.

> Pozdno. See 1148.

1163. Prints iz skazki (A chaparral prince). Trans. by Al.
Deich. Biblioteka Zhurnala "Ogonyok," M., 1926.
56 p., 14,000 c. KL 8046.26 (coll. s.)
From Heart of the West. Other titles not listed in KL.

> Printsessa i puma (The princess and the puma). See
> 1174.

1164. Proba (Proof of the pudding). Trans. by M. Bogo-
slovskaya. 30 Dnei (L.), 1937, No. 7, pp. 65-71.
ZL 35004.37 (s.)
From Strictly business.

1165. Puti kotoryie my izbirayem (Roads of destiny). V. A.
Azov, editor of translation. Atenei, P., 1923. 287
p., 4000 c. KL 10320.23 (coll. s.)

1166. Same. 1925. 296 p., 6000 c. KL 2290.25

1167. Rasskazy [short stories]. Trans. by N. Bryanski, L.
Gausman, S. Marshak, and O. Poddyacha. Edited
and with an introd. by Ye. Zamyatin. Vsemir Lit.,
M. & P., 1923. 251 p., 6000 c. KL 2961.23 (coll. s.)
Contents not listed in KL.

1168. Same. [no translator given]. Gudok, M., 1926. 64 p.,
26,000 c. KL 20369.26
Contents not listed in KL.

1169. Same. Goslitizdat., M., 1936. 289 p., 20,000 c.
KL 41627.36
Contents not listed in KL.

1170. Same. Goslitizdat., M., 1936. 332 p., 50,000 c.
KL 2839.37
Contents not listed in KL.

1171. Same. Edited by Ye. I. Klimenko. Uchpedgiz., M. &
L., 1937. 104 p., 10,000 c. KL 7152.37
A juvenile publication. Text in English and Russian.
Contents not listed in KL.

1172. Same. Selected, adapted and with an introd. by P.
Balashov. Goslitizdat., M., 1937. 48 p., 100,000 c.
KL 29456.37
Contents not listed in KL.

1173. Same. [no translator given]. Pravda, M., 1941. 48 p.,
100,000 c. KL 14098.41
Contents not listed in KL.

1174. Same. Introd. by T. Silman. Voyenmorizdat., M.,
1944. 164 p., 15,000 c. KL 11215.44 (coll. s.)
Contents: Zelyonnaya dver (The green door). Dary
volkhov (The gift of the Magi). Vykup [ransom; not
identified, but probably either The ransom of Mack,
or The ransom of Red Chief]. Klad (Buried treasure).
Spravochnik Gimeneya (The handbook of Hymen).
Durnoye pravilo (A poor rule). Mayatnik (The pendulum). Printsessa i puma (The princess and the puma).
Pimiyentskiye blinchiki (The Pimienta pancakes).
Drug Telemak (Telemachus, friend).
"The green door" and "The gift of the Magi" are from
The four million; "The handbook of Hymen," "The
princess and the puma," "The Pimienta pancakes"
and "Telemachus, friend" are from Heart of the West;
"Buried treasure" and "A poor rule" are from Options;
"The pendulum" is from The trimmed lamp; "The
ranson of Mack" is from Heart of the West, "The ran-
som of Red Chief" is from Whirligigs.

1175. Rasskazy lovkovo moshennika (The gentle grafter).

O. HENRY (William Sydney Porter) (Continued)

Trans. by A. A. Kashintsev. Nedra, M., 1925. 77 p.,
10,000 c. KL 18237.25 (coll. s.)
A selection. Titles not listed in KL.

1176. Rasskazy o zapade i yuge [stories of the West and
South; not identified, but possibly Heart of the West].
V. A. Azov, editor of translation. Petrograd, L. & M.,
1924. 253 p., 10,000 c. KL 12831.24 (coll. s.)

1177. Rasskazy zhulika (The gentle grafter). Trans. by K.
Chukovski. Sovremenny Zapad (L.), 1923, No. 4,
pp. 50-71. (coll. s.)
Contents: Dzheff Piters — kak lichny magnit (Jeff
Peters as a personal magnet). Supruzhestvo, kak
tochnaya nauka (The exact science of matrimony).
Trest, kotory lopnul (The octopus marooned).
Kafedra filantromatematiki (The chair of Philanthro-
mathematics).

1178. Same. Vsemir. Lit., M. & L., 1924. 95 p., 5150 c.
KL 3539.24
A selection. Titles not listed in KL.

1179. Roman birzhevovo maklera (The romance of a busy
broker). ZIF, M. & L., 1926. 32 p., 15,000 c.
KL 12711.26 (coll. s.)
From The four million. Other titles not listed in KL.

1180. Sherstyannaya koshechka (Roads of destiny). Trans.
by Zin. Lvovski. Mysl, L., 1924. 175 p., 8000 c.
KL 9125.24 (coll. s.)

1181. Shesterki-semerki (Sixes and sevens). Trans. by Zin.
Lvovski. Mysl, L., 1924. 208 p., 6000 c. KL 5296.24
(coll. s.)

1182. Same. Mysl, L., 1925. 207 p., 5000 c. Sob. soch.,
Vol. I. See 1111. KL 10396.25

1183. Shumi-gorodok nad podzemkoi (The voice of the city).
V. A. Azov, editor of translation. Petrograd, L. & M.,
1924. 288 p., 7000 c. KL 6741.24 (coll. s.)

1184. Sluchai iz departamentskoi praktiki (A departmental
case). Trans. by Ye. Brailovski. 30 Dnei (L.), 1938,
No. 9, pp. 71-80. ZL 48168.38 (s.)
From Roads of destiny.

1185. Soboli mekh (Vanity and some sables). Rabochaya
Moskva, M., 1925. 60 p., 25, 000 c. KL 9651.25
(coll. s.)
From The trimmed lamp. Other titles not listed in KL.

Spravochnik Gimeneya (The handbook of Hymen).
See 1174.

Spustya dvadtsat let (After twenty years). See 1.

Supruzhestvo, kak tochnaya nauka (The exact science of matrimony). See 1177.

1186. Sushchnost dela [the nature of the matter; not identi-
fied]. Trans. by Z. Lvovski. Seyatel, L., 1925. 96 p.,
15,000 c. KL 12222.25

1187. Tainstvenny maskarad (A midsummer masquerade).
Trans. by Zin. Lvovski. Novella, L. & M., 1924.
151 p., 5000 c. KL 6742.24 (coll. s.)
From The gentle grafter. Other titles not listed in
KL.

1188. Same. 1925. 163 p., 4000 c. KL 2292.25

Trest, kotory lopnul (The octopus marooned). See 1177.

1189. Trony vladyk (Seats of the haughty). Trans. by K.
Zhikhareva. Seyatel, L., 1925. 92 p., 15,000 c.
KL 12223. 25 (coll. s.)
From Heart of the West. Other titles not listed in
KL 12223.25

1190. Tysyacha dollarov (One thousand dollars). Trans. by
Zin. Lvovski. Novella, L. & M., 1925. 189 p., 5000
c. KL 12225.25 (coll. s.)
From The voice of the city. Other titles not listed in
KL.

1191. Villa Vereton (Vereton Villa). Trans. by G. Svobodin.
30 Dnei (L), 1937, No. 4, pp. 49-56. ZL 18360.37 (s.)
From Mary S. Harrell, O. Henry encore.

1192. Volchki (Whirligigs). Trans. by Zin. Lvovski. Mysl,
L., 1925. 208 p., 8000 c. KL 13654.24 (coll. s.)

1193. Volshebny profil (The enchanted profile). Trans. by
N. F. Davydova. Priboi, L., 1926. 28 p., 15,000 c.
KL 12710.26 (coll. s.)
From Roads of destiny. Other titles not listed in KL.

O. HENRY (William Sydney Porter) (Continued)

1194. Volya [will; not identified]. Trans. by Z. Lvovski. Seyatel, L., 1925. 48 p., 15,000 c. KL 15326.25

1195. Vozhd Krasnokozhikh (The ransom of Red Chief). Nizhegorodskaya Kommuna, N.N., 1927. 43 p., 3000 c. KL 1426.28 (coll. s.)
From Whirligigs. Other titles not listed in KL.

1196. Same. Trans. and adapted by L. Savelyeva. Gosizdat., M. & L., 1927. 28 p., 50,000 c. KL 19345.27 (s.)
A juvenile publication.

1197. Same. 1930. 24 p., 35,000 c.

1198. Same. [no translator given]. Introd. by A. Raskin. Detizdat., M. & L., 1937. 30 p., 100,300 c.
KL 20107.37
A juvenile publication.

Vykup. See 1148.

Same. See 1174.

1199. Vykup vozhdya krasnokozhikh (The ransom of Red Chief). Trans. by Z. Lvovski. Seyatel, L., 1925. 45 p., 15,000 c. KL 16546.25 (coll. s.)
From Whirligigs. Other titles not listed in KL.

1200. Zapisnaya knizhka [note-book; not identified]. Trans. by A. d'Aktil. Smekhach, L., 1926. 63 p., 30,000 c. KL 11215.26 (s.)

Zelyonaya dver (The green door). See 1174.

1201. Zhenshchina ("Girl"). Trans. by K. Chukovski, O. Poddyacha, N. Bryanski, L. M. Gausman. Kras. Prolet., M. & L., 1926. 61 p., 15,000 c. KL 222.26 (coll. s.)
From Whirligigs. Other titles not listed in KL.

O'NEILL, Eugene

1202. Anna Kristi (Anna Christie). Trans. by P. B. Zenkevich and N. M. Krymova. Vestnik Rabotnikov Iskusstv, M., 1925. 36 p., 3000 c. KL 1103.25 (pl.)

1203. "Koroleva Atlantiki" (Ile). Trans. and with an introd. by A. G. Movshenson. Teakinopechat, L. & M., 1929. 32 p., 6000 c. KL 12979.29 (pl.)

1204. Kosmataya obezyana (The hairy ape). Trans. by N.
M. Krymova and P. B. Zenkevich. Moskovskoye
Teatralnoye Izdatelstvo, M., 1925. 64 p., 3000 c.
KL 12476.24 (pl.)

1205. Lyubov pod vyazami (Desire under the elms). Trans.
by P. Zenkevich and N. Krymova. M.O.D.P. i K.,
M. & L., 1927. 48 p., 3000 c. KL 2515.27 (pl.)

1206. Na puti v Kardif (Bound east for Cardiff). Trans. by
Ye. Kalashnikova. Int. Lit. (M.), 1933, No. 5, pp.
92-98. (pl.)

1207. Negr (All God's chillun got wings). Trans. by N. M.
Krymova; adapted by P. B. Zenkevich and A. T.
M.O.D.P. i K., M. & L., 1930. 46 p., 3000 c.
KL 22819.29 (pl.)

1208. Volosotaya obezyana (The hairy ape). Trans. by M.
G. Volosov; edited by A. N. Gorlin. Gosizdat., L.,
1925. 84 p., 4000 c. KL 1629.25 (pl.)

1209. Zoloto (Gold). Trans. by N. M. Krymova; adapted by
P. B. Zenkevich. Teakinopechat, M., 1928. 80 p.,
3000 c. KL 11668.28 (pl.)

OPPENHEIM, James

1210. Khleba i roz [of bread and roses; not identified].
Trans. by T. Shchepkina-Kupernik. Zvezda (M. & L.),
1924, No. 3, p. 105. (p.)

OSTENSO, Martha

1211. Dikiye gusi (Wild geese). Trans. by M. I. Ratner.
Mysl, L., 1926. 240 p., 5000 c. KL 17144.26 (n.)

1212. Same. Trans. by Mark Volosov. ZIF, M. & L., 1926.
264 p., 4000 c. KL 18282.26 (n.)

1213. Shalnyie Keryu (The mad Carews). Trans. by N. N.
Shulgovski and B. P. Spiro. Vremya, L., 1928. 255
p., 4150 c. KL 7167.28 (n.)

1214. Tyomnaya zarya (The dark dawn). Trans. by Mark
Volosov. Mysl, L., 1927. 277 p., 5200 c.
KL 18564.27 (n.)

PARKER, Dorothy

1215. Soldaty respubliki (Soldiers of the republic). Trans. by V. Toper. Int. Lit. (M.), 1942, No. 6, pp. 77-79 (s.)
From Here lies: the collected stories of Dorothy Parker.

PEARL, Bertha

1216. Mat i doch (Sarah and her daughter). Trans. by D. Maizelis and V. Ilyichevaya. Vremya, L., 1928. 300 p., 3500 c. KL 17499.28 (n.)

PETERS, Paul

1217. Doroga v Souges [not identified]. Trans. by N. Krymova and N. Petrashkevich. Iskusstvo, M., 1938. 84 p., 5000 c. KL 24409.38 (pl.)

PHILLIPS, David Graham

1218. Vozvysheniye Syuzanny Lenoks (Susan Lenox: her fall and rise). Trans. by Mark Volosov. Vremya, L., 1928. 299 p., 4000 c. KL 19032.28 (n.)

PICKENS, William

1219. Negrityanskiye Yumoreski [Negro humoresques; not identified, but possibly excerpts from American Aesop: Negro and other humor]. Adapted by Ye. Lundberg. Biblioteka Zhurnala "Ogonyok," M., 1928. 32 p., 50,000 c. KL 19727.28

PINCHON, Edgcumb

1220. Zapata nepobedimy (Zapata, the unconquerable). Trans. by M. Kondratyeva and A. Krivtsova. Int. Lit. (M.), 1942, No. 3-4-5, pp. 35-132 (biog.)
The concluding chapters.

POE, Edgar Allan

Collected works

1221. Izbrannyie sochineniya [selected works]. Trans. by M. A. Engelgardt. Vsemir. Lit., Berlin, 1924. 3 vols,

299, 321 and 265 p., [no. of copies omitted].
KL 10150-52.24
Contents not listed in KL.

1222. Polnoye sobraniye poem i stikhotvoreni [complete
collected poetry]. Trans. and with an introd. by V.
Bryusov. Vsemir. Lit., M. & L., 1924. 128 p., 2150
c. KL 6406.24 (coll. p.)

Separate publications

Bochonok Amontilyado (The cask of Amontillado).
See 4.

1223. Izbrannyie rasskazy [selected stories]. S. S. Dinamov,
editor of translation, with an introd. by Dinamov.
Goslitizdat., M., 1936. 349 p., 15,000 c. KL 918.36
(coll. s.)
Contents not listed in KL

1224. Kolodez i mayatnik (The pit and the pendulum). Trans.
by Ye. Kalmeyer. Biblkoteka Zhurnala "Ogonyok,"
M., 1920. 44 p., 17,000 c. KL 14108.29 (coll. s.)
Other titles not listed in KL.

Nizverzheniye v Malstrem (A descent into the
Maelstrom). See 1234.

1225. Ochki (The spectacles). Argo, editor of translation.
ZIF, M. & L., 1926. 32 p., 15,000 c. KL 5510.26
(coll. s.)
Contents: Ochki. Zhulnichestvo, kak odna iz tochnykh
nauk (Diddling considered as one of the exact sciences).

1226. Poemy i stikhotvoreniya [poems]. Trans. by Vas.
Fedorov from the Oxford edition of 1909. Pervina,
M., 1923. 106 p., 2000 c. KL 4861.23 (coll. p.)
Contents not listed in KL.

1227. Poslednyaya shutka [the last joke; not identified].
Trans. by M. Viktorov. Biblioteka Zhurnala
"Ogonyok," M., 1927. 40 p., 15,500 c. KL 4856.27
(coll. s.)

1228. Priklyucheniya Artura Gordona Pima (The narrative
of Arthur Gordon Pym). Translated from a French
edition. Gosizdat., M. & L., 1928. 232 p., 15,000 c.
KL 2555.28 (coll. s.)
Other contents not listed in KL.

POE, Edgar Allan (Continued)

1229. Rasskazy [short stories]. Biblioteka Zhurnala
"Ogonyok," M., 1929. 32 p., 48,000 c. KL 16555.29
(coll. s.)
Contents not listed in KL.

1230. Ubistvo v ulitse Morg (The murders in the Rue
Morgue). Trans. by K. D. Balmont and M. N.
Engelgardt; introd. by A. Kamegulov. Priboi, L.,
1927. 185 p., 10,000 c. KL 16391.27 (coll. s.)
Other titles not listed in KL.

1231. Ulyalyum (Ulalume). Trans. by N. Chukovski. Zvezda
(M. & L.), 1939, No. 2, pp. 123-24. ZL 16338.39 (p.)

Zhulnichestvo, kak odna iz tochnykh nauk (Diddling
considered as one of the exact sciences). See 1225

1232. Zolotoi zhuk (The gold bug). Akvilon, P., 1922.
54 p., 800 c. KL 9684.22 (s.)

1233. Same. Voyenizdat., M., 1945. 66 p., [no. of copies
omitted]. KL 14978.45 (coll. s.)
Other titles not listed in KL.

Same. See 4.

1234. Zolotoi zhuk (The gold bug) and Nizverzheniye v
Malstrem (A descent into the Maelstrom). Introd. by
K. Paustovski. Detizdat., M. & L., 1946. 63 p.,
45,000 c. KL 7892.46 (coll. s.)
A juvenile publication.

1235. Zolotoi zhuk: zb. rasskasov Amer. klassikov [The
gold bug: a collection of American classic short
stories]. Compiled by A. Startsev. Detizdat.,
M. & L., 1943. 144 p., 25,000 c. KL 9322.43 (coll. s.)
A juvenile publication. This volume probably contains works by other authors, although the entry in
KL is not clear.

POLING, Dan

1236. Gorn (The furnace). Trans. by N. Chukovski. Nov.
Vsemir. Lit., L., 1927. 184 p., 4000 c. KL 7111.27
(n.)

POOLE, Ernest

1237. Gavan (The harbor). Trans. by L. Ya. Krukovskaya.
Seyatel, L., 1924. 319 p., 5000 c. KL 4957.24 (n.)

1238. Same. [no translator given]. Priboi, L., 1924. 310
p., 6000 c. Pechat i Rev., 1925, No. 2, p. 285.

1239. Same. V.Ts.S.P.S., M., 1924. 117 p., 5000 c.
KL 14024.24

1240. Same. Trans. and abridged by E. K. Pimenova.
Gosizdat., M. & L., 1926. 88 p., 15,000 c. KL 4970.26

1241. Opasnost (Danger). Trans. by V. Azov. Petrograd,
L. & M., 1925. 255 p., 4000 c. KL 13810.25 (n.)

QUINCE, Peter

1242. Vosstaniye v preispodnem (Revolt of the damned).
Trans. from the manuscript by Z. Gan. Int Lit. (M.),
1935, No. 11, pp. 71-78. (s.)
From International literature, Dec., 1935, p. 15.

REED, John

1243. Brodvei (Daughter of the revolution and other stories).
Trans. by M. Volosov. Priboi, L., 1928. 106 p.,
4000 c. KL 14731.28 (coll. s.)

1244. Desyat dnei kotoriye potryasli mir (Ten days that
shook the world). Trans. by V. Yarotski; with an
introd. by N. Lenin and N. Krupskaya and a short
biographical sketch of the author by A. R. Vilyams
[Albert Rhys Williams]. Kras. Nov, M., 1923. 316 p.,
10,000 c. KL 5507.23 (history)

1245. Same. 2nd revised ed., 1924, 324 p., 50,000 c.
KL 4352.24

1246. Same. 1924. 324 p., 25,000 c. KL 10731.24

1247. Same. Trans. by Dantziger, with an introd. by N.
Lenin and a short biographical sketch of the author
by Boris Reinshtein. Rabochaya Gazeta, M., 1924.
253 p., 150,000 c. KL 13224.24

1248. Same. [no translator given]. Rezets (L.), 1927, No.
43, pp. 1-3; No. 44, pp. 12-15.
Excerpts.

REED, John (Continued)

1249. 10 dnei kotoryie potryasli mir (Ten days that shook
the world). Trans. and edited by I. Vorobyev. Kras.
Prolet., M., 1924. [no. of pages omitted], [no. of
copies omitted]. KL 12519.24
KL notes that this is a special edition for peasant
readers.

1250. Doch revolyutsii (Daughter of the revolution and
other stories). Trans. by Ya. M. Chernyaka; foreword by N. Krupskaya. Moskovski Rabochi, M. & L.,
1928. 159 p., 5000 c. KL 16277.28 (coll. s.)

1251. Doch revolyutsii (Daughter of the revolution). Trans.
by Yak. Chernyaka. Oktyabr (M. & L.), 1928, No. 2,
pp. 3-15. ZL 5989.28 (s.)
From Daughter of the revolution and other stories.

1252. Kak oni voyevali [how they made war; not identified].
Trans. by I. Sablin. 30 Dnei (L.), 1927, No. 7, pp. 50-
63. (sk.)

Noch na Brodveye (Night on Broadway). See 5.

1253. Shturm otzhivshevo mira (Ten days that shook the
world). Priboi, P., 1923. 64 p., 5000 c. KL 11290.23
An adaptation.

REED, Mary

1254. Pervoye maya [the first of May; not identified].
Oktyabr (M.), 1928, No. 5, pp. 211-216. ZL 16972.28
(s.)

REYNOLDS, Quentin

1255. Tolko zvezdy neitralny (Only the stars are neutral).
Int. Lit. (M.), 1942, No. 12, pp. 93-106. (rep.)
An excerpt.

RICE, Elmer

1256. Nyu Iork (Street scene). Trans. and adapted by L.
Sheffer. Tsedram, M., 1935. 52 p., 190 c.
KL 38305.35 (pl.)

1257. V glukhom pereulke (Street scene). Trans. and

adapted by I. Rubinshtein. Iskusstvo, M., 1937. 121 p., 1000 c. KL 12936.37

1258. Same. 1938. 121 p., 10,000 c. KL 22383.38

RISKIN, Robert

1259. Ledi na den (Lady for a day). Trans. by N. Kumanova. Goskinoizdat, M., 1940. 116 p., 5000 c. KL 18204.40 (scenario)

1260. Mister Dids pereyezzhayet v bolshoi gorod (Mr. Deeds goes to town). Trans. by V. O. Bluvshtein; introd. by L. Trauberg. Goskinoizdat, M., 1940. 156 p., 5000 c. KL 13203.40 (scenario)

1261. Poteryanny gorizont (Lost horizon). Trans. by V. Bluvshtein. Goskinoizdat, M., 1940. 152 p., 5000 c. KL 26184.40 (scenario)

ROBINSON, Edwin Arlington

1262. Ben Dzhonson zanimayet gostya iz Stretforda (Ben Johnson entertains a man from Stratford). Trans. by Ivan Kashkin. Int. Lit. (M.), 1936, No. 1, pp. 41-45. (p.)
From The man against the sky.

ROLLINS, William

1263. Ten vperedi (The shadow before). Trans. by Ye. Romanova. Int. Lit. (M.), 1934, No. 6, pp. 5-24. (n.)
An excerpt.

1264. Same. Trans. by M. Bogoslavskaya; foreword by N. Gorin. Goslitizdat., M., 1935. 395 p., 10,000 c. KL 42051.35

ROOSEVELT, Elliot

1265. Yevo glazami (As he saw it). Trans. by A. D. Gurevich and D. E. Kunina. Zvezda (L.), 1947, No. 4, pp. 100-128; No. 5, pp. 78-167. (biog.)

RUSSELL, John

1266. Chetvyorty chelovek (The fourth man). Trans. by P. Okhrimenko. 30 Dnei (L.), 1939, No. 4, pp. 70-80. ZL 23647.39 (s.)
From The red mark and other stories.

RYERSON, Florence, and Colin Clements
  Takov Gollivud (That's Hollywood). See 9.

SALINAS, Marcelo
  Zashchitnik (The protector). See 8.

SANDBURG, Carl
  Broshen. See 1271.

  Chikago (Chicago). See 1268.

1267. Dmitriyu Shostokovichu — tvortsu Sedmoi Simfonii
  [to Dmitri Shostokovich — creator of the Seventh
  Symphony; not identified]. Trans. by M. Zenkevich.
  Int. Lit. (M.), 1942, No. 11, pp. 109-110. (p.)

  Dym (Smoke). See 1269.

  Same. See 1271.

  Dym i stal (Smoke and steel). See 1271.

  Lyudi i loshadi v dozhd (Horses and men in rain).
  See 1271.

  Lyuks. See 1271.

  Na detskikh nozhkakh (Baby toes). See 1270.

  Okno (Window). See 1271.

  Palach u sebya doma (The hangman at home). See
  1270.

  Pokinuty (Lost). See 1270.

  Portret avtomobilya (Portrait of a motor car).
  See 1268.

  Psalom tem, kto vykhodit na rassvete (Psalm of
  those who go forth before daylight). See 1271.

1268. Pustynya (Wilderness), Chikago (Chicago), and Portret
  avtomobilya (Portrait of a motor car). Znamya
  (M.), 1936, No. 8, pp. 131-133. ZL 49791.36 (coll. p.)
  "Wilderness" and "Portrait of a motor car" are from
  Cornhuskers; "Chicago" is from Chicago poems.

1269. Rabochiye vatagi (Work gangs), Dym (Smoke), and
  Shlyapy (Hats). Trans. by Grig Petnikov. Lit. Sov.
  (L.), 1935, No. 5, pp. 88-92. ZL 28655.35 (coll. p.)

"Work gangs" and "Hats" are from <u>Smoke and steel</u>;
"Smoke" is from <u>Cornhuskers</u>.

1270. Shest stikhotvoreni [six poems]. Trans. and with an
introd. by D. Vygodski. <u>Zvezda</u> (M.), 1935, No. 3,
pp. 133-135. ZL 28656.35 (coll. s.)
Contents: Na detskikh nozhkakh (Baby toes). Trava
(Grass). Pokinuty (Lost). Sup (Soup). Palach u
sebya doma (The hangman at home). Skolzyashka
(Slippery).
"Baby toes," "Soup," "The hangman at home," and
"Slippery" are from <u>Smoke and steel</u>; "Grass" is
from <u>Cornhuskers</u>; "Lost" is from <u>Chicago poems</u>.

Shlyapy (Hats). See 1269.

Skolzyashka (Slippery). See 1270.

1271. Stikhi [poems]. Trans. by I. Kashkin. <u>Int. Lit.</u> (M.),
1936, No. 8, pp. 54-57. (coll. p.)
Contents: Dym i stal (Smoke and steel). Psalom
tem, kto vykhodit na rassvete (Psalm of those who
go forth before daylight). Lyudi i loshadi v dozhd
(Horses and men in rain). Zemlekopy (The shovel
man). Dym (Smoke). V Kholstedskom tramvaye
(Halsted street car). Broshen [deserted; not identi-
fied]. Tuman (Fog). Okno (Window). Lyuks [not
identified].
"Smoke and steel" is a selection from <u>Smoke and
steel</u>; "Psalm of those who go forth before daylight,"
"Horses and men in rain," and "Smoke" are from
<u>Cornhuskers</u>; "The shovel man," "Halsted street
car," "Fog," and "Window" are from <u>Chicago poems</u>.

Sup (Soup). See 1270.

Trava (Grass). See 1270.

Tuman (Fog). See 1271.

V Kholstedskom tramvaye (Halsted street car).
See 1271.

Zemlekopy (The shovel man). See 1271.

SAROYAN, William

1272. Besstrashny yunets na trapetsii (The daring young
man on the flying trapeze). Trans. by I. Romano-

SAROYAN, William (Continued)

vich. Int. Lit. (M.), 1935, No. 8, pp. 110-113. (s.)
From The daring young man on the flying trapeze.

SCHULTZ, James Willard

Collected works

1273. Sobraniye sochineni [collected works]. Edited by Yev.
Lann. Gosizdat., M. & L., 1929, 1930.

Separate publications

1274. Lovets orlov (Seizer of eagles). Trans. and adapted
by A. V. Krivtsova. Gosizdat., M. & L., 1930. 158
p., 10,000 c. Sob. soch., Vol. VIII. See 1273.
KL 31252.30 (n.)

1275. Oshibka odinokovo Bizona (Lone Bull's mistake). Trans.
by A. V. Krivtsova. Gosizdat., M. & L., 1930. 174 p.,
7000 c. Sob. soch., Vol. IV. See 1273. KL 19561.30 (n.)

Same. See 1279.

1276. S Indeitsami v skalistykh gorakh (With the Indians in
the Rockies). Trans. and adapted by A. V. Krivtsova.
Gosizdat., M. & L., 1930. 160 p., 10,000 c. Sob. soch.,
Vol. VI. See 1273. KL 17534.30 (n.)

Same. See 1279.

1277. Syn plemeni Navakhov (A son of the Navahos). Trans.
and adapted by A. V. Krivtsova. Gosizdat., M. & L.,
1929. 178 p., 7000 c. Sob. soch., Vol. II. See 1273.
KL 173.29 (n.)

1278. Same. 1930. 124 p., 15,000 c. KL 26298.30

Same. See 1279.

1279. V skalistykh gorakh [in the Rocky Mountains]. Trans.
and adapted by A. V. Krivtsova. Detizdat., M. & L.,
1940. 368 p., 10,000 c. KL 2719.40 (coll. n.)
Contents: S Indeitsami v skalistykh gorakh (With the
Indians in the Rockies). Syn plemeni Navakhov (A son
of the Navahos). Oshibka odinokovo Bizona (Lone
Bull's mistake).
A juvenile publication.

SCOTT, Leroy

1280. Sekretar professionalnovo soyuza (The walking dele-

gate). Trans. by S. Tsederbaum. Gosizdat., M., 1922.
440 p., 6000 c. KL 4927.22 (n.)

1281. Same. 1922. 440 p., 6000 c. KL 495.23

1282. Same. V.Ts.S.P.S., M., 1924. 93 p., 8000 c. KL 2056.24
Abridged.

1283. Same. 1924. 116 p., 5000 c. KL 21979.25

1284. Same. Abridged by Ye. V. Aleksandrova; foreword by
D. Gorbov. Novaya Moskva, M., 1925. 164 p., 8000 c.
KL 3747.25

1285. Same. Trans. by S. Tsederbaum. Kniga, M. & L., 1925.
284 p., 4150 c. KL 20305.25

1286. Same. Gosizdat., M. & L., 1927. 440 p., 50,000 c.
KL 10179.27

SHAW, Irwin

Moi butonchik (My green flower). See 1287.

1287. Novelly [short stories]. Trans. by N. Daruzes; introd.
by A. Abramov. Int. Lit. (M.), 1941, No. 3, pp. 68-86.
(coll. s.)
Contents: Uimis, Roki (Stop pushing, Rocky).
Zemlyanichnoye morozhenoye (Strawberry ice cream
soda). Pomoshchnik sherifa (Deputy sheriff). Moi
butonchik (My green flower).
From Sailor off The Bremen.

Pomoshchnik sherifa (Deputy sheriff). See 1287.

Uimis, Roki (Stop pushing, Rocky). See 1287.

Zemlyanichnoye morozhenoye (Strawberry ice cream
soda). See 1287.

Same. See 12.

SHERWOOD, Robert E., and Eric Keown

1288. Dvukhsotletiye trusa (The ghost goes west). Trans. and
adapted by V. Bluvshtein and N. Otten. Iskusstvo, M.,
1940. 98 p., 1075 c. KL 23356.40 (scenario)

1289. Privideniye otpravlyayetsya na zapad (The ghost goes
west). Trans. by V. O. Bluvshtein. Goskinoizdat, M.,
1940. 104 p., 5000 c. KL 13205.40 (scenario)

SHNEIDER [sic.]

1290. Amerikanskiye kinotsenarii: sbornik [American movie scenarios: a collection]. Trans. by Atasheva. Goskinoizdat, M., 1940. 260 p., 3000 c. KL 7575.40 This writer not identified. This is probably the name of the Russian compiler, since a collection of this kind does not seem to have been published in the United States.

SINCLAIR, Upton

Collected works

1291. Sobraniye sochineni [collected works]. Edited by V. A. Azov and A. N. Gorlin. Gosizdat., L., 1924, 1925, 1926. 12 vols.

1292. Sobraniye sochineni [collected works]. Mysl, L., 1925. 2 vols.
No editor was given. There are other Sinclair titles published by Mysl in this period which are probably part of this edition, but they were not so listed in KL.

1293. Polnoye sobraniye sochineni [complete collected works Introd. by V. M. Friche. ZIF, M. & L., 1925. Only one volume was listed in KL. See 1416.

1294. Sobraniye sochineni [collected works]. Edited by V. A. Aleksandrov and A. N. Gorlin. Priboi and Goslitizdat., L. & M., 1930, 1931, 1932, 1933. 11 vols.

Separate publications

1295. Ad (Hell). Trans. by S. V. Sh., edited by M. Lozinski and Yev. Zamyatin. Vsemir. Lit., M. & P., 1923. 165 p., 7150 c. KL 8705.23 (pl.)

1296. Same. Trans. from the manuscript by Vl. Morits; edited and with a foreword by P. S. Kogan. Krasnaya Nov, M., 1923. 157 p., 10,000 c. KL 13047.23

Same. See 1363 and 1291.

1297. Agent prezidenta (Presidential agent). Trans. by V. Stanevich. Novy Mir (M.), 1946, No. 7-8, pp. 137-183. (n.)
An excerpt.

1298. Amerikanskaya krov — sto protsentov (100%: the story

of a patriot). Trans. and abridged by I. I. Yasinski.
Krasnaya Nov, M., 1923. 110 p., 10,000 c. KL 6163.23
(n.)

1299. Amerikanskiye birzheviki (The moneychangers). Trans.
by E. K. Pimenova. Petrograd, P., 1923. 200 p.,
4000 c. KL 11800.23 (n.)

1300. Same. 1924. 199 p., 5000 c. KL 10218.24

1301. Artur Stirling — dolina tenei (The journal of Arthur
Stirling). Trans. by V. I. Smetanich. Mysl, L. & M.,
1924. 200 p., 6000 c. KL 6455.24 (n.)

1302. Same. 1925. 172 p., 7000 c. KL 1112.25

1303. Avtomobilny korol (The flivver king). Trans. by S.
Gurevich. Goslitizdat., M., 1938. 220 p., 20,000 c.
KL 22910.38 (n.)

1304. Same. Trans. by M. Urnov. Int. Lit. (M.), 1938. No. 5,
pp. 3-88.
An excerpt.

1305. Same. Goslitizdat., M., 1939. 268 p., 10,000 c.
KL 15202.39

1306. Bill Porter (Bill Porter: a drama of O. Henry in
prison). Kras. Prolet., M. & L., 1926. 95 p., 15,000
c. KL 3944.26 (pl.)

1307. Boston (Boston). Trans. by Z. Vershinina and A. V.
Krivtsova; foreword by Dzh. Dzhermanetto. Gosizdat.,
M. & L., 1930. 2 vols., 467 and 441 p., 10,000 c.
KL 7892.30 (n.)

1308. Chashcha (The jungle). Trans. and adapted by P.
Konstantinov. Krasnaya Nov, M., 1923. 148 p.,
25,000 c. KL 4937.23 (n.)

1309. Chelovek vtorykh etazhe (The second-story man).
Trans. by N. Galperin. Mol. Gvard. (M.), 1926, No. 6,
pp. 3-10. (pl.)
From Plays of protest.

1310. Chetyresta (The metropolis). Edited by V. A. Azov.
Petrograd, P. & M., 1924. 228 p., 5000 c. KL 980.24
(n.)

1311. Same. 1924. 228 p., 5000 c. KL 3850.24

SINCLAIR, Upton (Continued)

1312. Same. 1925. 228 p., 6000 c. KL 3098.25

1313. Chyorny vlastelin (King Coal). With an introd. by Dr.
Georg Brandes. Trans. by D. I. Nosovich. Gosizdat.,
L., 1926. 427 p., 5000 c. Sob. soch., Vol. VI.
See 1291. KL 7475.26 (n.)

1314. Same. 1927. 424 p., 2500 c. KL 15026.27

1315. Same. 1927. 424 p., 2500 c. KL 16394.27

1316. Same. [no translator given]. Ts.K.S.T., M., 1928.
103 p., 120,000 c. KL 4861.28
Abridged

1317. Same. 1928. 103 p., 20,000 c. KL 5929.28

1318. Same. With an introd. by Georg Brandes. Trans. by
D. I. Nosovich. Priboi, L., 1930. 432 p., 10,000 c.
Sob. soch., Vol. III. See 1294. KL 18411.30

1319. Debri (The jungle). Proletari, Kharkov, 1923. 306 p.,
5000 c. Pechat i Rev., 1924, No. 3, p. 256.

1320. Same. Trans. by I. D. Markuson. Mysl, L., 1924.
236 p., 8000 c. KL 12549.24

1321. Same. Trud i Kniga, M., 1925. 236 p., 8000 c.
KL 14099.24

1322. Same. Trans. and abridged by P. Zaitsev. V.Ts.S.P.S.
M., 1925. 155 p., 5000 c. KL 5577.25

1323. Same. [no translator given]. Priboi, L., 1925. 269
p., 10,000 c. KL 12297.25

1324. Dengi (The moneychangers). Priboi, P., 1923. 144
p., 10,000 c. KL 12405.23 (n.)

1325. Same. 1924. 144 p., 6000 c. KL 137.24

1326. Same. 1924. 144 p., 8000 c. KL 13271.24

1327. Same. Trud i Kniga, M., 1925. 201 p., 8000 c. KL 1635.25

1328. Same. Mysl, L., 1925. 201 p., 5000 c. KL 2337.25

1329. Dengi pishut! (Money writes). Trans. from the manu-
script by B. Ya. Zhukovetski; foreword by S. S.
Dinamov. Gosizdat., M. & L., 1928. 296 p., 4000 c.
KL 15477.28 (coll. essays)

1330. 2000-i god (The millenium: a comedy of the year
       2000). Trans. by B. L.   Vsemir. Lit., M., 1924. 207
       p., 7000 c. KL 10219.24 (n.)

Dvoye. See 1.

1331. Dzhimmi Khiggins (Jimmie Higgins). Trans. by M. A.
       Dyakonov. Gosizdat., P., 1921. 328 p., 15,000 c.
       KL 2468.22 (n.)

1332. Same. 1923. 315 p., 7000 c. KL 7672.23

1333. Same. Trans. by M. A. Dyakonov. A new illustrated
       edition. Krasnaya Nov, M., 1922. 242 p., 10,000 c.
       KL 9984.22

1334. Same. 1924. 236 p., 10,000 c. KL 3194.24

1335. Same. Trans. by M. A. Dyakonov. Volna, Arkangelsk,
       1923. 32 p., [no. of copies omitted]. KL 1732.23
       An excerpt.

1336. Same. Gosizdat., L., 1924. 320 p., 10,000 c. Sob. soch.,
       Vol. I. See 1291. KL 13272.24

1337. Same. 1927. 320 p., 1750 c. KL 18570.27

1338. Same. 1927. 320 p., 3250 c. KL 19326.27

1339. Same. Trud, Klintsy, 1925. In two parts; 129 p. and
       144 p., 4000 c. each. KL 8556.25, KL 13833.25

1340. Same. Trans. by E. K. Pimenova. Mysl, L., 1925.
       357 p., 10,000 c. KL 14102.25

1341. Same. Trans. and abridged by P. Zaitsev. V.Ts.S.P.S.,
       M., 1925. 155 p., 5000 c. KL 3096.25

1342. Same. Trans. by E. K. Brodersen. Priboi, L., 1925.
       224 p., 10,000 c. KL 13834.25

1343. Same. Trans. and abridged by M. A. Dyakonov. Gosiz-
       dat., M. & L., 1928. 181 p., 20,000 c. KL 5928.28

1344. Same. [no translator given]. Ts.K.S.T., M., 1928.
       109 p., 100,000 c. KL 20639.28

1345. Same. Trans. by M. A. Dyakonov; foreword by G.
       Munblit. Gosizdat., M. & L., 1930. 362 p., 100,000 c.
       KL 15183.30

1346. Same. Trans. by M. A. Dyakonov. Priboi, L., 1930.

SINCLAIR, Upton (Continued)

398 p., 10,000 c. Sob. soch., Vol. I. See 1294.
KL 1650.30

1347. Same. Goslitizdat., L. & M., 1933. 198 p., 40,250 c.
KL 21247.33

1348. Dzhimmi Khiggins v Rossii [Jimmie Higgins in
Russia]. Gudok, M., 1925. 32 p., 40,000 c. KL 4679.25
An excerpt from Jimmie Higgins.

1349. Dzhungli (The jungle). 2nd edition. Gosizdat., M. & P.,
1923. 179 p., 7000 c. KL 4936.23 (n.)

1350. Same. Introd. by N. Raivid. Uralskaya Kniga, Yekater-
inburg, 1924. 288 p., 5000 c. KL 8212.24

1351. Same. Trans. by D. M. Gorfinkel. Gosizdat., L., 1925.
384 p., 10,000 c. Sob. soch., Vol. IV. See 1291. KL 15451.25

1352. Same. Trans. and abridged by D. Gorfinkel. Gosizdat.,
M. & L., 1928. 142 p., 15,000 c. KL 9939.28

1353 Same. [no translator given]. Gudok, M., 1928. In
three parts, published separately: Part 1, pp. 1-128;
Part 2, pp. 129-256; Part 3, pp. 257-365; 40,000 c.
each. KL 15504.28, KL 15874.28, KL 17004.28

1354. Same. Trans. by D. M. Gorfinkel. Priboi, L., 1930.
456 p., 10,000 c. Sob. soch., Vol. IV. See 1294.
KL 24200.30

1355. Gusiny shag (The goose-step). Trans. from the man-
uscript. Krasnaya Nov, M., 1924. 210 p., 8000 c.
KL 4996.24 (coll. essays).
Abridged.

1356. Gusyata (The goslings). Trans. and abridged by Ye. I.
Fortunato. Ye. V. Vysotski, L., 1924. 182 p., 4000 c.
KL 10759.24 (coll. essays)

Gvozd. See 1363 and 1291.

1357. "I votsarilos na tysyachu let" (The millenium). Kniga,
L. & M., 1925. 148 p., 4000 c. KL 14099.24 (n.)

1358. Iskatel pravdy (Samuel the seeker) and Tyuremnyie
solovushki (Singing jailbirds). Trans. by V. A. Azov
and A. N. Gorlin. Gosizdat., L., 1925. 334 p., 10,000
c. Sob. soch., Vol. III. See 1291. KL 13839.25 (coll.
n., pl.)

1359. Iskatel pravdy (Samuel the seeker). Trans. by V. A.
Aleksandrov. Tsar Midas (King Midas). Trans. by
M. N. Matveyeva. Priboi, L., 1930. 414 p., 10,000 c.
Sob. soch., Vol. VI. See 1294. KL 29865.30 (coll. n.)

1360. Iskusstvo mammony (Mammonart). Priboi, L., 1925.
278 p., 10,000 c. KL 18303.25 (coll. essays)

1361. Ispytaniya lyubvi (Love's pilgrimage). Trans. by
M. I. Brusyanina; edited by Shtakelberg-Popova.
Vsemir. Lit., M. & P., 1923. 260 p., 7150 c.
KL 10642.23 (n.)
Abridged.

1362. Same. Trans. by I. D. Markuson. Mysl, L., 1925.
295 p., 8000 c. KL 10444.25

1363. Ispytaniya lyubvi (Love's pilgrimage). Trans. by M. I.
Brusyanina. Ad (Hell). Trans. by S. V. Sh. Gvozd
[nail; not identified]. Trans. by K. M. Zhikhareva.
Gosizdat., M. & L., 1926. 544 p., 5000 c. Sob. soch.,
Vol. VIII. See 1291. KL 13229.26 (coll. n., pl.)

1364. Same. 1927. 544 p., 2500 c. KJ. 10889.27

1365. Same. 1927. 544 p., 2500 c. KL 11189.27

1366. Ispytaniya lyubvi (Love's pilgrimage). Trans. by M.
Volosov. Len. GIKhL., L. & M., 1932. 350 p., 5140 c.
KL 18148.32

1367. Istoriya amerikanskovo millionera (A captain of industry). Polyarnaya Zvezda, P., 1923. 85 p., 5000 c.
KL 4300.23 (n.)

1368. Same. Trans. by S. K-ova. Krasnaya Nov, L., 1924.
83 p., 5000 c. KL 3849.24 (n.)

Same. See 1457 and 1291.

Same. See 1447 and 1294.

1369. Khristos v Uestern-Siti (They call me Carpenter).
Trans. by Anna Ostrogorskaya. Petrograd, P. & M.,
1923. 132 p., 8000 c. KL 4935.23 (n.)

1370. Kipyashchi gorshok (The pot boiler). Trans. by K.
Zhikhareva; edited by K. Chukovski. Vsemir. Lit.,
M., 1925. 111 p., 5000 c. KL 1113.25 (pl.)

1371. Kniga o zhizni (The book of life). Trans. by O. Ya.
Skitalits-Ukovlev. Vopl o spravedlivosti (The cry

SINCLAIR, Upton (Continued)

for justice). Trans. by E. I. Vygodskaya. Gosizdat., M. & L., 1926. 464 p., 5000 c. Sob. soch., Vol. IX. See 1291. KL 16146.26 (coll. essays, anthology) The cry for justice is an anthology of the literature of social protest edited by Sinclair.

1372. Same. 1927. 464 p., 2500 c. KL 10529.27

1373. Same. 1927. 464 p., 2500 c. KL 11483.27

1374. Komicheskaya utopiya: 2000-i god (The millenium: a comedy of the year 2000). M. Yu. Levidov, editor of translation. Mezhrabpom, M., 1924. 174 p., 15,000 c. KL 11451.24 (n.)

1375. Korol Midas (King Midas). Trans. by M. N. Matveyeva Mysl, L., 1924. 195 p., 4000 c. KL 3851.24 (n.)

1376. Same. 1925. Introd. by A. Danilov. 208. p., 8000 c. KL 16627.25

1377. Korol Ugol (King Coal). Trans. by S. S. Nesterova. Gosizdat., M. & P., 1923. 437 p., 15,000 c. KL 4933.23 (n.)

1378. Same. Trans. by B. Yanovski; edited by Gr. Nemnikov. Trud i Kniga, M., 1924. 420 p., 3000 c. KL 11449.24 (n.)

1379. Same. 1925. 420 p., 5000 c. KL 6513.25

1380. Same. Mysl, L., 1924. 420 p., 7000 c. KL 11453.24

1381. Same. Mysl, L., 1925. 420 p., 5000 c. Sob. soch., Vol. V. See 1292. KL 6514.25

1382. Same. Trans. by S. S. Nesterova. Trud, Klintsy, 1925. In three parts, published separately: Part 1, pp. 1-96; Part 2, pp. 97-192; Part 3, pp. 193-288; 3500 c. each. KL 20301-02.25, KL 21976.25

1383. Same. [no translator given]. V.Ts.S.P.S., M., 1925. 211 p., 5000 c. KL 4678.25

1384. Same. Trans. and revised by Z. V. Rabochaya Gazeta, M., 1925. 208 p., 60,000 c. KL 3800.25

1385. Same. [no translator given]. Introd. by Georg Brandes. Priboi, L., 1925. 260 p., 10,130 c. KL 13835.25 The introduction by George Brandes is part of the

American edition (New York: Macmillan, 1917) from which this translation was made.

1386. Same. Trans. by S. G. Zaimovski. Goslitizdat., M. & L., 1931. 413 p., 100,000 c. KL 12147.31

1387. Malaya stal (Little steel). Industriya sotsializma (M.), 1939, No. 1, pp. 53-57. ZL 16341.39 (n.) An excerpt.

1388. Manassa (Manassas). Trans. by I. Ye. Khorodchinskaya. Petrograd, L. & M., 1925. 252 p., 5000 c. KL 336.25 (n.)

1389. Mashina (The machine). Trans. by P. Mandelshtat. Gosizdat., M. & P., 1923. 84 p., 3000 c. KL 1733.23 (pl.) From Plays of protest.

1390. Same. Trans. by A. V. Krivtsova; edited by Yev. Lann. ZIF, M., 1924. 85 p., 5000 c. KL 3195.24

1391. Maunten-Siti (Mountain City). Trans. by M. Volosov. Goslitizdat., M. & L., 1931. 481 p., 10,000 c. KL 13313.31 (n.)

1392. Same. 1932. 442 p., 8200 c. Sob. soch., Vol. X. See 1294. KL 29420.32

1393. Menya zovut plotnikom (They call me Carpenter). Trans. by S. I. Tsederbaum. Kniga, M. & P., 1923. 252 p., 5000 c. KL 4934.23 (n.)

1394. Same. Trans. by M. M. Birinski. Mysl, L., 1925. 171 p., 8000 c. KL 14103.24

1395. Millioner i pisatel (A millionaire and an author). Mol. Gvard., (M.), 1922, No. 4-5, pp. 295-298. (essay) A chapter from The brass check.

Moi sobralya po peru (The brass check). See 1453 and 1291.

1396. Neft (Oil!). Trans. by V. A. Barbasheva and Ye. K. Gdaleva; edited by Z. A. Vershinina. Gosizdat., M. & L., 1926. Part I, 307 p., 4000 c. KL 15495.26 (n.)

1397. Same. 1928. 315 p., 7000 c. KL 3505.28

1398. Same. 1928. Part II, 539 p., 10,000 c. KL 6799.28

Same. See 1457. and 1291.

SINCLAIR, Upton (Continued)

1399. Same. Trans. by V. A. Barbasheva. Goslitizdat., L. & M., 1932. 739 p., 7200 c. Sob. soch., Vol. XI-XII. See 1294. KL 277.33

1400. No pasaran: oni ne proidut! (No pasaran! They shall not pass). Trans. by A. Gavrilova. Goslitizdat., M., 1937. 157 p., 50,000 c. KL 24232.37 (n.)

1401. Same. [no translator given]. 1937. 68 p., 210,000 c. KL 26543.37
Probably an excerpt or an abridgment.

1402. Same. Trans. by A. Gavrilova. Znamya (M.), 1937, No. 6, pp. 35-132. ZL 28972.37

1403. Same. Trans. by S. Gurevich; postscript by A. Mingulin. Zhurn. Gaz. Obyed., M., 1937. 206 p., [no. of copies omitted]. KL 22252.37

1404. Same. Trans. by A. Gavrilova. Oblastnoye Izdatelstvo (Arkhangelsk), Arkhangelsk, 1937. 147 p., 5000 c. KL 2313.37

1405. Okovy sbrosheny (The jungle). Trans. by Zin. Lvovski. Mysl, P., 1923. 237 p., 4000 c. KL 13048.23 (n.) According to a note in KL, this volume is the conclusion of The jungle.

1406. Otets semeistva (The pot boiler). Mezhrabpom., M., 1925. 180 p., 10,000 c. KL 11223.25 (pl.)

1407. Porchennyie (Damaged goods). Trans. by D. P. Nosovich; introd. by L. M. Vasilevski. Mysl, L., 1925. 146 p., 8000 c. KL 3801.25 (n.)

1408. Poyushchiye uzniki (Singing jailbirds). Trans. by B. I. Yarkho. Krug, M., 1925. 108 p., 6000 c. KL 5578.25 (pl.)

1409. Predatel (100%: the story of a patriot). Trans. and adapted by Petrova. Gosizdat., M., 1924. 64 p., 25,000 c. KL 13271.24 (n.)
Abridged.

1410. Priklyucheniya malenkovo sotsialista (Jimmie Higgins). Trans. and abridged by Yu. Slyozkin. Rabochaya Moskva, M., 1926. 68 p., 9000 c. KL 8695.26 (n.)

1411. Prints Gagen (Prince Hagen). Trans. by A. V.
Luchinskaya. Petrograd, P. & M., 1923. 99 p., 5000
c. KL 6162.23 (pl.)
From Plays of protest.

Same. See 1451 and 1291.

1412. Prishestviye Khrista v leto 1921-e (They call me
Carpenter). Mol. Gvard., M., 1924. 148 p., 5000 c.
KL 10217.24 (n.)

1413. Pyesy [plays]. Trans. by A. d'Aktil. Priboi, L.,
1925. 199 p., 6000 c. KL 335.25 (coll. pl.)
Contents not listed in KL.

1414. Rimskiye kanikuly (Roman holiday). Introd. by S.
Rodzevich. Len. GIKhL., L. & M., 1933. 290 p.,
5200 c. KL 7889.33 (n.)

1415. Samuel iskatel (Samuel, the seeker). Trans. by A. V.
Krivtsova; edited by Yev. Lann. Novaya Moskva, M.,
1924. 284 p., 4000 c. KL 2054.24 (n.)

1416. Same. ZIF, M. & L., 1925. 320 p., 10,000 c. Pol. sob.
soch., Vol. III., Book I. See 1293. KL 7617.25

1417. Same. [no translator given]. V.Ts.S.P.S., M., 1925.
129 p., 10,000 c. KL 1111.25

1418. Same. [no translator given]. Preface by A. Ts.
Gudok, M., 1925. In three parts: Part 1, 30 p.; Part
2, 30 p.; Part 3, 31 p.; 50,000 c. KL 13836.25

1419. Sekretar govoruna — pisma Mem k mame (The spokes-
man's secretary; being the letters of Mame to mom).
Trans. by L. N. Vsevolodskaya; edited by S. A.
Lopatov. Gosizdat., M. & L., 1927. 191 p., 15,000 c.
KL 6780.28 (coll. essays)

1420. Semyuel — iskatel (Samuel, the seeker). Trans. by D.
Ye. Leikhtenberg; edited by D. O. Glikman. Mysl,
L., 1924. 204 p., 5000 c. KL 4378.24

1421. Same. 1925. 227 p., 10,000 c. KL 2338.25

1422. Sever i yug (Manassas). Trans. by N. F. Davydova.
Gosizdat., M. & L., 1926. 368 p., 5000 c. Sob. soch.,
Vol. XI. See 1291. KL 17971.26 (n.)

1423. Same. 1927. 368 p., 2500 c. KL 11747.27

SINCLAIR, Upton (Continued)

1424. Same. 1927. 368 p., 2500 c. KL 11744.27

1425. Same. Adatped and annotated by R. Bershadski. ZIF, M., 1928. 168 p., 50,000 c. KL 15127.28

1426. Same. Trans. by N. Davydova. Goslitizdat., L. & M., 1931. 444 p., 10,000 c. Sob soch., Vol. VIII. See 1294. KL 11737.31

1427. Silviya (Sylvia). Trans. by A. F. Damanskaya. Gosizdat., M., 1922. 273 p., 3000 c. KL 5890.22 (n.)

1428. Same. 1923. 271 p., 7000 c. KL 1279.23

1429. Same. Trans. by L. Vsevolodskaya. Petrograd, L. & M., 1925. 350 p., 6000 c. KL 15450.25

1430. Silviya (Sylvia). Trans. by A. F. Damanskaya. Zamuzhestvo Silvii (Sylvia's marriage). Trans. by N. F. Davydova. Gosizdat., M. & L., 1926. 436 p., 5000 c. Sob. soch., Vol. X. See 1291. KL 16796.26 (coll. n.)

1431. Same. 1927. 436 p., 2500 c. KL 11746.27

1432. Same. 1927. 436 p., 2500 c. KL 11745.27

1433. Silviya (Sylvia). Trans. by A. F. Damanskaya. Priboi, L., 1927. 375 p., 15,000 c. KL 17932.27

1434. Silviya (Sylvia). A. N. Gorlin, editor of translation. Silviya zamuzhem (Sylvia's marriage). Trans. by N. F. Davydova. Goslitizdat., L. & M., 1931. 510 p., 10,000 c. Sob. soch., Vol. VII. See 1294. KL 29983.31 (coll. n.)

1435. Silviya zamuzhem (Sylvia's marriage). Trans. by N. D. Volnin. Mysl, L., 1925. 232 p., 8000 c. Sob. soch., Vol. II. See 1292. KL 10445.25 (n.)

Same. See 1434 and 1294.

Solovi tyuremnyie (Singing jailbirds). See 1455 and 1294.

Spekulyanty (The moneychangers). See 1453 and 1291.

1436. Same. Trans. by D. M. Gorfinkel, Ye. I. Patterson, N. M. Rachinskaya. Gosizdat., M. & L., 1927. 498 p., 2500 c. KL 11484.27 (n.)

1437. Srazheniye [battle]. Propaganda i Agitatsiya (L.), 1938,
No. 5, pp. 41-45. ZL 14932.38
An excerpt from No pasaran!

1438. Sto protsentov (100%: the story of a patriot). Trans.
by L. Gausman; edited by D. M. Gorfinkel and K. I.
Chukovski. Vsemir. Lit., M. & P., 1923. 315 p.,
10,000 c. KL 2649.23 (n.)

1439. Same. 2nd revised ed., 1924. 316 p., 7150 c.
KL 12550.24

1440. Same. Trans. by K. N. Chetverikov. Trud i Kniga,
M., 1924. 293 p., 3000 c. KL 11450.24 (n.)

1441. Same. 1925. 293 p., 5000 c. KL 10442.25

1442. Same. Mysl, L., 1924. 293 p., 7000 c. KL 11452.24

1443. Same. 1925. 293 p., 5000 c. KL 10443.25

1444. Same. Trans. by L. M. Gausman. Gosizdat., L. & M.,
1925. 299 p., 10,000 c. Sob. soch., Vol. II, See 1291.
KL 7616.25

1445. Same. [no translator given]. Foreword by G. Yakubov-
ski. V.Ts.S.P.S., M., 1926. 161 p., 5000 c.
KL 16626.25
Abridged.

1446. Same. Edited by P. S. Kogan, I. N. Kubikov, and N. K.
Piksanov. Gosizdat., M. & L., 1928. 178 p., 20,000 c.
KL 5453.28

1447. Sto protsentov (100%: the story of a patriot). Trans.
by L. M. Gausman. Istoriya amerikanskovo millionera
(A captain of industry). Trans. by I. R. Gerbach.
Priboi, L., 1930. 394 p., 5000 c. Sob. soch., Vol. II.
See 1294. KL 4498.30

1448. Same. 1930. 394 p., 5000 c. KL 18411.30

1449. Sto protsentov: istoriya amerikanskovo patriota
(100%: the story of a patriot). S. S. Zayaitski, editor of
translation. Moskovski Rabochi, M., 1922. 230 p.,
10,000 c. KL 9983.22

1450. Stolitsa (The metropolis). Trans. by M. V. Vatson
and S. Titova. Mysl, L., 1925. 271 p., 8000 c.
KL 10446.25 (n.)

SINCLAIR, Upton (Continued)

1451. Stolitsa (The metropolis). Trans. by I. R. Gerbach. Prints Gagen (Prince Hagen). Trans. by M. N. Matveyeva. Gosizdat., L., 1925. 432 p., 10,000 c. Sob. soch., Vol. V. See 1291. KL 20303.25 (coll. n., pl.)

1452. Stolitsa (The metropolis). Trans. by I. R. Gerbach. Priboi, L., 1930. 372 p., 10,000 c. Sob. soch., Vol. V. See 1294. KL 1430.31

1453. Strannoye proisshestviye v Uestern-Siti (They call me Carpenter). Trans. by D. M. Gorfinkel. Spekulyanty (The moneychangers). Trans. by Ye. I. Patterson and N. M. Rachinskaya. Moi sobratya po peru (The brass check). Trans. by D. M. Gorfinkel. Gosizdat., L., 1926. 498 p., 5000 c. Sob. soch., Vol. VII. See 1291. KL 7476.26 (coll. n., essays)

1454. Same. 1927. 498 p., 2500 c. KL 10528.27

1455. Strannoye proisshestviye v Uestern-Siti (They call me Carpenter). Zolotoi vek (The millenium: a comedy of the year 2000). Solovi tyuremnyie (Singing jailbirds). Trans. by D. M. Gorfinkel. Goslitizdat., L. & M., 1931. 469 p., 10,000 c. Sob. soch., Vol. IX. See 1294. KL 2455.32 (coll. n., pl.)

1456. Svetoprestavleniye: komediya 2000-vo goda (The millenium: a comedy of the year 2000). Trans. by S. Fortunato. Seyatel, L., 1925. 206 p., 5000 c. KL 14101.24 (n.)

1457. Tsar Midas (King Midas). Zolotoi vek (The millenium: a comedy of the year 2000). Istoriya amerikanskovo millionera (A captain of industry). Neft (Oil!). With a biographical sketch of Sinclair by L. M. Vaisenberg. Gosizdat., M. & L., 1927. 631 p., 5000 c. Sob. soch., Vol. XII. See 1291. KL 11190.27 (coll. n.)

1458. Same. 1927. 631 p., 2500 c. KL 1324.27

Tsar Midas (King Midas). See 1359 and 1294.

1459. Tsarstvo korolya uglya (King Coal). Novaya Moskva, M., 1925. 248 p., 8000 c. KL 10441.25 (n.) An adaptation.

1460. Tyuremnyie ptitsy poyut (Singing jailbirds). With a postscript by Upton Sinclair. Trans. by A. Shtusser;

foreword by V. Friche; songs adapted by D. Gorbov.
Trud i Kniga, M., 1925. 94 p., 500 c. KL 13840.25
(pl.)

1461. Tyuremnyie solovushki (Singing jailbirds). Trans. by
V. A. Azov and A. N. Gorlin. Gosizdat., L., 1925.
171 p., 7000 c. KL 12298.25 (pl.)

Same. See 1358 and 1291.

1462. V poiskakh pravdy (Samuel, the seeker). Priboi, L.,
1924. 130 p., 10,000 c. KL 3848.24 (n.)

1463. Same. 1924. 130 p., 6000 c. KL 10757.24

1464. Vor (The second-story man). Trans. by Zelikov.
Teakinopechat, M., 1928. 16 p., 10,000 c.
KL 17949.28 (pl.)
From Plays of protest.

1465. Vygody religii (The profits of religion). Trans. by A.
I. Yakovlev; foreword by V. S. Rozhitsyn. Krasnaya
Nov, M., 1924. 155 p., 7000 c. KL 981.24 (coll.
essays)

1466. Same. 1924. 153 p., 15,000 c. KL 7638.24

1467. Yug i sever (Manassas). Priboi, L., 1924. 212 p.,
10,000 c. KL 10758.24 (n.)

1468. Same. 1925. 212 p., 10,000 c. KL 7615.25

1469. Same. Kras. Gaz., L., 1929. In two parts, published
separately: Part 1, 162 p.; Part 2, 148 p.; 105,000 c.
each. KL 4477.29, KL 5265.29

1470. Za khlebom i schastyem (Samuel, the seeker). Adapted
by A. Ostrogorskaya-Malkina. Gosizdat., M. & L.,
1926. 61 p., 35,000 c. KL 8694.26 (n.)

1471. Zamuzhestvo Silvii (Sylvia's marriage). Trans. by
E. K. Pimenova. Petrograd, L. & M., 1924. 240 p.,
6000 c. KL 4377.24 (n.)

1472. Same. 1924. 240 p., 5000 c. KL 6993.24

1473. Same. Trans. by Ye. Blagoveshchenskaya. Gosizdat.,
M., 1924. 337 p., 3000 c. KL 6994.24

Same. See 1430 and 1291.

1474. Zhizn na razvalinakh: komediya 2000-vo goda (The

SINCLAIR, Upton (Continued)

millenium: a comedy of the year 2000). Trans. by
A. d'Aktil. Priboi, L., 1925. 109 p., 7000 c.
KL 3097.25 (n.)

1475. Same. 1925. 109 p., 6000 c. KL 17375.25

1476. Zolotoi vek (The millenium: a comedy of the year 2000).
Trans. by N. M. Rachinskaya, M. N. Matveyeva, I. P.
Gerbach, Ye. K. Gdaleva, V. A. Barbasheva. Gosizdat.,
M. & L., 1927. 598 p., 2500 c. KL 11482.27 (coll. n.)
According to Kl this volume contains other novels, but
the titles are not listed.

Same. See 1457 and 1291.

Same. See 1455 and 1294.

1477. Zuby drakona (Dragon's teeth). Trans. by D. Gorbov
and V. Kurell. Int. Lit. (M.), 1942, No. 11, pp. 12-65
(n.)
An excerpt.

1478. Same. Sovetskaya Kolyma, Magadan, 1943. 192 p.,
5000 c. KL 9144.44

1479. Zverinets [menagerie; not identified]. Trans. by T.
Shchepkina-Kupernik. Zvezda (M. & L.), 1924, No. 3,
p. 104.

SINCLAIR, Upton (editor)

1480. Krik o spravedlivosti (The cry for justice). Trans. by
E. K. Pimenova and T. A. Bogdanovich. Mysl, L.,
1925. 296 p., 5100 c. KL 15452
An anthology of the literature of social protest, edited
by Sinclair.

Vopl o spravedlivosti (The cry for justice). See 1371
and 1291.

SMEDLEY, Agnes

Ballada o semi mostakh (Ballad of the seven bridges).
See 1489.

1481. Bandit (The bandit). Trans. by P. Okhrimenko. Kras.
Nov (M.), 1934, No. 1, pp. 134-46. ZL 11491.34 (sk.)
From Chinese destinies.

Banditskaya territoriya (A commissar makes a report). See 1489.

1482. Doch zemli (Daughter of earth). Trans. by P. Okhrimenko. ZIF, M. & L., 1930. 294 p., 10,000 c. KL 9290.30 (n.)

1483. Same. Goslitizdat., M. & L., 1930. 280 p., 5000 c. KL 14917.31

Dva epizoda (White episode). See 1493.

1484. Geroi sovetskovo Kitaya [heroes of Red China]. Trans. by P. Okhrimenko; introd. by A. Khamadana. Goslitizdat., M., 1936. 365 p., 50,000 c. KL 18670.36 (coll. sk.) Contains Chinese destines and China's Red Army marches.

1485. Kitaiskiye sudby (Chinese destinies). Trans. by P. Okhrimenko. Goslitizdat., M. & L., 1934. 186 p., 7000 c. KL 12858.34 (coll. sk.)

1486. Padeniye Shanpo (The fall of Shangpo). Trans. by L. Kislova. Int. Lit. (M.), 1933, No. 5, pp. 83-91. (sk.) From Chinese destinies.

1487. Pyat let (The five years). Trans. from the manuscript by N. Georgelevskaya. Int. Lit. (M.), 1933, No. 2, pp. 87-93. (sk.) From Chinese destines.

1488. Rasskazy o Kitaiskoi krasnoi armii (China's Red Army marches). Trans. by P. Okhrimenko. Znamya (M.), 1934, No. 6, pp. 68-91. ZL 35142.34 (coll. sk.) Selections. Titles not listed in ZL

1489. Same. Kras. Nov (M.), 1934, No. 5, pp. 142-170. ZL 37848.34 Contents: Razvedchiki (Scouts). Banditskaya territoriya (A commissar makes a report). Shinkanshan (Ching-Kangshan). Ballada o semi mostakh (Ballad of the seven bridges).

1490. Same. [no translator given]. In. Rab., M., 1935. 191 p., [no. of copies omitted]. KL 945.36 Contents not listed in KL.

1491. Same. Trans. by P. Okhrimenko. Goslitizdat., M., 1935. 328 p., 15,000 c. KL 7257.35

SMEDLEY, Agnes (Continued)

1492. Same. Goslitizdat., M., 1935. 95 p., 150,000 c.
      KL 16088.35
      Selections. Titles not listed in KL.

1493. Razvedchiki (Scouts) and Dva epizoda (White episode).
      Inter. Molodyozhi (M.), 1934, No. 11-12, pp. 61-64.
      ZL 1852.35 (coll. sk.)
      From China's Red Army marches.

      Razvedchiki (Scouts). See 1489.

1494. Shankhaiski kaleidoskop (A moving picture of
      Shanghai). Trans. by P. Okhrimenko. 30 Dnei (L.), 1934,
      No. 3, pp. 3-8. ZL 19199.34 (sk.)
      From Chinese destinies.

      Shinkanshan (Ching-Kangshan). See 1489.

1495. Smert Li-Keya (The death of Li-Kwei). Trans. by
      P. Okhrimenko. Izvestiya (M.), 1934, No. 102, p. 6.
      ZL 120.34 (sk.)
      From China's Red Army marches.

1496. Soldaty (Soldiers). Trans. by P. Okhrimenko. Znamya
      (M.), 1934, No. 3, pp. 135-144. ZL 23774.34 (sk.)
      From Chinese destinies.

      Synovni bunt (A Chinese son rebels). See 5.

      Vdova muchenika (The martyr's widow). See 5.

SMITTER, Wessel

1497. Detroit (F.O.B. Detroit). Trans. by P. Vladimirov.
      Industriya Sotsializma (M.), 1940, No. 4, pp. 48-55;
      No. 5, pp. 48-55; No. 6, pp. 50-56. ZL 23053.40 (n.)
      Excerpts.

SPIVAK, John

1498. Negr iz Dzhordzhii (Georgia nigger). With a foreword
      by Walt Carmon and an introd. by Langston Hughes.
      Trans. by A. A. Gavrilova. Goslitizdat., M., 1933.
      175 p., 7000 c. KL 25735.33 (n.)

STEELE, Wilbur Daniel

1499. Syn ubitsy (The killer's son). Trans. by A. Krivtsova.

30 Dnei (L.), 1936, No. 2, pp. 37-49. ZL 16028.36
(s.)
From Land's end and other stories.

1500. Zima belovo konya (White horse winter). Trans. by
A. V. Krivtsova. Int. Lit. (M.), 1936, No. 2, pp. 74-
81. (s.)
From Land's end and other stories.

ŠTEFFENS, Lincoln

1501. Iz avtobiografii [from the autobiography]. Trans. by
N. Daruzes. Int. Lit. (M.), 1937, No. 12, pp. 146-166.
An excerpt from The autobiography of Lincoln Steffens.

1502. Malchik na loshadi (Boy on horseback). Detizdat., M.
& L., 1939. 96 p., 15,000 c. KL 23033.39 (autobiog.)
A juvenile publication. From The autobiography of
Lincoln Steffens.

STEINBECK, John

1503. Grozdya gneva (The grapes of wrath). Trans. by N.
Volzhina. Int. Lit. (M.), 1940, No. 1, pp. 5-85; No. 2,
pp. 87-133; No. 3-4, pp. 26-140. (n.)

1504. Same. Trans. by R. Rait. Zvezda (M. & L.), 1940, No.
3-4, pp. 159-186. ZL 35420.40
The concluding chapters.

1505. Same. Trans. by N. Volzhina; postscript by I.
Anisimov. Goslitizdat., M., 1940. 504 p., 25,000 c.
KL 2899.41

1506. Same. Trans. by N. Volzhina. Goslitizdat., M., 1941.
198 p., 300,000 c. KL 7641.41

1507. Luna zashla (The moon is down). Trans. by N.
Volzhina. Znamya (M.), 1943, No. 5-6, pp. 34-97. (n.)

1508. Same. Trans. by A. Belyayev. Ogonyok (M.), 1943,
No. 4, pp. 9-10; No. 5, pp. 11-12; No. 6, pp. 13-14;
No. 9, pp. 11-12; No. 10-11, pp. 11-12.
Excerpts.

1509. Nalyot (Raid). Trans. by Yu. Smirnov. Mol. Gvard.
(M.), 1940, No. 12, pp. 62-68. ZL 64133.40 (s.)
From The long valley.

STEINBECK, John (Continued)

1510. Nalyot (Raid) and Presvyataya Keti — devstvennitsa
(St. Katy the virgin). Trans. by R. Rait. Zvezda
(M. & L.), 1940, No. 1, pp. 109-119. ZL 25478.40 (coll. s.)
From The long valley.

Presvyataya Keti — devstvennitsa (St. Katy the virgin).
See 1510.

1511. Pyat tsentov za yashchik [five cents a box]. Trans.
by L. Nikitina. 30 Dnei (L.), 1940, No. 1, pp. 64-68.
ZL 15345.40
An excerpt from The grapes of wrath.

Ryzhi poni (The red pony). See 12.

STEVENS, James

Amerikanski gerkules. See 12.

1512. Drovosek Benyan (Paul Bunyan). Trans. by M. G.
Volosov and M. Ye. Levberg; edited by A. N. Gorlin.
Gosizdat., L., 1927. 330 p., 5000 c. KL 19328.27
(coll. s.)

1513. Sorvi-golova (Brawnyman). N. F. Davydova, editor
of translation. Priboi, L., 1927. 297 p., 7000 c.
KL 10180.27 (n.)

STEWART, Donald Ogden

1514. Istoriya chelovechestva v islozhennii tyoti Polli
(Aunt Polly's story of mankind). Trans. by Yev.
Lann. Gosizdat., M. & L., 1928. 152 p., 4000 c.
KL 6782.28 (coll. s.)

STOCKTON, Frank R.

1515. "Pokoinaya sestra yevo zheny" (His wife's deceased
sister). Trans. by P. Okhrimenko. Int. Lit. (M.),
1937, No. 2, pp. 132-137. (s.)
From The lady or the tiger.

1516. Reis vdovi (The widow's cruise). Trans. by P.
Okhrimenko. 30 Dnei (L.), 1937, No. 8, pp. 67-75.
ZL 38938.37 (s.)
From A story-teller's pack.

STONE, Irving

1517. Moryak v sedle (Sailor on horseback). Trans. by Ye.
      Kalashnikova. Int. Lit. (M.), 1939, No. 7-8, pp. 237-
      268. ZL 47521.39 (biog.)
      An excerpt.

STOWE, Harriet Beecher

1518. Begletsy (Uncle Tom's cabin). Trans. and adapted
      by N. Moguchi. Mol. Gvard., M. & L., 1930. 181 p.,
      10,000 c. KL 10764.30 (n.)
      Selected episodes.

1519. Khizhina dyadi Toma (Uncle Tom's cabin). Adapted
      by Ye. N. Vinogradskaya. Gosizdat., M. & L., 1926.
      80 p., 35,000 c. KL 1154.26 (n.)
      A juvenile publication. Abridged.

1520. Same. Adapted by A. Deich. Biblioteka Zhurnala
      "Ogonyok," M., 1928. 42 p., 3000 c. KL 2956.28
      Selected episodes.

1521. Same. Trans. and abridged by N. and M. Chukovski.
      Edited and with a foreword by K. Chukovski. Detizdat.,
      M. & L., 1941. 360 p., 50,000 c. KL 26188.40

STRIBLING, T. S.

1522. Drama krovi (Birthright). Trans. by V. Barbasheva.
      Gosizdat., M. & L., 1927. 256 p., 4000 c. KL 11485.27
      (n.)

1523. Krasny pesok (Red sand). Trans. by M. Volosov.
      Vremya, L., 1927. 245 p., 5150 c. KL 19329.27 (n.)

1524. Megafon (The sound wagon). Trans. by A. M.
      Karnaukhova. Int. Lit. (M.), 1940, No. 11-12, pp. 24-
      149 (n.)

1525. Tiftalou (Teeftallow). Trans. by M. G. Volosov.
      Vremya, L., 1926. 266 p., 4150 c. KL 21766.26 (n.)

1526. General Fombombo (Fombombo). Trans. by K.
      Syromyatnikov. Petrograd, L. & M., 1925. 280 p.,
      4000 c. KL 21980.25 (n.)

      Vyborny vagon (The sound wagon). See 13.

STRIBLING, T. S. (Continued)

1527. Yarki metall (Bright metal). Trans. by Mark Volosov. ZIF, M. & L., 1929. 320 p., 5000 c. KL 17425.29 (n.)

STRONG, Anna Louise

1528. Nepobedimy Kitai (One-fifth of mankind). Trans. by M. Volosov; edited by M. Bogoslovskaya. Goslitizdat., M., 1939. 274 p., 20,000 c. KL 5410.39 (history)

1529. Same. 1939. 68 p., 275,000 c. KL 7526.39 Excerpts.

STUART, Jesse

1530. Paltsy na nogakh (Toes). Trans. by P. Okhrimenko. 30 Dnei (L.), 1938, No. 6 pp. 71-79. ZL 28679.38 (s.) From Head o' W-Hollow.

SUBLETTE, Clifford MacClellan

1531. Krasny petushok (The scarlet cockerel). Trans. by A. F. Ravinskaya. Mysl, L., 1927. 232 p., 5000 c. KL 4160.27 (n.)

TARKINGTON, Booth

1532. Priklyucheniya Penroda (Penrod). Trans. by M. Gershenzon. Gosizdat., M. & L., 1929. 200 p., 7000 c. KL 5788.29 (n.) A juvenile publication

THORPE, T. B.

Bolshoi medved iz Arkanzasa (The big bear of Arkansaw). See 4.

TRAIN, Arthur

1533. Vtoraya luna [the second moon; not identified]. Trans. by D. G. Malis. Izdatelstvo Doma Kommuny Trudovoi Molodyozhi, L., 1924. 94 p., 5000 c. KL 13329.24 (n.)

TREADWELL, Sophie

1534. Mashinal (The life machine). Trans. from the manuscript by S. L. Bertenson; edited and with a foreword by Yu. Yuzovski. Vsekdram, M., 1933. 88 p., 500 c. KL 24448.33 (pl.)

1535. Same. [no translator given]. Teatr i dramaturgiya
(M.), 1933, No. 1, pp. 1-24. ZL 32280.33

TULLY, Jim

1536. Avtobiografiya brodyagi (Beggars of life). Trans. by
E. Patterson; edited by A. N. Gorlin. Gosizdat.,
M. & L., 1926. 196 p., 5000 c. KL 6179.26 (autobiog.)

1537. Teni lyudei (Shadows of men). Trans. by A. V. Krivtsova. Goslitizdat., M. & L., 1931. 200 p., 5000 c.
KL 23479.31 (coll. sk.)

1538. Ukratitel lvov (Circus parade). Trans. by A. V.
Krivtsova. Rabochaya Moskva, M., 1928. 64 p.,
170,000 c. KL 5461.28 (coll. sk.)
Selections. Contents not listed in KL.

TUPPER, Tristram

1539. Dzhorgensen (Jorgensen). Trans. by Mark Volosov.
Vremya, L., 1927. 164 p., 4150 c. KL 9835.27 (n.)

TWAIN, Mark (Samuel Langhorne Clemens)

Collected works

1540. Sobraniye sochineni [collected works]. Edited by
P. K. Guber and K. I. Chukovski. Gosizdat., M. & L.,
1927, 1928, 1929. 6 vols.

Separate publications

1541. Amerikanski pretendent (The American claimant).
Trans. by N. Kazas and I. Rents; foreword by S.
Dinamov. Biblioteka Zhurnala "Ogonyok," M., 1930.
160 p., 45,070 c. KL 809.31 (n.)

1542. Amerikanskiye rasskazy [American stories]. Introd.
by T. Silman. Goslitizdat., L., 1938. 68 p., 100,000 c.
KL 12876.38 (coll. s.)
Contents not listed in KL.

1543. Avtobiografiya (Mark Twain's autobiography). Trans.
by N. Daruzes. Int. Lit. (M.), 1935, No. 11, pp. 85-97;
1936, No. 1, pp. 92-103. ZL 2020.36
Excerpts.

1544. Bankovy bilet v million funtov sterlingov (The £1,000,-
000 bank-note). Trans. by A. Deich. Zhurn. Gaz.
Obyed., M., 1934. 62 p., 40,000 c. KL 25331.34 (s.)

TWAIN, Mark (Samuel Langhorne Clemens) (Continued)

1545. Bankovy bilet v 1000000 funtov sterlingov (The £1,000,000 bank-note). See 4.

1546. Chelovek podkupivshi Gedliburg (The man that corrupted Hadleyburg). Trans. by K. M. Zhikhareva. Seyatel, L., 1925. 80 p., 15,000 c. KL 21981.25 (n.)

1547. Dzhim Vulf i koty (Jim Wolf and the cats). Trans. by N. Daruzes. 30 Dnei (L.), 1936, No. 5, pp. 58-60. ZL 32381.36 (sk.)
From Mark Twain's autobiography.

1548. Fartuk na kabriolete: neskolko neskromny rasskaz [the apron on the cabriolet: a somewhat immodest story; not identified]. Trans. by N. Treneva. Int. Lit. (M.), 1935, No. 6, pp. 96-99. (s.)

1549. Gody uchenichestva (Mr. Clemens as apprentice to Mr. Ament). Trans. by N. Daruzes. Int. Lit. (M.), 1936, No. 4, pp. 119-122.
From Mark Twain's autobiography.

1550. Iz "Avtobiografii" [from the autobiography]. Trans. by N. Daruzes. Int. Lit. (M.), 1936, No. 5, pp. 144-150.
An excerpt from Mark Twain's autobiography.

1551. Same. Trans. by L. Nikitina. 30 Dnei (L.), 1940, No. 3-4, pp. 40-43. ZL 35421.40

1552. Izbrannyie proizvedeniya [selected words]. Introd. by A. Startsev. Goslitizdat., M., 1937. 508 p., 30,000 c. KL 8885.38 (coll. n., memoirs)
Contents: Priklyucheniya Toma Soiyera (The adventures of Tom Sawyer). Priklyucheniya Geklberri Finna (The adventures of Huckleberry Finn). Zhizn na Mississippi (Life on the Mississippi). This volume also contains a critical article, Mark Tven i Amerika [Mark Twain and America], by A. Startsev.

1553. Izbrannyie rasskazy [selected stories]. Trans. by S. G. Zaimovski. Goslitizdat., M., 1936. 413 p., 20,000 c. KL 2265.37 (coll. s.)
Contents not listed in KL.

1554. Same. [no translator given]. Detizdat., M. & L., 1939. 240 p., 15,000 c. KL 11267.39 (coll. s.)
A juvenile publication. Contents not listed in KL.

Kak menya vybirali v gubernatory (Running for governor). See 13.

Kak ya redaktiroval selsko-khozyaistvennuyu gazetu
(How I once edited an agricultural paper). See 1624.

1555. Lyubopytnaya uveselitelnaya ekskursiya (A curious
pleasure excursion). Trans. by P. Okhrimenko. 30
Dnei (L.), 1940, No. 3, pp. 37-39. ZL 35422.40 (s.)
From Sketches new and old.

1556. Lyudoyedstvo v poyezde (Cannibalism in the cars). M.
Senkevich, editor of translation. ZIF, M. & L., 1926.
32 p., 15,000 c. KL 4488.26 (coll. s.)
From Sketches new and old. Other titles not listed in
KL.

1557. Moi chasy (The great revolution in Pitcairn). Biblioteka Zhurnala "Ogonyok," M., 1929. 30 p., 65,000 c.
KL 8168.29 (coll. s.)
From The stolen white elephant. Other titles not
listed in KL.

Same. See 1624.

1558. Neizdannyie rasskazy [unpublished stories]. Trans.
by S. Zaimovski. Smekhach, L., 1926. 59 p., 30,000 c.
KL 17976.26 (coll. s.)
Contents not listed in KL.

1559. O duelyakh (About dueling). Trans. by N. Daruzes.
Int. Lit. (M.), 1936, No. 2, pp. 90-94. (sk.)
From Mark Twain's autobiography.

Pochemu ya podal v otstavku (The facts concerning
the recent resignation). See 1612.

1560. Pokhishcheniye belovo slona (The stolen white elephant).
Trans. by E. Vygodskaya. Gosizdat., M. & L., 1930.
48 p., 25,000 c. KL 28600.30 (coll. s.)
A juvenile publication. Other titles not listed in KL.

1561. Same. [no translator given]. Zhurn. Gaz. Obyed., M.,
1935. 46 p., 50,000 c. KL 25525.35 (coll. s.)
A juvenile publication. Other titles not listed in KL.

1562. Priklyucheniya Finna (The adventures of Huckleberry
Finn). V. Dinze, editor of translation. Kras. Gaz., L.,
1927. 252 p., 20,000 c. KL 17196.27 (n.)
A juvenile publication.

TWAIN, Mark (Samuel Langhorne Clemens) (Continued)

1563. Priklyucheniya Gekkelberri Finna (The adventures of Huckleberry Finn). Trans. by K. Chukovski. Gosizdat., M. & L., 1928. 372 p., 10,000 c. KL 1010.28

1564. Same. 1930. 372 p., 15,000 c. KL 26308.30

1565. Priklyucheniya Gekkelberri Finna i beglovo negra Dzhima (The adventures of Huckleberry Finn). Mol. Gvard., L., 1926. 206 p., 10,000 c. KL 14064.26 (n.) A juvenile publication. Abridged.

1566. Priklyucheniya Geklberri Finna (The adventures of Huckleberry Finn). P. K. Guber, editor of translation. Gosizdat., M. & L., 1927. 319 p., 7000 c. Sob. soch., Vol. II. See 1540. KL 17560.27

1567. Same. Trans. by K. Chukovski. Mol. Gvard., M., 1933. 252 p., 75,325 c. KL 25325.23

1568. Same. Oblastnoye Izdatelstvo (Saratov), Saratov, 1937. 204 p., 10,000 c. KL 34130.37 A juvenile publication.

1569. Same. K. Chukovski, editor of translation. Detizdat., M. & L., 1936. 296 p., 25,000 c. KL 32081.36 A juvenile publication.

1570. Same. 1937. 295 p., 120,000 c. KL 15763.37

Same. See 1552.

1571. Same. K. Chukovski, editor of translation. Detizdat., M. & L., 1942. 208 p., 40,000 c. KL 12216.42 A juvenile publication.

1572. Priklyucheniya Toma (The adventures of Tom Sawyer). Trans. by Z. Zhuravskaya; edited and with an introd. by K. Chukovski. Vsemir. Lit., P., 1919. 272 p., [no. of copies omitted]. KL 3120.21 (n.)

1573. Same. Vsemir. Lit., M. & P., 1923. 258 p., 8150 c. KL 7686.23

1574. Same. V. Dinze, editor of translation. Vokrug Sveta, L., 1927. 219 p., 20,000 c. KL 17947.27 A juvenile publication.

1575. Same. Trans. by K. I. Chukovski. Gosizdat., M. & L.,

1928. 312 p., 7000 c. Sob. soch., Vol. I. See 1540.
KL 2568.28

1576. Priklyucheniya Toma Soiyera (The adventures of Tom
Sawyer). K. Chukovski, editor of translation. Gosiz-
dat., M. & L., 1927. 328 p., 10,000 c. KL 17948.27
A juvenile publication.

1577. Same. 1929. 328 p., 10,000 c. KL 2750.29

1578. Same. 1930. 328 p., 10,000 c. KL 5800.30

1579. Same. 1931. 328 p., 20,000 c. KL 26149.30

1580. Same. Trans. and abridged by L. Rakilin. Biblioteka
Zhurnala "Ogonyok," M., 1928. 48 p., 16,000 c.
KL 17952.28

1581. Same. K. Chukovski, editor of translation. Mol. Gvard.,
L. & M., 1933. 213 p., 20,325 c. KL 14230.33
A juvenile publication.

1582. Same. Detizdat., L., 1934. 214 p., 100,350 c.
KL 21262.34
A juvenile publication.

1583. Same. Trans. by K. Chukovski. Detizdat., L., 1935.
286 p., 75,000 c. KL 41191.35
A juvenile publication. According to KL this is a
"new, complete translation."

1584. Same. Detizdat., M. & L., 1936. 291 p., 25,000 c.
KL 31424.36

1585. Same. [no translator given]. Edited by B. A. Ilish.
Uchpedgiz., M. & L., 1936. 104 p., 5000 c. KL 6057.37
A juvenile publication. Selected excerpts; text in Eng-
lish and Russian.

1586. Same. Trans. by K. Chukovski. Oblastnoye Izdatelstvo
(Kirov), Kirov, 1937. 216 p., 4000 c. KL 4426.38
A juvenile publication.

1587. Same. K. Chukovski, editor of translation. Oblastnoye
Izdatelstvo (Saratov), Saratov, 1937. 224 p., 10,000 c.
KL 25447.37

Same. See 1552.

1588. Same. Trans. by K. Chukovski. Detizdat., M. & L.,
1938. 248 p., 8000 c. KL 5782.38
A juvenile publication.

TWAIN, Mark (Samuel Langhorne Clemens) (Continued)

1589. Same. 1938. 248 p., 8000 c. KL 15344.38

1590. Same. Uchpedgiz., M., 1938. 4 vols., 72, 70, 71 and 69 p. 200 c. each. KL 14011.38
A juvenile publication. In braille.

1591. Same. Dalgiz., Khabarovsk, 1939. 196 p., 15,000 c. KL 4737.40
A juvenile publication.

1592. Same. Detizdat., M. & L., 1940. 232 p., 50,000 c. KL 22717.40
A juvenile publication.

1593. Same. 1945. 227 p., [no. of copies omitted]. MLRA, 1951, No. 11, p. 742.

1594. Same. Lenizdat., L., 1946. 223 p., 20,000 c. KL 4560.47
A juvenile publication.

1595. Prints i nishchi (The prince and the pauper). Trans. by M. A. Shishmareva. Priroda i Lyudi, P., 1918. 128 p., [no. of copies omitted]. KL 1214.19 (n.)

1596. Same. Trans. and adapted by S. Bure. I. D. Sytin, M., 1918. 176 p., 10,000 c. KL 3793.18

1597. Same. Trans. by L. Umants. I. D. Sytin, M., 1918. 279 p., 6000 c. KL 4379.18

1598. Same. Trans. by Z. N. Zhuravskaya; edited and with an introd. by K. Chukovski. Gosizdat., P., 1922. 323 p., 7000 c. KL 4960.22

1599. Prints i nishchi (The prince and the pauper). Trans. by Ye. Zhuravskaya. Zhizn na Missisipi (Life on the Mississippi). Trans. by Ye. Svemlovski. Gosizdat., M. & L., 1929. 395 p., 7000 c. Sob. soch., Vol. V. See 1540. KL 2728.29 (coll. n., memoirs)

1600. Prints i nishchi (The prince and the pauper). Trans. by K. and N. Chukovski. Detizdat., M. & L., 1936. 296 p., 25,000 c. KL 35315.36
A juvenile publication.

1601. Same. 1937. 290 p., 25,000 c. KL 16501.37

1602. Same. 1937. 290 p., 120,000 c. KL 20783.37

1603. Same. Oblastnoye Izdatelstvo (Kuibyshev), Kuibyshev, 1938. 184 p., 20,000 c. KL 6242.38
A juvenile publication.

1604. Same. Detizdat., M. & L., 1941. 232 p., 50,000 c. KL 11274.41
A juvenile publication.

1605. Same. 1946. 272 p., 25,000 c. KL 668.47

1606. Prostaki za granitsei ili novoye stranstviye pilgrima (The innocents abroad). Trans. by M. A. Engelgardt; edited by P. K. Guber. Gosizdat., M. & L., 1928. 503 p., 7000 c. Sob. soch., Vol. IV. See 1540. KL 13276.28 (coll. sk.)

1607. Prostaki za granitsei (The innocents abroad). Edited by B. M. Margolin, with an introd. by the editor. Goslitizdat., M., 1936. 40 p., 100,000 c. KL 38992.36
Excerpts.

1608. Prygayushchaya lyagushka (The celebrated jumping frog of Calaveras county). Trans. by N. and K. Chukovski. Detizdat., M. & L., 1937. 30 p., 100,300 c. KL 32867.37 (coll. s.)
A juvenile publication. Other titles not listed in KL.

1609. Pustogolovy Uilson (Pudd'nhead Wilson). Trans. by Ye. V. Voznesenskaya. Kras. Gaz., L., 1929. 146 p., 120,000 c. KL 19209.29 (n.)

1610. Puteshestviye kapitana Stormfilda na nebo (Captain Stormfield's visit to heaven). Trans. by N. K. Chukovski. Seyatel, L., 1926. 47 p., 15,000 c. KL 3947.26 (s.)

1611. Same. Trans. and with an introd. by Z. Vershinina. Goslitizdat., M., 1935. 48 p., 100,000 c. KL 24813.35

Puteshestviye Kapitana Stormfilda na nebesa (Captain Stormfield's visit to heaven). See 1624.

1612. Rasskazy [short stories] with an introd. by Upton Sinclair. Trans. by Al. Deich. Biblioteka Zhurnala "Ogonyok," M., 1926. 48 p., 15,000 c. KL 11720.26 (coll. s.)
Contents: Pochemu ya podal v otstavku (The facts concerning the recent resignation). Other titles not listed in KL.

TWAIN, Mark (Samuel Langhorne Clemens) (Continued)

"The facts concerning the recent resignation" is from Sketches new and old.

1613. Same. [no translator given]. Kras. Gaz., L., 1928. 135 p., 50,000 c. KL 5456.28
Contents not listed in KL.

1614. Same. Trans. by S. G. Zaimovski. Goslitizdat., M., 1937. 48 p., 150,000 c. KL 3271.38
Contents not listed in KL.

1615. Same. Trans. by Ye. Shlosberg. Pravda, M., 1940. 48 p., 50,000 c. KL 20992.40
Contents not listed in KL.

1616. Same. [no translator given]. Introd. by A. Startsev. Detizdat., M. & L., 1947. 175 p., 45,000 c. KL 8536.47
A juvenile publication. Contents not listed in KL.

1617. Razgovor s intervyurom i drugiye yumoristicheskiye rasskazy (An encounter with an interviewer and other humorous stories). Trans. by E. Pimenova. Univ. Bib., M., 1918. 119 p., 10,000 c. (coll. s.)
"An encounter with an interviewer" is from The stolen white elephant. Other titles not listed in KL.

1618. Repa ili podlinnaya perepiska mezhdu Grili i Eriksonom [the turnip, or the original correspondence between Greeley and Erickson]. Trans. by G. Yarros. 30 Dnei (L.), 1936, No. 5, pp. 53–57. ZL 32382.36
An excerpt from Roughing it.

1619. Roman eskimoski (The Esquimau maiden's romance). Trans. by K. Zhikhareva. Seyatel, L., 1926. 79 p., 15,250 c. KL 14879.26 (coll. s.)
From The man that corrupted Hadleyburg and other stories and essays. Other titles not listed in KL.

Sobaka. See 1624.

1620. Strashnoye proisshestviye [a frightful incident; not identified]. Trans. by K. Zhikhareva. Seyatel, L., 1925. 46 p., 15,000 c. KL 12308.25 (s.)

1621. Tom Soiyer — syshchik (Tom Sawyer, detective). Trans by N. Gorvits. Gosizdat., M. & L., 1928. 109 p., 10,000 c. KL 12531.28 (n.)

1622. Tom Soiyer — syshchik (Tom Sawyer, detective), and
Tom Soiyer — za granitsei (Tom Sawyer abroad).
Trans. by Ye. Zhurovskaya. Gosizdat., M. & L., 1929.
336 p., 7000 c. Sob. soch., Vol. VI. See 1540.
KL 11578.29 (coll. n.)

Tom Soiyer — za granitsei (Tom Sawyer abroad). See
1622 and 1540.

1623. Ukroshcheniye velosipeda (Taming the bicycle). Trans.
by N. Daruzes. Int. Lit. (M.), 1936, No. 3, pp. 128-
132. (sk.)
From What is man?

1624. Same. [no translator given]. Voyenmorizdat., M.,
1944. 128 p., [no. of copies omitted]. KL 9471.44
(coll. s., sk.)
Contents: Znamenitaya skachushchaya lyagushka iz
Kalaverasa (The celebrated jumping frog of Calaveras
country). Kak ya redaktiroval selskokhozyaistvennuyu
gazetu (How I once edited an agricultural paper). Moi
chasy (The great revolution in Pitcairn). Ukroshcheniye
velosipeda (Taming the bicycle). Sobaka [the dog; not
identified, but possibly A dog's tale]. Puteshestviye
Kapitana Stormfilda na nebesa (Captain Stormfield's
visit to heaven).
"How I once edited an agricultural paper" is from
Sketches new and old; "The great revolution in
Pitcairn" is from The stolen white elephant; "Taming
the bicycle" is from What is man?; "A dog's tale" is
from The $30,000 bequest.

1625. Vizit kapitana Stormfilda na nebesa (Captain Stormfield's visit to heaven). Mol. Gvard., M., 1938. 79 p.,
40,000 c. KL 14840.38 (s.)

1626. Same. Voyenizdat., M., 1940. 40 p., [no. of copies
omitted]. KL 10194.40

1627. Yanki iz Konnektikuta pri dvore korolya Artura (A
Connecticut Yankee in King Arthur's court). Trans.
by Z. Zhuravskaya; edited by P. K. Guber. Gosizdat.,
M. & L., 1928. 357 p., 7000 c. Sob. soch., Vol. III.
See 1540. KL 8895.28 (n.)

1628. Yanki pri dvore korolya Artura (A Connecticut Yankee
in King Arthur's court). Trans. by T. L. Shchepkina-

TWAIN, Mark (Samuel Langhorne Clemens) (Continued)

Kupernik. Petrograd, L. & M., 1926. 205 p., 4000 c. KL 12203.26

1629. Same. Adapted by E. Sholok; foreword by A. Tsingovatov. ZIF, M., 1928. 160 p., 35,000 c. KL 6349.28

1630. Same. [no translator given]. Kras. Gaz., L., 1928. In two parts; published separately: Part 1, 200 p.; Part 2, 200 p.; 60,000 c. each. KL 12115.28, KL 12869.28

1631. Same. Trans. by N. K. Chukovski. Detizdat., M. & L., 1945. 359 p., 25,000 c. KL 2803.46
A juvenile publication

Zhizn na Missisipi (Life on the Mississippi). See 1599 and 1540.

Same. See 1552.

Zhurnalistika v Tenessi (Journalism in Tennessee). See 4.

Znamenitaya skachushchaya lyagushka (The celebrated jumping frog of Calaveras country). See 4.

1632. Znamenitaya skachushchaya lyagushka i drugiye rasskazy [The celebrated jumping frog of Calaveras county and other stories]. A. Startsev, editor of translation. Goslitizdat., M., 1943. 136 p., 25,000 c. KL 7866.43 (coll. s.)
Other titles not listed in KL.

Znamenitaya skachushchaya lyagushka iz Kalaverasa (The celebrated jumping frog of Calaveras county). See 1624.

VAN DINE, Warren L.

1633. Poet (The poet). Trans by P. Okhrimenko. 30 Dnei (L.), 1940, No. 2, pp. 70-74. ZL 26741.40 (s.)
From O'Brien, The best short stories of 1924.

VAN VECHTEN, Carl

1634. Negrityanski rai (Nigger heaven). Trans. by A. V. Shvyrov; edited by A. N. Gorlin. Gosizdat., L., 1928. 318 p., 4000 c. KL 10868.28 (n.)

VOGEL, Joseph

1635. Muzhestvo (Man's courage). Trans. by N. Daruzes.
Int. Lit. (M), 1939, No. 3-4, pp. 15-113. (n.)

1636. Same. Trans. by N. Daruzes; foreword by P. Balashov.
Goslitizdat., M., 1940. 276 p., 25,000 c. KL 17608.40

1637. Vozvrashcheniye [the return]. Sputnik Agitatora (M.),
1939, No. 10, pp. 32-34. ZL 31467.39
An excerpt from Man's courage.

VORSE, Mary Heaton

1638. Desyat dnei i chetyrnadtsat nochei [ten days and fourteen nights; not identified]. Mol. Gvard. (M.), 1929,
No. 6, pp. 38-41. (s.)

1639. Stachka (Strike!). Trans. by M. Volosov; foreword by
K. Gendriks. Goslitizdat., M. & L., 1932. 256 p.,
10,000 c. KL 2541.32 (n.)

Zabastovka (Strike!). See 14.

WALSH, Ernest

Lyubovnaya pesn (A love song). See 22.

WARD, Artemus (Charles Farrar Browne)

1640. Dryguny (The Shakers). Trans. by P. Okhrimenko.
ZIF, M. & L., 1926. 31 p., 15,000 c. KL 13235.26 (s.)

WATKINS, Maurine

1641. Reklama: Chikago (Chicago). Trans. by N. D. Volkov
and A. A. Arian. Tsedram, M., 1936. 81 p., 190 c.
KL 11835.36 (pl.)

1642. Same. Iskusstvo, M., 1938. 99 p., 550 c. KL 2833.38

WATKINS, Richard Howell

1643. U norvezhskovo fiorda [by a Norwegian fiord; not
identified]. Trans. by Yu. Smirnov. Krasnoflotets
(M.), 1945, No. 6, pp. 17-19. KL 8547.45 (s.)

WEBSTER, Jean

1644. Dlinnonogi dyadyushka (Daddy-Long-Legs). Trans. by
N. N. Guk. Gosizdat., M. & L., 1926. 198 p., 15,000 c.
KL 17148.26 (n.)

WEBSTER, Jean (Continued)

1645. Dlinnonogi papochka (Daddy-Long-Legs). Knizhny Ugol, L. & M., 1924. 233 p., 3000 c. KL 9518.24

1646. Mily nedrug (Dear enemy). Trans. by V. Dugovskaya and E. Shteinberg. Kosmos, Kharkov, 1929. 253 p., 6000 c. KL 1491.29 (n.)

WEXLEY, John

Shosse No. 51 (Southern Highway 51). See 8.

WHITE, Stewart Edward

1647. Pogonya v strane molchaniya (The silent places). Trans. by O. N. Annenkova. Mol. Gvard., M. & L., 1930. 128 p., 10,100 c. KL 16390.30 (n.)
A juvenile publication.

1648. Zavoyevateli lesov [conquerors of the forests; not identified]. Trans. by Z. Lvovski. Mysl, L., 1927. 322 p., 6200 c. KL 17177.27 (n.)

WHITE, Walter Francis

1649. Ogon iz kremnya (The fire in the flint). Trans. by Sviyazheninov. Nedra, M., 1926. 218 p., 5000 c. KL 4981.26 (n.)

1650. Udar po kremnyu (The fire in the flint). Foreword by D. Zislavski. Priboi, L., 1925. 194 p., 5000 c. KL 2617.26
Abridged.

1651. Pobeg (Flight). Trans. by L. Vsevolodskaya. Mysl, L., 1927. 258 p., 5200 c. KL 19837.27 (n.)

WHITMAN, Walt

Armeiski korpus v pokhode (An army corps on the march). See 1661.

Bei! bei baraban! (Beat! beat! drums!). See 11.

Bivuak na sklone gory (Bivouac on a mountain side). See 1661.

Budushchiye puti demokratii (Democratic vistas). See 1654.

Dlya tebya, demokratiya (For you O democracy). See 1662.

Drob barabana. See 1661.

Druzhelyubny i pokladisty dikar (Song of myself, section 39). See 1662.

Gody sovremennyie (Years of the modern). See 11.

Ispaniya v 1873-1874 godu (Spain, 1873-74). See 1662.

1652. Izbrannyie stikhotvoreniya [selected poetry]. Trans. and with a biographical sketch of Whitman by K. Chukovski; introd. by A. Lunacharski. Goslitizdat., M. & L., 1932. 125 p., 3000 c. KL 3296.33 (coll. p.) Contents not listed in KL.

1653. Izbrannyie stikhotvoreniya i proza [selected poetry and prose]. Translated, edited and with an introd. by K. Chukovski. Goslitizdat., M., 1944. 216 p., 10,000 c. KL 4050.45
Contents not listed in KL. The title of Chukovski's introductory article is "Uolt Vitman, yevo zhizn i tvorchestvo" [Walt Whitman, his life and art].

Kavaleriya perekhodit v brod (Cavalry crossing a ford). See 1661.

Khochesh poslushat kak dralis v starinu na moryakh (Song of myself, section 35). See 1662.

Kogda vo dvore pered domom tsvela etoi vesnoyu siren (When lilacs last in the dooryard bloom'd). See 1662.

Kogda ya skitalsya v virginskikh lesakh (As toilsome I wander'd Virginia's woods). See 1661.

1654. Listya travy (Leaves of grass). Trans. and with an introd. by K. Chukovski. Gosizdat., P., 1922. 260 p., 4000 c. KL 4990.22 (coll. p., essays)
Contents: Listya travy. Iz dnevnika [from the diary; not identified]. Budushchiye puti demokratii (Democratic vistas). Uitman v russkoi literature [Whitman in Russian literature].

1655. Same. Trans. and with an introd. by K. Chukovski. Biblioteka Zhurnala "Ogonyok," M., 1931. 43 p., 20,000 c. KL 13677.31 (coll. p.)

WHITMAN, Walt (Continued)

Selections. Contents not listed in KL. The title of Chukovski's introductory article is "Predtecha revolyutsionnykh poetov" [forerunner of the revolutionary poets].

1656. Same. Trans. and edited by K. I. Chukovski; introd. by D. Mirski. Goslitizdat., L., 1935. 229 p., 10,300 c. KL 31380.35 (coll. p.)

Mir pod morskoi vodoi (The world below the brine). See 1662.

Ne zakryvaite vashikh dverei (Shut not your doors). See 1662.

Nochyu na morskom beregu (On the beach at night). See 1662.

Odnomu shtatskomu (To a certain civilian). See 1662.

1657. Peredovyie boitsy [foremost soldiers; not identified]. Trans. by K. Chukovski. Gosizdat., P., 1923. 4 p., 3000 c. KL 4981.23 (p.)

1658. Pesni o samom sebe (Song of myself). Trans. by D. Maizels. Mol. Gvard. (M.), 1935, No. 7, pp. 26-27. ZL 38829.35 (p.)
An excerpt.

1659. Pionery (Pioneers! O Pioneers!). Trans. by M. S. Tsentralnaya tipografiya, P., 1918. 4 p., 1000 c. KL 1475.18 (p.)

1660. Same. Trans. by Dm. Maizels. Mol. Gvard. (M.), 1935, No. 7, pp. 32-34. ZL 38829.35

Ruchnoye zerkalo (A hand-mirror). See 1662.

Starikovskoye spasibo, poka ya ne umer (Thanks in old age). See 1662.

1661. Stikhi o voine [poems of war]. Trans. by M. Zenkevich. Int. Lit. (M.), 1942, No. 12, pp. 107-110. (coll. p.)
Contents: Drob barabana [roll of the drum; not identified]. Armeiski korpus v pokhode (An army corps on the march). Kavaleriya perekhodit v brod (Cavalry crossing a ford). Ya videl generala v boyu (I saw Old General at bay). Bivuak na sklone gory (Bivouac

on a mountain side). U mertsayushchevo kostra
bivuaka (By the bivouac's fitful flame). Strannoye
bdenye provyol ya na pole boya (Vigil strange I kept
on the field one night). Kogda ya skitalsya v virginskikh lesakh (As toilsome I wander'd Virginia's
woods).

1662. Stikhotvoreniya [poems]. Int. Lit. (M.), 1941, No. 2,
pp. 179-187. (coll. p.)
Contents: Dlya tebya, demokratiya (For you O dem-
ocracy). V myslyakh moikh prokhoda — posle chteniya
Gegelya (Roaming in thought — after reading Hegel).
Vo sne mne prisnilsya gorod (I dreamed in a dream).
Vy, lodyri, tam na karaule (Song of myself, section 37).
Ne zakryvaite vashikh dverei (Shut not your doors).
Nochyu na morskom beregu (On the beach at night).
Ispaniya v 1873-1874 godu (Spain, 1873-74). Mir pod
morskoi vodoi (The world below the brine). Ruchnoye
zerkalo (A hand-mirror). Druzhelyubny i pokladisty
dikar (Song of myself, section 39). Odnomu shtatskomu
(To a certain civilian). Khochesh poslushat, kak
dralis v starinu na moryakh (Song of myself, section
35). Starikovskoye spasibo, poka ya ne umer (Thanks
in old age). Kogda vo dvore pered domom tsvela etoi
vesnoyu siren (When lilacs last in the dooryard
bloom'd).

Strannoye bdenye provyol ya na pole boya (Vigil strange
I kept on the field one night). See 1661.

U mertsayushchevo kostra bivuaka (By the bivouac's
fitful flame). See 1661.

V boi pospeshim my skorei [into battle we hasten; not
identified]. [no publisher given], Totma, 1918. 1 p.,
1000 c. KL 217.19 (p.)

V myslyakh moikh prokhoda — posle chteniya Gegelya
(Roaming in thought — after reading Hegel). See 1661.

Vo sne mne prisnilsya gorod (I dreamed in a dream).
See 1662.

Vy, lodyri, tam na karaule (Song of myself, section
37). See 1662.

Ya videl generala v boyu (I saw Old General at bay).
See 1661.

WHITMAN, Walt (Continued)

1663. Yevropa (Europe). Upravleniye Belomorskovo
Voyennovo Okruga, Arkhangelsk, 1920. 10 p., 1000 c.
KL 193.21 (coll. p.)
Other titles not listed in KL.

WILLIAMS, Albert Rhys

1664. Narodnyie massy v russkoi revolutsii [the masses of
people in the Russian revolution; not identified, but
possibly selections from Through the Russian revo-
lution]. With a foreword by Upton Sinclair. Gosizdat.,
M., 1924. 189 p., 6000 c. KL 13612.24

1665. Ocherki russkoi revolutsii (Through the Russian revolution). Gosizdat., M., 1924. 203 p., 5000 c.
KL 4080.24 (history)

WILLIAMS, William Carlos

Metricheskaya figura (Metric figure). See 22.

Rassvet (Dawn). See 22.

WOODFORD, Jack

Kniga (The book). See 1666.

Otzyv (Testimonial). See 1666.

1666. Rasskazy Dzheka Vudforda [stories of Jack Woodford].
Trans. by P. Okhrimenko. 30 Dnei (L.), 1933, No. 8,
pp. 48-51. ZL 41428.33 (coll. s.)
Contents: Otzyv (Testimonial). Kniga (The book).
From Evangelical cockroach.

WOODWARD, William E.

1667. Khleba i zrelishch (Bread and circuses). Trans. by
A. V. Krivtsova; foreword by Yev. Lann. Gosizdat.,
M. & L., 1927. 379 p., 10,000 c. KL 13950.27 (n.)

1668. Lotereya (Lottery). Trans. by A. V. Krivtsova; foreword by Yev. Lann. Gosizdat., M. & L., 1926. 399 p.,
4000 c. KL 22277.26 (n.)

1669. Vzdor (Bunk). Trans. by S. A. Polyakov and L. I.
Nekrasova; edited by Yev. Lann. Gosizdat., M. & L.,
1927. 352 p., 4000 c. KL 934.27 (n.)

1670. Same. 1927. 335 p., 5000 c. KL 13345.27

WRIGHT, Richard

    Big boi pokidayet dom (Big boy leaves home). See 1671.

1671. Deti dyadi Toma (Uncle Tom's children). Int. Lit. (M.), 1938, No. 7, pp. 3-85. (coll. s.) Contents: Big boi pokidayet dom (Big boy leaves home). Trans. by V. Toper. Na beregu reki (Down by the riverside). Trans. by Yev. Kalashnikova. Tuchi i plamya (Fire and cloud). Trans. by T. Ozerskaya. Utrennyaya zvezda (Bright and morning star). Trans. by N. Daruzes.

1672. Same. Trans. and with an introd. by A. Shneider. Goslitizdat., M., 1939. 224 p., 25,000 c. KL 14124.39

1673. Kak rodilsya "Bigger" (How "Bigger" was born). Trans. from the manuscript by Ye. Kalashnikova. Int. Lit. (M.), 1941, No. 1, pp. 145-156. (essay)

    Na beregu reki (Down by the riverside). See 1671.

1674. Syn Ameriki (Native son). Trans. by Ye. Kalashnikova. Int. Lit. (M.), 1941, No. 1, pp. 3-44; No. 2, pp. 4-153. (n.)

    Tuchi i plamya (Fire and cloud). See 1671.

1675. Utrennyaya zvezda (Bright and morning star). Trans. by N. Daruzes. Pravda, M., 1938. 48 p., 50,000 c. KL 977.39 (s.) From Uncle Tom's children, 2nd edition, 1938.

    Same. See 1671.

WRIGHT, Richard, and Langston Hughes

1676. Pesnya o krasnoi zemle (Red clay blues). Trans. by M. Zenkevich. Int. Lit. (M.), 1940, No. 1, p. 86 (p.) From New Masses, Aug. 1, 1939, p. 14.

WYLIE, Elinor

    Pesenka bezumnovo (Madman's song). See 22.

ZINBERG, Len

    Bolshiye ruki (Big hands). See 8.

ZINBERG, Len (Continued)

1677. Bolshiye ruki (Big hands), Eto ved Amerika [this is indeed America; not identified], and Sovety Miss Lovlorn [advice to Miss Lovelorn; not identified. Trans. by Yu. Smirnov. Mol. Gvard. (M.), 1937, No. 10-11, pp. 26-51. ZL 45530.37 (coll. s.) "Big hands" is from New Masses, July 2, 1935, p. 22.

Eto ved Amerika. See 1677.

Sovety Miss Lovlorn. See 1677.

ZUGSMITH, Leane

1678. Dom — eto tam gde proshlo detstvo (Home is where you hang your childhood) and Mesto v zhizni (Room in the world). Trans. by M. Lariye. Int. Lit. (M.), 1938, No. 4, pp. 122-130. (coll. s.) "Home is where you hang your childhood" is from O'Brien, The best short stories, 1934; "Room in the world" is from O'Brien, The best short stories, 1937.

Mesto v zhizni (Room in the world). See 1678.

TABLES

TABLE I

Authors Most Widely Published in Russian Translation in Book
Form in the USSR, According to Number of Copies Printed

Each unit represents 1,000 copies. Asterisks indicate years in
which authors were published only in periodicals, or in which
there were editions of unknown size. Anthologies are not included.

	Jack London	Mark Twain	Upton Sinclair	O. Henry	Bret Harte	James Oliver Curwood
Total	7,640	2,534	2,292	1,430	801	645
1917	152					
1918	262	26			*	
1919	25	*				
1920	*					
1921			15			
1922	59	7	23			
1923	224	8	154	33		
1924	479		244	111		
1925	769	30	496	303	11	17
1926	643	104	103	257		51
1927	548	57	70	110	90	131
1928	961	202	416	1	555	446
1929	1,347	209	105			
1930	342	95	165	35		
1931		20	140			
1932	20		21	10		
1933	50	96	45			
1934		140				
1935	68	225				
1936	545	200		70		
1937	731	569	260	210	100	
1938	255	231	20	25	*	
1939	125	30	10	50	20	
1940		100				
1941	25	50		100		
1942		40	*			
1943		25	5	*		
1944	*	*		15		
1945	10	25			25	
1946		45	*	100		
1947	*					

Table I (Continued)

	Joel Chandler Harris	David Freedman	Theodore Dreiser	John Steinbeck	James Fenimore Cooper	Anna Louise Strong
Total	450	447	381	365	362	295
1917						
1918						
1919						
1920						
1921						
1922						
1923					*	
1924						
1925		9	34			
1926		318				
1927		120	31		75	
1928			30		71	
1929			15		15	
1930			35		15	
1931						
1932						
1933			55			
1934			*			
1935			*			
1936	25		71		25	
1937	151		10			
1938			50		111	
1939	274					295
1940				25		
1941			50	300		
1942						
1943				*		
1944						
1945				40		
1946					50	
1947			*			

Table I (Continued)

	John Reed	Agnes Smedley	Erskine Caldwell	Edgar Allan Poe	Sinclair Lewis	Jim Tully
Total	249	240	224	210	204	180
1917						
1918						
1919						
1920						
1921						
1922				1		
1923	15			2		
1924	225			2	16	
1925					18	
1926				15	14	5
1927	*			25	53	
1928	9			15	38	170
1929				65	25	
1930		15				
1931						5
1932						
1933		*			*	
1934		7	*		*	
1935		168	*			
1936		50		15	20	
1937			4		20	
1938			10			
1939			50	*		
1940			*			
1941			50			
1942						
1943				25		
1944			10			
1945				*		
1946				45		
1947			100			

Table I (Continued)

	Henry Wadsworth Longfellow	Pearl Buck	Washington Irving	Konrad Bercovici	Edgar Rice Burroughs	Ernest Hemingway
Total	175	170	150	135	135	130
1917						
1918	10					
1919	10					
1920						
1921						
1922					10	
1923					98	
1924					27	
1925				5		
1926				63		
1927				67		
1928	7					
1929						
1930						
1931	7					
1932						
1933	20					
1934		5				8
1935	50	105				10
1936	1	60				10
1937		*	100			70
1938			*			10
1939	*		25			22
1940	*		25			
1941	70					
1942						
1943						*
1944						
1945						
1946						
1947						

Table I (Continued)

	Leroy Scott	John Dos Passos	Michael Gold	Harriet Beecher Stowe	Martha Dodd	Richard Wright
Total	125	117	101	98	78	75
1917						
1918						
1919						
1920						
1921						
1922						
1923						
1924	8	3				
1925	17					
1926				35		
1927	100	5				
1928				3		
1929						
1930		5	5	10		
1931		15	61			
1932		40	30			
1933		10				
1934		3	*			
1935			*			
1936		36				
1937			5			
1938						50
1939						25
1940						
1941				50		
1942					75	
1943					3	
1944						
1945						
1946						
1947						

Table I (Continued)

	Sherwood Anderson	Waldo Frank	Angelo Herndon	Claude McKay	James Willard Schultz	Fannie Hurst
Total	69	69	60	59	59	53
1917						
1918						
1919						
1920						
1921						
1922						
1923						
1924	6					
1925	10			50		4
1926	18	9				5
1927	20					24
1928						
1929				5	7	
1930				4	42	20
1931						
1932						
1933	5					
1934						
1935						
1936	10	60				
1937						
1938			60			
1939						
1940					10	
1941						
1942						
1943						
1944						
1945						
1946						
1947						

Table I (Continued)

	Frank Norris	Walt Whitman	Albert Maltz	Joseph Hergesheimer
Total	53	53	44	38
1917				
1918		2		
1010				
1920		1		
1921				
1922		4		
1923		3		
1924				
1925	23			13
1926	20			12
1927	5			13
1928	5			
1929				
1930				
1931		20		
1932		3		
1933				
1934		10		
1935				
1936				
1937				
1938			19	
1939				
1940				
1941			25	
1942				
1943				
1944		10		
1945				
1946				
1947				

TABLE II

Yearly Summaries of Book Publication

Year	Number of authors published in book form	Number of anthologies	Number of printings of known size	Number of printings of unknown size	Number of known copies printed
1917	1	0	11	0	151,500
1918	6	0	27	3	300,450
1919	4	0	3	2	35,000
1920	2	0	1	1	1,000
1921	1	0	1	0	15,000
1922	9	0	24	0	125,600
1923	9	1	72	4	537,700
1924	16	1	137	1	1,208,600
1925	23	0	192	0	1,859,580
1926	34	0	163	0	1,838,800
1927	52	1	177	0	1,783,350
1928	41	4	118	2	3,117,050
1929	21	0	54	0	1,935,200
1930	23	0	45	1	868,740
1931	11	0	18	1	287,780
1932	9	1	14	0	153,980
1933	10	0	13	0	292,125
1934	7	1	8	0	200,925
1935	14	0	24	1	679,245
1936	20	1	39	0	1,277,430
1937	18	1	39	1	2,350,800
1938	22	1	34	0	1,037,180
1939	13	2	18	0	966,000
1940	12	1	17	1	275,150
1941	9	0	9	0	720,000
1942	2	0	3	0	115,000
1943	6	0	4	2	58,000
1944	6	1	4	3	30,200
1945	6	0	5	3	110,100
1946	3	2	4	0	225,000
1947	5	0	4	2	205,000
Totals		18	1,282	28	22,761,485

INDEXES

INDEX OF AUTHORS

Author references are to page numbers

INDEX OF AMERICAN TITLES

Title references are to item numbers

Oh, the Cobbs an' Mc Farlands are
    fightin', 17
Oil!,1396, 1397, 1398, 1399
Old man at the bridge, 507
Old man's folly, an, 271
Ol' man Adam an' his chillun, 88
One-fifth of mankind, 1528, 1529
120 million, 418
100%: the story of a patriot, 1298,
    1409, 1438, 1439, 1440, 1441,
    1442, 1443, 1444, 1445, 1446,
    1447, 1448, 1449
One kind of officer, 75
One man's initiation-1917, 305
£ 1,000,000 banknote, the, 4, 1544
One thousand dollars, 1190
One thousand dozen, the, 1031, 1032
Only the stars are neutral, 1255
On the American dead in Spain, 476,
    493
On the beach at night, 1662
On the Makaloa mat, 847
Open boat, the, 5
Open letter to the South, 544
Open window, 272
Our comrade Munn, 173
Our Mr. Wrenn, 623, 624
Our spring, 559
Outcasts of Poker Flat, the, 458,
    462
'Out, out-', 401
Oyster's son, 557

Pace of youth, the, 220
Passage in the life of Mr. John Oak-
    hurst, a, 462
Passing of Marcus O'Brien, the,
    742, 743
Pathfinder, the, 210, 211, 212
Paths of glory, 175
Paul Bunyan: in work of John Dos
    Passos, 14, 306; James Stevens,
    1512
Paving gang-on a job in Missouri, 5
Pen, the, 989
Pendulum, the, 1174
Penrod, 1532
People of the abyss, the, 768, 769,
    786, 840, 841, 842, 861, 1026
People's choice, 155
Piece of paper, the, 1069
Piece of steak, a, 756, 766
Pigs is pigs, 136

Pilot, the, 196
Pimienta pancakes, the, 1119, 1174
Pioneers, the, 213
Pioneers! O Pioneers!, 1659, 1660
Pit, the, 1097
Pit and the pendulum, the, 1224
Pity is not enough, 512
Plains of Abraham, the, 259
Plant in the sun, 55
Playboy, 298
Poems of Joe Hill, 536
Poems on slavery, 1049
Poet, the, 1633
Poor rule, a, 1174
Porgy, 534
Portrait of a motor car, 1268
Posson Jone', 4
Postscripts, 1149
Pot boiler, the, 1370, 1406
Prairie, the, 205, 206
Preface to a life, 402
Presidential agent, 1297
Prince and the pauper, the, 1595,
    1596, 1597, 1598, 1599, 1600,
    1601, 1602, 1603, 1604, 1605
Prince Hagen, 1411, 1451
Prince has the mumps, the, 187
Princess, the, 888, 982, 983
Princess and the puma, the, 1174
Princess of Mars, a, 117
Private Hicks, 1072
Professor, 551
Profits of religion, the, 1465, 1466
Proof of the pudding, 1164
Protector, the, 8
Psalm of those who go forth before
    daylight, 1271
Pudd'nhead Wilson, 1609

Quest of the silver fleece, the, 350

Rachel, 162
Raid, 1509, 1510
Ransom of Mack, the, 1148, 1174
Ransom of Red Chief, the, 1148,
    1174, 1195, 1196, 1197, 1198,
    1199
Red badge of courage, the, 218, 219
Red clay blues, 1676
Red one, the, 761
Red pony, the, 12
Red roses of Tonia, the, 1148
Red rover, the, 194

R